Table of Contents

ACT® Mastery English

Student Workbook

4th Edition

MasteryPrep

Inquiries concerning this publication should be mailed to:

MasteryPrep
7117 Florida Blvd.
Baton Rouge, LA 70806

10 9 8 7 6 5 4 3 2 1

ISBN-13: 978-1-948846-04-2

Get ready to master the ACT® test!

You are about to take part in the most effective and broadly used ACT prep program in the nation! With ACT Mastery, you will learn the most frequently tested content on the ACT test and develop the skills and strategies necessary to achieve the score you desire.

With practice in all four subjects, you will be fully prepared.

The ACT Mastery English workbook is just one part of a larger program that includes four core subject books, each in line with a subtest found on the ACT: English, math, reading, and science. Each book works to build your mastery of the content most frequently tested on the ACT by providing thorough subject reviews and hundreds of ACT practice questions. By completing this book, you will be prepared for the English subtest; the rest of the program will prepare you for the math, reading, and science subtests.

Test prep is a team effort.

Although you may be tempted to jump ahead, this workbook should be used in conjunction with your teacher's instructions and is not intended for self-guided practice. Each lesson is designed so that the majority of the direction and some of the content is delivered by an instructor either verbally or visually by way of slide presentations or whiteboards. Working ahead will limit your understanding of the ACT content and may actually lead to confusion. Follow your teacher's instructions during the lesson and only work on practice as directed. This will maximize your understanding of the material and, ultimately, your score.

The score you want is within your reach!

The ACT test is a rigorous, challenging marathon of an exam. It can be intimidating. Of the more than two million students who take the test each year, many feel that it is uncoachable—that whatever score they earn on the test is the best they can do. The ACT Mastery program has proven this assumption to be *completely false.* Students dedicated to the program routinely see substantial improvement on their test scores. It will take hard work and determination, but with the content and strategies available to you, anything is possible.

You *can* master the ACT test.

The keys to success with ACT preparation are content, practice, and strategy. As your teacher leads you through the lessons, focus on the content. Take notes on all of the definitions and rules, ask questions to clarify any points of confusion, and participate in all of the activities.

Once you begin to master the content, practice the problems in your workbook. Give your best effort on every question no matter how hard or easy it may seem. Complete any homework your teacher assigns and make sure you ask questions if you don't fully understand a concept.

Finally, as you develop content mastery and practice the ACT questions, work on building your test-day strategy. Look for trends in the questions and answer choices, determine your strongest and weakest areas, and decide how you will pace yourself on the day of the test.

Good luck!

Lesson 1

Ambiguity and Series

CAPTION:

1.1 Entrance Ticket

How does the location of the comma affect the sentence's meaning? Write a short paragraph explaining the image. Use complete sentences.

1.2 Learning Targets

1. Identify several different strategies to use in comma usage conflicts

2. Use commas for different purposes in several types of sentences

Self-Assessment

Circle the number that corresponds to your confidence level in your knowledge of this subject before beginning the lesson. A score of 1 means you are completely lost, and a score of 4 means you have mastered the skills. After you finish the lesson, return to the bottom of this page and circle your new confidence level to show your improvement.

Before Lesson

1 2 3 4

After Lesson

1 2 3 4

1.3.1 FANBOYS

1. The five-foot gorilla lives at the zoo but it is originally from Africa.
2. My music teacher from high school was at the restaurant and I ran over to say hello as soon as I saw him.
3. We started the music and immediately the baby started to dance!

Comma Rule 1:

---

1. I prefer the color purple but Kevin likes red better.
2. My grandmother came to America hoping to escape the terrors of war in her native country and I'm glad she did because it was here she met my grandfather!
3. My friend Bella and I recently took a ballet class so one night we went to the Bass Performance Hall to see a show by the ballerina Kristina Haronoff.
4. The man paid me twenty dollars for the book and he said he would have paid twice as much if it had been a first edition.
5. The very idea of spiders and even just the word spiders terrify us and both tend to give us chills.
6. The two types of cats are short-haired and long-haired and each has different grooming requirements.

English Tip

Sounds Right: If a comma causes you to pause your reading at an awkward location, it's almost always wrong. Try the "secret agent move" to sound out comma pauses and determine if the comma is misplaced. Place a finger over one ear and whisper the answers. Using this technique, you will hear your whispers loud and clear without disrupting the others testing around you.

1.3.2 Lists and Series

1. Kim ordered a large coffee pancakes eggs and hashbrowns for breakfast.
2. Brandon had homework in geometry world history Spanish and even PE!
3. Azalea lived at home with her parents her grandma one brother one sister and a dog.

Comma Rule 2:

---

1. Old McDonald raises various livestock poultry and some domestic animals on his farm.
2. Miriam decided to try out for the softball swimming and cross country teams at her school.
3. He stopped by the grocery store to pick up fruit and crackers to bring to the party.
4. The Himalayan teapots are quite rare exceedingly lovely and richly intricate.
5. Mike snuck into the kitchen scarfed down some cookies swept away the crumbs that might give him away and was out in a flash.

1.3.2 Lists and Series

1. Jamie snuck into the kitchen and scarfed down some cookies.

2. Her trip abroad was both incredibly enlightening and overwhelmingly exhausting.

3. After the speech, congressman and presidential candidate Ford Peterson took some time to answer questions from reporters in the audience.

Comma Rule 3:

1.3.3 Introductory Words and Phrases

1. Even though I don't like pickles I ate a spoonful of relish when my friend dared me.
2. Growling and barking the dog warned the mailman not to come any closer.
3. As if being grounded weren't enough her mom also took away her cell phone.

Comma Rule 4:

---

1. After we won regionals the entire basketball team went out for pizza.
2. While I didn't practice piano much in middle school I've come to love it now that I'm in high school.
3. Running late for school Marcus didn't brush his teeth this morning.
4. One sweltering Texas day in 1956 a Dallas gym teacher pondered how to handle a difficult problem.
5. It was early morning when my parents and I arrived at the museum a huge building in the middle of town.
6. When singer Ally King Scott sings everyone listens.

English Tip

Decoding: Look for giveaway words, such as *when*, *while*, *even though*, and *although*. These words create dependent clauses. If the dependent clause comes first in the sentence, you will need to use a comma to separate the dependent clause from the independent clause.

1 1

1.4.1 Set One

My friend and I wanted to go to the beach, so we gathered our change together and got on the bus.

1. A. NO CHANGE
   B. the beach so we
   C. the beach so, we
   D. the beach; so we

The explorers reached the edge of the forest, where they collected water and they decided to set up camp for the night.

2. F. NO CHANGE
   G. water and, they decided
   H. water, and they decided
   J. water and, they decided,

Next, my sister and I, braided each other's hair.

3. A. NO CHANGE
   B. Next my sister and I,
   C. Next my sister, and I
   D. Next, my sister and I

END OF SET ONE
STOP! DO NOT GO ON TO THE NEXT PAGE
UNTIL TOLD TO DO SO.

1 1

1.4.2 Set Two

I can see him now, standing in the hallway, <u>sweat dripping from his forehead,</u> hands worn from the day's work.

4. **F.** NO CHANGE
   G. sweat dripping, from his forehead
   H. sweat, dripping from his, forehead
   J. sweat dripping from his forehead

We ordered in French, so it took the waiter a few minutes to <u>understand</u> and bring out our drinks.

5. **A.** NO CHANGE
   B. take the order,
   C. take the order;
   D. understand them

Once she started the car, she pulled out of the driveway and <u>then, drove around the block</u> and went to the store.

6. **F.** NO CHANGE
   G. then, drove around, the block
   H. then drove around the block,
   J. then drove around the block

END OF SET TWO

STOP! DO NOT GO ON TO THE NEXT PAGE UNTIL TOLD TO DO SO.

1.4.3 Set Three

Even though she hadn't practiced the piano <u>in years she still remembered</u> how to play the piece almost perfectly.

7. **A.** NO CHANGE
   B. in years; she still remembered
   C. in years she, still remembered
   D. in years, she still remembered

Growing <u>up, in Florida, in the 1990s</u> Sara developed a deep appreciation for video games.

8. **F.** NO CHANGE
   G. up in Florida in the 1990s
   H. up, in Florida in the 1990s
   J. up in Florida in the 1990s,

Every winter, <u>thousands of tourists,</u> come to Colorado. They enjoy the snowy mountains and scenic views.

9. **A.** NO CHANGE
   B. thousands, of tourists
   C. thousands of tourists
   D. thousands of tourists'

END OF SET THREE

STOP! DO NOT GO ON TO THE NEXT PAGE
UNTIL TOLD TO DO SO.

1.4.4 Set Four

Ms. Barnes, the librarian, then decorated a banner with red, white, and blue stripes; hung it; and began pouring soda for the class.

10. **F.** NO CHANGE
G. stripes, hung it,
H. stripes hung it,
J. stripes, hung it;

In desert sands and sweltering canyons once thought too hot, too dangerous or too secluded to support a community, there exist small villages determined to fight for survival.

11. **A.** NO CHANGE
B. too hot, too dangerous, or too secluded
C. too hot, too dangerous, or too secluded,
D. too hot, too dangerous, or to secluded

What's already clear, is that the image of coal miners as rough men fails to take into account the great diversity within the profession.

12. **F.** NO CHANGE
G. clear is that,
H. clear is, that
J. clear is that

END OF SET FOUR
STOP! DO NOT GO ON TO THE NEXT PAGE
UNTIL TOLD TO DO SO.

1.4.5 Set Five

The school day was over, the children had returned home; and everyone was sitting in the kitchen waiting for dinner.

13. **A.** NO CHANGE
    B. over, the children had returned home,
    C. over the children had returned home,
    D. over the children had returned home;

In the mythology, of the ancient tribes of Ireland, selkies live as seals in the sea and become human on land.

14. **F.** NO CHANGE
    G. mythology of the ancient tribes, of Ireland
    H. mythology, of the ancient tribes, of Ireland
    J. mythology of the ancient tribes of Ireland,

The heart-shaped, dark-brown chocolates sat waiting for my valentine on his desk.

15. **A.** NO CHANGE
    B. heart-shaped, dark-brown, chocolates
    C. heart-shaped, dark-brown chocolates,
    D. heart-shaped dark-brown chocolates,

END OF SET FIVE
STOP! DO NOT GO ON TO THE NEXT PAGE
UNTIL TOLD TO DO SO.

Sum It Up

Ambiguity and Series

Clause
A phrase with a subject and predicate

Independent Clause
A clause that can stand on its own as a complete sentence

Dependent Clause
A clause that is not a complete idea and so cannot stand on its own as a complete sentence

---

Conjunction
A word used to connect words, phrases, clauses, or sentences

Tips and Techniques

Sounds Right: Remember to eliminate any commas that create awkward-sounding pauses or otherwise seem misplaced.

Lesson 2

Unnecessary Commas

CAPTION:

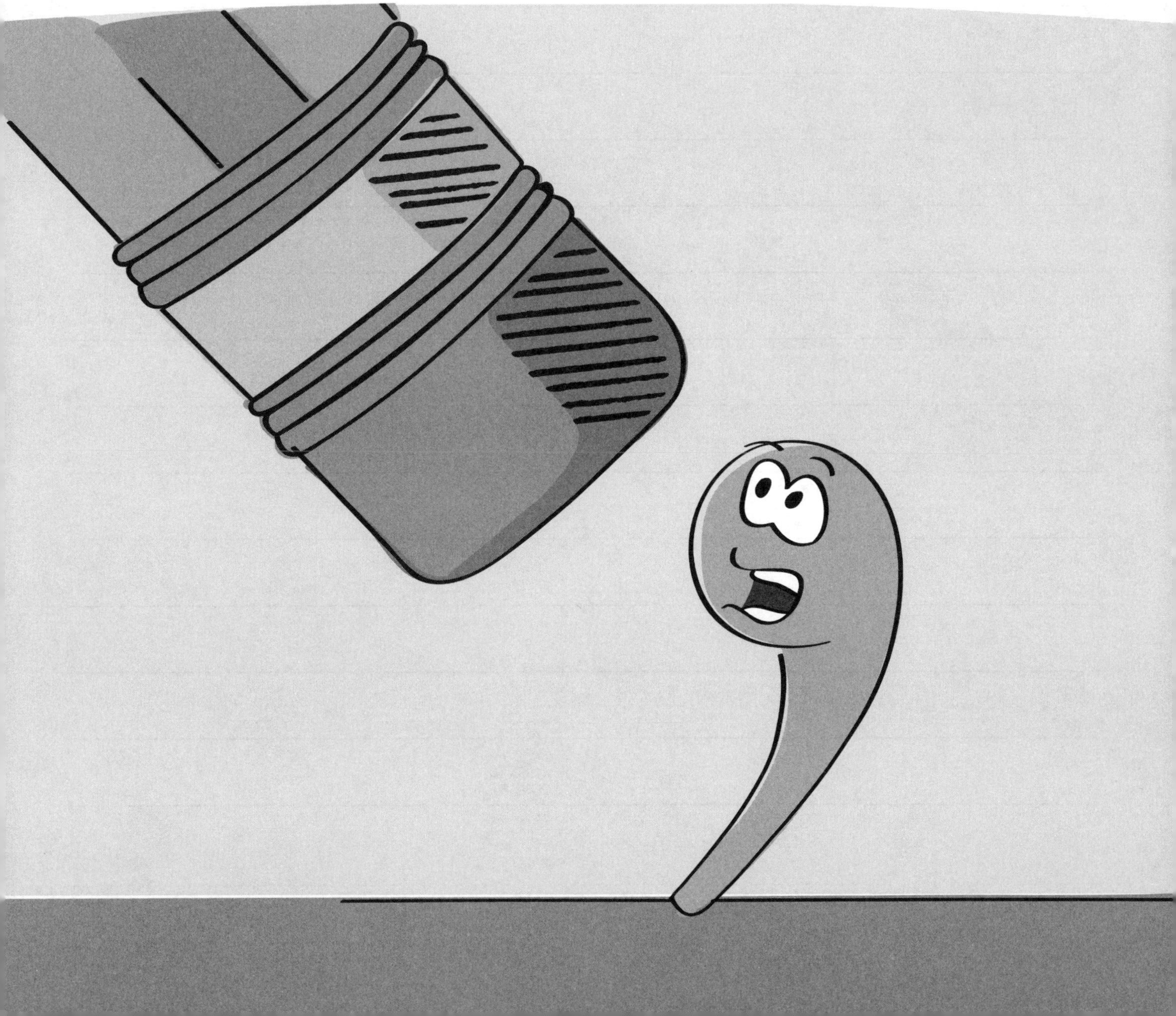

2.1 Entrance Ticket

Describe a time when an obstacle got in the way of something you were trying to accomplish. What steps did you take to remove the obstacle?

2.2 Learning Target

1. Recognize when to delete unnecessary commas

Self-Assessment

Circle the number that corresponds to your confidence level in your knowledge of this subject before beginning the lesson. A score of 1 means you are completely lost, and a score of 4 means you have mastered the skills. After you finish the lesson, return to the bottom of this page and circle your new confidence level to show your improvement.

Before Lesson

1 2 3 4

After Lesson

1 2 3 4

2.3.2 Deleting Commas

Comma Rule 1:

____

____

Comma Rule 2:

____

____

____

1. So, biologists decided, to dissect the mutated frogs themselves.

____

2. Growing up, on the beaches of Australia, Adrian Buchan would one day become a world-renowned surfer.

____

3. Athletes, typically, find, that getting enough sleep at night plays a huge role in their endurance.

____

English Tip

Go with the Flow: When you read, you should be able to go with the flow. There should be a normal rhythm and cadence to the writing. Remove commas that disrupt the flow of a sentence or confuse its meaning.

2.3.2 Deleting Commas

Suddenly he felt himself whirl round, and round—spinning like a top. The water, the banks, the forests, the now distant bridge, fort, and men all were commingled and blurred. Objects, were represented by their colors only; circular horizontal streaks of, color—that was all he saw. He had been caught in a vortex, and was being whirled on with a velocity of advance and gyration that made him giddy and sick. In a few moments he was flung upon, the gravel at the foot of the left bank of the stream—the southern bank—and behind a projecting point, which concealed him from his, enemies. The sudden arrest of his motion, the abrasion of one, of his hands on the gravel, restored him, and he wept with delight. He dug, his fingers into the sand, threw it over himself in handfuls, and audibly blessed it. It looked like diamonds, rubies, emeralds; he could think of nothing beautiful which it, did not resemble. The trees, upon the bank were giant garden plants; he noted a definite order in their arrangement, inhaled the fragrance, of their blooms. A strange roseate light shone through the spaces among their trunks and the wind, made in their branches the music of Aeolian, harps. He had no wish to perfect his escape—he was content to remain in that enchanting, spot until retaken.

Source: Bierce, Ambrose. "An Occurrence at Owl Creek Bridge." *Tales of Soldiers and Civilians*. San Francisco: San Francisco Examiner, 1890. N. pag. Project Gutenberg. 19 Mar. 2008. Web.

English Tip

When in Doubt, Leave It Out: The ACT English test measures your ability to recognize when commas included in the text do not need to be there. If you do not have a specific reason to keep it, leave it out.

2.4.1 Set One

It didn't take long, though for the grumpy Rottweiler to trot back to his bed to protect his mammoth-sized chew toy.

1. **A.** NO CHANGE
   B. take, long though,
   C. take long though
   D. take long, though,

In other words, the man equipped with the sword sharp enough, to slay a dragon, will save the kingdom.

2. **F.** NO CHANGE
   G. enough to slay a dragon
   H. enough, to slay a dragon
   J. enough to slay a dragon,

I'm afraid those of us, who ate at the Chinese buffet last night, will likely have an upset stomach.

3. **A.** NO CHANGE
   B. us who ate at the Chinese buffet, last night,
   C. us who ate at the Chinese buffet last night,
   D. us who ate at the Chinese buffet last night

END OF SET ONE

STOP! DO NOT GO ON TO THE NEXT PAGE UNTIL TOLD TO DO SO.

2.4.2 Set Two

In other words, the camp was outfitted with the emergency rations needed, to survive the blizzard, the hikers were soon to face.

4. **F.** NO CHANGE
   G. rations needed to survive the blizzard
   H. rations, needed to survive the blizzard
   J. rations needed to survive the blizzard,

Wearing athletic shoes, admittedly, sounds like a trivial issue to discuss in a dress code meeting.

5. **A.** NO CHANGE
   B. shoes, admittedly sounds
   C. shoes admittedly, sounds
   D. shoes admittedly sounds,

It took the athletic community many years to understand and publicly recognize that women were a force to be reckoned with in the sport of boxing.

6. **F.** NO CHANGE
   G. understand,
   H. understand:
   J. understand them

END OF SET TWO
STOP! DO NOT GO ON TO THE NEXT PAGE
UNTIL TOLD TO DO SO.

1 1

2.4.3 Set Three

Fans, hundreds of them lined up for blocks to see the arrival of the rapper.

7. A. NO CHANGE
   B. Fans hundreds of them
   C. Fans, hundreds, of them
   D. Fans, hundreds of them,

Even though most people like the idea of a quiet and seemingly peaceful baby, an infant who rarely cries often has a hidden illness that needs to be quickly diagnosed.

8. F. NO CHANGE
   G. hidden illness,
   H. hidden, illness
   J. hidden; illness,

The Road Runners Club of America; has a main office in Arlington, Virginia, with a beautiful view of the Potomac River.

9. A. NO CHANGE
   B. Club, of America
   C. Club of America
   D. Club of America,

END OF SET THREE
STOP! DO NOT GO ON TO THE NEXT PAGE
UNTIL TOLD TO DO SO.

2.4.4 Set Four

<u>Musicians, often, find</u> that best-selling albums need at least three months in production.

10. **F.** NO CHANGE
G. Musicians often find
H. Musicians often, find
J. Musicians, often find

At the same time, surrealist artists and expatriates emigrating from the <u>United States;</u> left a tangible influence on modern art in Europe.

11. **A.** NO CHANGE
B. United States
C. United States:
D. United States,

Air-conditioned <u>seating at the ballpark</u> and other stadiums helps fans stay cool during the hottest summer days.

12. **F.** NO CHANGE
G. seating, at the ballpark,
H. seating, at the ballpark
J. seating at the ballpark,

END OF SET FOUR
STOP! DO NOT GO ON TO THE NEXT PAGE UNTIL TOLD TO DO SO.

2.4.5 Set Five

It was late summer when my family and I arrived, at the vacation cottage, a quaint house on the edge of the lake.

13. **A.** NO CHANGE
    B. family, and I, arrived
    C. family and I arrived
    D. family, and I arrived

The two main types of cake are: the dense pound cake and the more airy sponge cake.

14. **F.** NO CHANGE
    G. cake are,
    H. cake, are
    J. cake are

However, all painters can appreciate the beauty of primary colors mixed with black in this graceful, but simple work of art.

15. **A.** NO CHANGE
    B. graceful
    C. graceful—
    D. graceful:

END OF SET FIVE

STOP! DO NOT GO ON TO THE NEXT PAGE UNTIL TOLD TO DO SO.

Sum It Up

Unnecessary Commas

When to use commas:

1. With conjunctions to connect two independent clauses
2. To separate items in a series
3. To set off parenthetical elements
4. After an introductory word or phase
5. To link two equal modifiers not joined by a conjunction

When to delete commas:

1. When the comma disrupts correct sentence structure
2. When the comma disrupts the sentence flow
3. When the comma confuses meaning

Tips and Techniques

Go with the Flow: When you read, you should be able to go with the flow. There should be a normal rhythm and cadence to the writing. Remove commas that disrupt the flow of a sentence or confuse its meaning.

When in Doubt, Leave It Out: The ACT English test measures your ability to recognize when commas included in the text do not need to be there. If you do not have a specific reason to keep it, leave it out.

Parenthetical Elements

Larry
fell in the hole.
, who is clumsy,

CAPTION:

3.1 Entrance Ticket

Select the best alternative to the underlined portion in each sentence below. If no change is necessary, select NO CHANGE.

<u>Social media, admittedly seems</u> like a rather inconsequential topic for the board of directors' meeting tomorrow.

1. A. NO CHANGE
   B. Social media, admittedly, seems
   C. Social media admittedly, seems
   D. Social media admittedly seems

Many <u>students, at Middleton Valley High School</u> take their lunch break away from campus, usually stopping at one of the nearby fast food restaurants.

2. F. NO CHANGE
   G. students at Middleton Valley High School,
   H. students at, Middleton Valley High School,
   J. students at Middleton Valley High School

A month <u>later, his son Tim,</u> made the varsity baseball team after training vigorously all summer.

3. A. NO CHANGE
   B. later, his son, Tim,
   C. later, his son, Tim
   D. later his son Tim,

3.2 Learning Targets

1. Know when independent and dependent clauses need commas

2. Identify essential information and non-essential information

Self-Assessment

Circle the number that corresponds to your confidence level in your knowledge of this subject before beginning the lesson. A score of 1 means you are completely lost, and a score of 4 means you have mastered the skills. After you finish the lesson, return to the bottom of this page and circle your new confidence level to show your improvement.

Before Lesson

1 2 3 4

After Lesson

1 2 3 4

3.3.1 Using Commas to Offset

- I failed the test, the most important one of the year, because I didn't study.
- My boyfriend picked me up, late as usual, to take me to the movie.
- Power was out everywhere, even at the hospital, after the storm hit.
- Swimming laps each morning, though, energized and strengthened him while he was recovering from the accident.

Comma Rule:

____

____

1. My cat Morton is hiding under the bed.
2. The surgery she needed however was dangerous and had some risks she didn't feel were worth taking.
3. Mrs. Little the school librarian showed me how to access online databases so I could do research for my term paper.
4. I saw my first sequoia an enormous redwood tree when I went on a roadtrip to California.

3.3.1 Using Commas to Offset

My grandmother however; has no pets because she has an allergy to all types of animal hair.

1. A. NO CHANGE
   B. grandmother; however,
   C. grandmother, however,
   D. grandmother, however

The following year, 1558, Mary died in an influenza epidemic, and Elizabeth, then twenty-four, assumed the throne of England.

2. F. NO CHANGE
   G. 1558, and
   H. 1558;
   J. 1558

Neither one, in my opinion possessed the leadership skills or the commitment necessary to be the club president.

3. A. NO CHANGE
   B. Neither one, in my opinion,
   C. Neither one in my opinion;
   D. Neither one in my opinion,

Ballads can be long or short, but most rely on varying verses that alternate with an unchanging refrain or, chorus, to tell a story.

4. F. NO CHANGE
   G. refrain, or chorus, to
   H. refrain or chorus to,
   J. refrain or, chorus to

English Tip

Keep Your Pencil Moving: If you are not sure whether you need to put commas around a word or phrase, cross out the word or phrase with your pencil. If the sentence is still complete and gets the same meaning across, you should put commas around the part you crossed out.

3.3.2 Essential and Nonessential Information

Three of us kids excitedly took our places in line for the roller coaster, but <u>Ray, being too young to ride</u> had to settle for an ice cream with Mom instead.

1. **A.** NO CHANGE
   B. Ray, being too young to ride,
   C. Ray, being too young, to ride
   D. Ray being too young to ride,

The names we had picked out in advance—Shadow, Scamp, and <u>Skip,</u> didn't seem to fit once we met the puppies in person.

2. **F.** NO CHANGE
   G. Skip—
   H. Skip:
   J. Skip

These days, with information so easily available via the <u>Internet; it's</u> easy to forget that library card catalogs were once the starting point for research projects.

3. **A.** NO CHANGE
   B. Internet, its
   C. Internet; its
   D. Internet, it's

3.3.2 Essential and Nonessential Information

These adherents of Sikhism, millions of whom live in the Punjab region of the Indian subcontinent—classify service in three forms: physical service, mental service, and material service.

○ Essential ○ Nonessential | Punctuation: ____

1. A. NO CHANGE
   B. Sikhism—
   C. Sikhism;
   D. Sikhism

Mrs. Zervoudakis, our next-door neighbor for many years never shared the recipe for her delicious baklava, preferring to keep it a family secret.

○ Essential ○ Nonessential | Punctuation: ____

2. F. NO CHANGE
   G. neighbor, for many years,
   H. neighbor for many years,
   J. neighbor, for many years

Franco Corelli, revered by opera lovers, appeared regularly with the Metropolitan Opera between 1961 and 1975.

○ Essential ○ Nonessential | Punctuation: ____

3. A. NO CHANGE
   B. Corelli, revered by opera lovers
   C. Corelli revered by opera lovers,
   D. Corelli revered by opera lovers

English Tip

Consistent, Clear, and Concise: Any time you are adding punctuation to a sentence, especially for parenthetical elements, make sure that it is consistent with the rest of the sentence, not just the underlined portion.

3.3.2 Essential and Nonessential Information

In 1946, British mathematician, Alan Turing presented a paper on what is now regarded as the first stored-program computer.

1. A. NO CHANGE
   B. mathematician Alan Turing,
   C. mathematician, Alan Turing,
   D. mathematician Alan Turing

Approximately 300 crew members from the U.S. Navy cruiser *Indianapolis* were rescued at sea after their ship went down on July 30, 1945.

2. F. NO CHANGE
   G. cruiser, *Indianapolis*;
   H. cruiser *Indianapolis*,
   J. cruiser, *Indianapolis*

The continued usage of several English words, coined in the early seventeenth century, can be directly attributed to the influence of Shakespeare's works on the spoken language.

3. A. NO CHANGE
   B. words, coined in the early seventeenth century
   C. words coined in the early seventeenth century,
   D. words coined in the early seventeenth century

On the first day of class, the professor emphasized that those students, who fall behind early in the semester, would have a hard time getting through the course.

4. F. NO CHANGE
   G. students who fall behind, early in the semester,
   H. students who fall behind early in the semester,
   J. students who fall behind early in the semester

English Tip

Consistent, Clear, and Concise: If you think a word or phrase is nonessential to the sentence, you should set it off with some form of punctuation. However, if it is necessary to make the sentence clear, you should not use any punctuation at all.

3.4.1 Set One

It took longer, though for me to realize that Spark needed quite a bit of training, as well as love and affection.

1. A. NO CHANGE
   B. took, longer though,
   C. took longer though,
   D. took longer, though,

Although Graham died in 1991, her namesake: the Martha Graham Dance Company—continues to serve as an innovative force in the world of contemporary dance.

2. F. NO CHANGE
   G. namesake,
   H. namesake—
   J. namesake

My siblings and I spent our summers at our grandparents' farm, where Grandpa's firefly hunting expeditions kept us up long past our bedtimes.

3. A. NO CHANGE
   B. kept us up long, past,
   C. kept us up, long past,
   D. kept us up, long, past

END OF SET ONE
STOP! DO NOT GO ON TO THE NEXT PAGE
UNTIL TOLD TO DO SO.

3.4.2 Set Two

Although parents found the code hard to distinguish, emoticons and acronyms became a <u>prevalent or, popular, language</u> among texting and instant-messaging teenagers.

4. **F.** NO CHANGE
   G. prevalent, or popular, language
   H. prevalent or popular,
   J. prevalent or, popular language

On the few occasions Missy ate vegetables, she liked them roasted or <u>fried rather, then</u> in the raw form her brother preferred.

5. **A.** NO CHANGE
   B. fried, rather then
   C. fried rather than
   D. fried rather, than

After his knee gave out during the last lap, Jake was motivated to finish the race by the <u>teammates, who ran alongside him,</u> to the finish line.

6. **F.** NO CHANGE
   G. teammates who, ran alongside him
   H. teammates, who ran alongside, him
   J. teammates who ran alongside him

END OF SET TWO
STOP! DO NOT GO ON TO THE NEXT PAGE
UNTIL TOLD TO DO SO.

3.4.3 Set Three

The dog seemed shy, like Jenna, herself but his tail burst into motion every time she came into view.

7. **A.** NO CHANGE
   B. Jenna, herself,
   C. Jenna herself,
   D. Jenna herself

Where Nicholas excelled at math and science, his younger brother Freddie preferred subjects that involved extensive reading and writing such as, history and English.

8. **F.** NO CHANGE
   G. writing; such as, history;
   H. writing, such as history
   J. writing such as history

Along with fellow, magician, Roy Horn, Siegfried performed for over a decade at the Mirage resort in Las Vegas.

9. **A.** NO CHANGE
   B. fellow magician,
   C. fellow, magician
   D. fellow magician

END OF SET THREE
STOP! DO NOT GO ON TO THE NEXT PAGE
UNTIL TOLD TO DO SO.

3.4.4 Set Four

In the same year, 1971, three artists of diverse ethnic backgrounds received national awards for their contributions to performance art, gaining large strides in the diversification of the medium.

10. F. NO CHANGE
    G. 1971, and
    H. 1971;
    J. 1971

Dozens of people, many of them hikers in the national park reported seeing large bear pawprints, hearing deep growling, and finding grizzly droppings along one of the major trails.

11. A. NO CHANGE
    B. people—many of them hikers in the national park—
    C. people; most of them hikers in the national park,
    D. people most of them having hiked in the national park

Civil engineer, Joseph Bazalgette was chosen to design the London underground sewage system.

12. F. NO CHANGE
    G. engineer—Joseph Bazalgette
    H. engineer Joseph Bazalgette,
    J. engineer Joseph Bazalgette

END OF SET FOUR
STOP! DO NOT GO ON TO THE NEXT PAGE UNTIL TOLD TO DO SO.

3.4.5 Set Five

At the university gym, students can volunteer for say, five hours of work at the reception desk per week, and in return, they receive a few hours of fitness class privileges.

13. A. NO CHANGE
    B. volunteer for, say
    C. volunteer, for say,
    D. volunteer for, say,

Even though my cousin, now the president of a major accounting firm struggled with math in school, she didn't give up on herself and was determined to earn a dual degree in mathematics and business.

14. F. NO CHANGE
    G. president, of a major accounting firm,
    H. president of a major accounting firm,
    J. president, of a major accounting firm

Harper Lee published her novel *To Kill a Mockingbird* in 1960 after a group of friends gave her a sum of money to support her work as a full-time writer.

15. A. NO CHANGE
    B. her, novel *To Kill a Mockingbird*, in 1960,
    C. her, novel, *To Kill a Mockingbird* in 1960,
    D. her novel: *To Kill a Mockingbird*, in 1960

END OF SET FIVE

STOP! DO NOT GO ON TO THE NEXT PAGE UNTIL TOLD TO DO SO.

Sum It Up

Parenthetical Elements

Parenthetical Elements
Words or phrases that are not essential to the meaning of a sentence

---

Parenthetical elements are always offset with two punctuation marks on either side:

two commas
two dashes
two parentheses

If an answer option leaves a parenthetical element set off with just one punctuation mark, you know it is wrong!

Tips and Techniques

Keep Your Pencil Moving: Cover up or cross out the portion you think may be nonessential and read the sentence to yourself without it. If the sentence is still complete and makes sense, you know the information is parenthetical.

Lesson 4

Pronoun-Antecedent Agreement

CAPTION:

4.1 Entrance Ticket

Write for five minutes on the following topic. Use complete sentences.

What did you do last weekend?

4.2 Learning Targets

1. Identify and correct pronoun-antecedent agreements

2. Strategize multiple ways to identify antecedents and create pronoun agreement

3. Revise sentences for clarity, including linking pronouns with antecedents

Self-Assessment

Circle the number that corresponds to your confidence level in your knowledge of this subject before beginning the lesson. A score of 1 means you are completely lost, and a score of 4 means you have mastered the skills. After you finish the lesson, return to the bottom of this page and circle your new confidence level to show your improvement.

Before Lesson

1 2 3 4

After Lesson

1 2 3 4

4.3.1 Pronoun–Antecedent Agreement

1. Rex buried the bone in the backyard next to his dog house. (masculine, singular, third person)

2. My mom is a nurse, but she prefers gardening to working any day. (feminine, singular, third person)

3. Early computers were large; some required whole rooms to be housed. (neutral, plural, third person)

---

1. A helmet from the German Army had found its way into the school; it was used as a prop for a history lesson.

antecedent: ____________________

pronoun: ____________________

gender: ____________________

number: ____________________

person: ____________________

2. Max found his guitar, the one he got from his parents.

antecedent: ____________________

pronoun: ____________________

gender: ____________________

number: ____________________

person: ____________________

4.3.1 Pronoun–Antecedent Agreement

3. Michael Jordan, the greatest basketball player to ever live, always played his best when needed.

antecedent: ______________________________

pronoun: ______________________________

gender: ______________________________

number: ______________________________

person: ______________________________

In each sentence, circle the antecedent and underline the pronoun that agrees with it.

1. Roger is coming for dinner tonight; please do not embarrass him.

2. Sierra is staying up late to be one of the first customers in the store on Black Friday; she is either truly dedicated or nuts.

3. In the 1990s, there had been rumors in Major League Baseball of steroid use, but it took years for the journalists and fans to realize just how many players were involved.

4.3.2 Types of Pronouns

Type	What They Do	Examples
Personal		I, you, he, she, it, we, they
Possessive	Show ownership	
Indefinite		All, anyone, many, more, some
Demonstrative	Show whether something is close or far away	
Reflexive		Myself, himself, herself, ourselves

4.3.2 Types of Pronouns

Type	Example Sentence
Personal	
Possessive	
Indefinite	
Demonstrative	
Reflexive	

English Tip

The Big Three: Any time you are dealing with pronouns and antecedents, be sure they agree in gender, number, and person.

4.3.3 Ambiguity

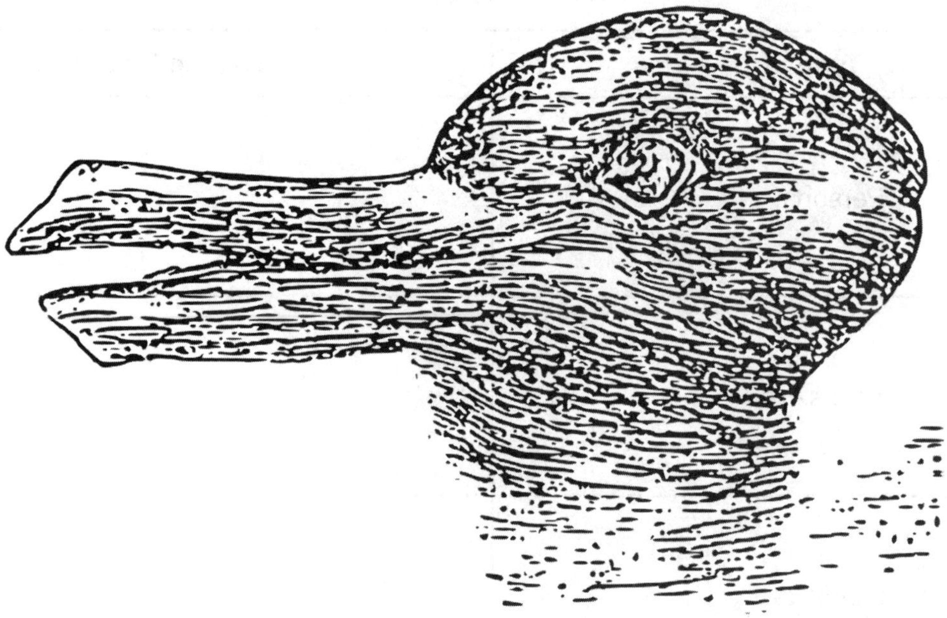

1. Elizabeth and Esther are going down to the boat this afternoon. It is bright red and easy to recognize.

2. I felt bad about walking away from the cat, but I'm allergic. Besides, who knows if it has fleas?

3. The donut shop was running a special on chocolate-covered éclairs. The soccer team rushed over after school to buy them.

4. The politician gave a lengthy speech on the importance of holding more frequent town assemblies with all representatives present. The audience, however, soon tired of listening to him.

5. It is unlikely that the new debate team won last week's competition. That is typically the most difficult one of the season.

English Tip

Consistent, Clear, and Concise: Anytime you are working with pronouns, remember the three C's. Choose the answer that wastes no words (concise), eliminates any ambiguity (clear), and has all pronouns agreeing with their antecedents (consistent).

4.3.3 Ambiguity

1. They say the ACT considers vague pronouns to be grammatically incorrect.

 ____

2. He gave him money for the completed job.

 ____

3. I need to speak with the head supervisor; they never seem to help, however.

 ____

4. The teacher gave the student her notes.

 ____

5. Tyrone's computer, which has a new monitor, is expensive. It is not working properly.

 ____

6. The mailman had a letter for Mary, but he couldn't make it to the door because he was barking very loudly.

 ____

4.3.4 Pronoun–Antecedent Pyramid Game

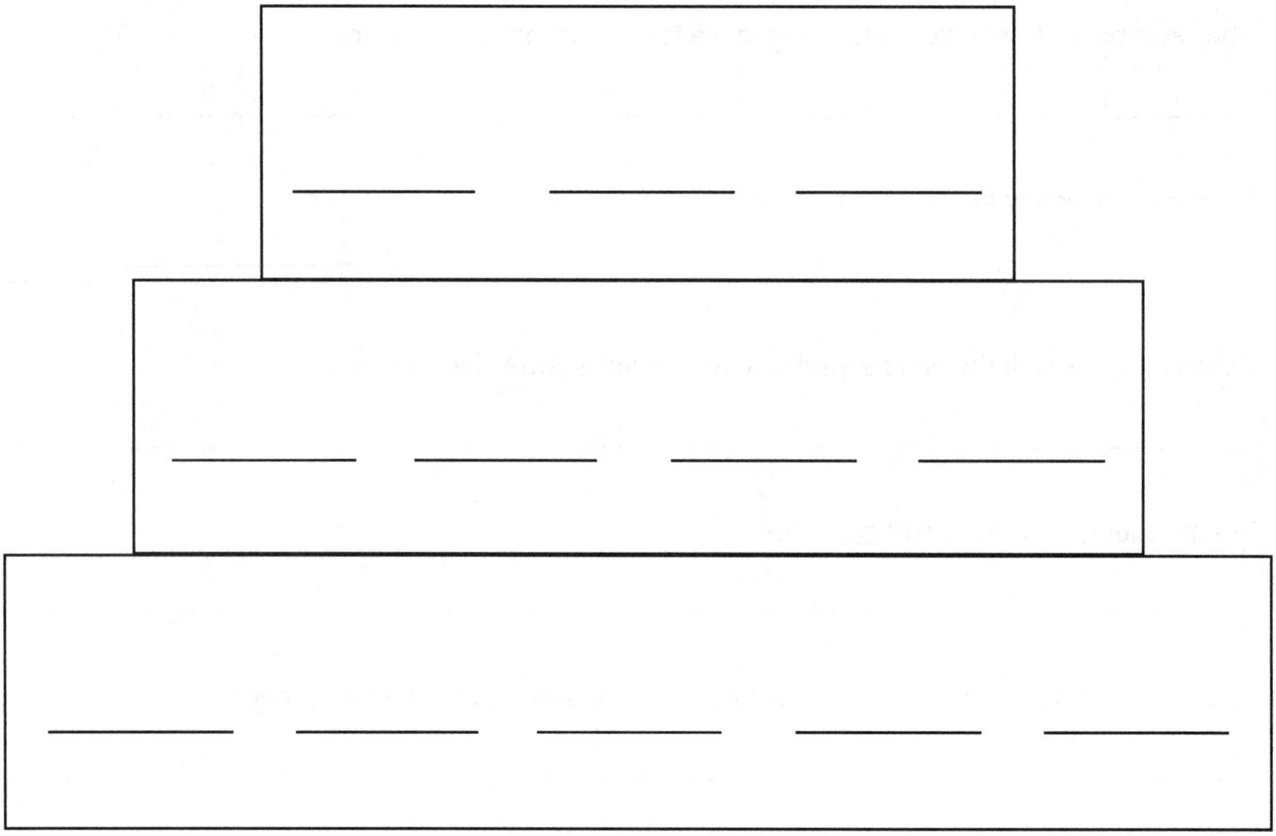

4.4.1 Set One

The two often discussed their mutual hobby. After talking about Pierre's books, Sharon then received <u>feedback on their</u> own work.

1. A. NO CHANGE
   B. feedback on his
   C. his feedback on her
   D. feedback on it

On rainy days I love to watch horror movies, but <u>one was still</u> scared to death by the time they are over.

2. F. NO CHANGE
   G. one still is
   H. you still are
   J. I am still

Jared and I leave home at eight o'clock sharp, heading out on our long-awaited vacation to California. <u>He or she drives</u> so far that the highway seems like it must be infinite.

3. A. NO CHANGE
   B. We drive
   C. You drive
   D. People drive

END OF SET ONE
STOP! DO NOT GO ON TO THE NEXT PAGE UNTIL TOLD TO DO SO.

4.4.2 Set Two

Before bathing regularly became the norm, strong perfume was used to mask <u>its</u> body odor.

4. **F.** NO CHANGE
   G. one's
   H. their
   J. it's

In 1894, <u>alarmed about being endangered,</u> John F. Lacey sponsored legislation aimed at protecting Yellowstone National Park from poachers, stating firmly, "Prompt action is necessary, or this last remaining herd of buffalo will be destroyed."

5. **A.** NO CHANGE
   B. alarmed that the wildlife was endangered,
   C. in the face of endangerment,
   D. alarmed and endangered,

Her bright, sunny smile always causes many to return it, <u>having chosen</u> to comfort the little ones in her preschool classroom.

6. **F.** NO CHANGE
   G. being creative enough
   H. sometimes deciding
   J. particularly when she uses it

END OF SET TWO
STOP! DO NOT GO ON TO THE NEXT PAGE
UNTIL TOLD TO DO SO.

4.4.3 Set Three

One must first understand the plight of industrial laborers in 1890s Chicago before one can grasp the particular struggle of <u>that</u> desperate, unlucky factory workers—the Dobrevas.

7. **A.** NO CHANGE
   B. those
   C. a lot of
   D. one of the

Mario is thirteen, living in that space of time when <u>they</u> project a solid understanding of the way the world works but have yet to really experience anything of adult life, such as loss, heartache, and speeding tickets.

8. **F.** NO CHANGE
   G. young people
   H. he
   J. some of them

<u>Their</u> culture became apparent when our star point guard, who had recently come back from an ankle injury, was forced to play the entire game.

9. **A.** NO CHANGE
   B. One's
   C. Its
   D. This

END OF SET THREE

STOP! DO NOT GO ON TO THE NEXT PAGE UNTIL TOLD TO DO SO.

4.4.4 Set Four

Every once in a while, one gardener or another would kneel as if you were praying as he tended the colorful flower garden.

10. A. NO CHANGE
    B. when it was bent
    C. in the posture that is
    D. in the position of someone

Being a city dweller, I often take the subway to work, but sometimes I take the bus to enjoy the sights as one of its passengers.

11. A. NO CHANGE
    B. her
    C. their
    D. there

During the 1960s, many people protested the war, but that took many years of protesting, lobbying, and voting to actually end the conflict.

12. F. NO CHANGE
    G. it
    H. they
    J. which

END OF SET FOUR

STOP! DO NOT GO ON TO THE NEXT PAGE UNTIL TOLD TO DO SO.

1 ■ ■ ■ ■ ■ ■ ■ ■ ■ 1

4.4.5 Set Five

Once you have grasped a language, the challenge is gone, and you must hunt for a new language to master.

13. **A.** NO CHANGE
B. you then hunted
C. one then hunts
D. one must hunt

On rainy days I love to watch horror movies, but one was still scared to death by the time they are over.

14. **F.** NO CHANGE
G. one still is
H. you still are
J. I am still

The second day, the storm clouds brought heavy winds and rain, and the pair drifted at least 100 miles over the next four nights.

15. Which of the following alternatives to the underlined portion would be LEAST acceptable?
A. the two
B. Johnson and Patterson
C. the men
D. these

END OF SET FIVE
STOP! DO NOT GO ON TO THE NEXT PAGE
UNTIL TOLD TO DO SO.

Sum It Up

Pronoun-Antecedent Agreement

Antecedent
The noun that the pronoun replaces

Pronoun
A word that replaces a previously mentioned noun

Person
Refers to the point of view used in writing

Tips and Techniques

Consistent, Clear, and Concise: Keep pronouns clear, and don't be afraid to drop the pronoun if the sentence is too confusing.

The Big Three: Focus on gender, number, and person when using pronouns and antecedents.

Apostrophes

CAPTION:

5.1 Entrance Ticket

Select the best alternative to the underlined portion in each section below. If no change is necessary, select NO CHANGE.

Salvador Dali, a painter who lived from 1904 to 1989, was <u>one of Spains</u> most celebrated artists.

1. **A.** NO CHANGE
B. one, of Spain's
C. one, of Spains
D. one of Spain's

On the afternoon of December 1, 1955, Rosa Parks refused to give up her seat on a bus after a hard <u>days</u> work.

2. **F.** NO CHANGE
G. days'
H. day's
J. days's

Many of them tasted the salted caramel—one of the <u>company's fastest-selling</u> flavors.

3. **A.** NO CHANGE
B. company's fastly selling
C. companies fastest-selling
D. companies' fastest-selling

5.2 Learning Targets

1. Delete apostrophes used incorrectly when forming plural nouns

2. Use apostrophes correctly to form possessives

Self-Assessment

Circle the number that corresponds to your confidence level in your knowledge of this subject before beginning the lesson. A score of 1 means you are completely lost, and a score of 4 means you have mastered the skills. After you finish the lesson, return to the bottom of this page and circle your new confidence level to show your improvement.

Before Lesson

1 2 3 4

After Lesson

1 2 3 4

5.3.1 Apostrophe Rules

5.3.1 Apostrophe Rules

1. The bikes tires were destroyed when I ran over the nails.

2. The congressman was a firm believer in the peoples power to choose.

3. The classs projects were displayed in the hallway.

4. The childrens play was enjoyed by everyone.

5. The leaves yellow and green colors were wonderful to see.

6. Both bananas peels were brown.

English Tip

The "Of Test": Many times you can use the "of test" to determine if an apostrophe is needed to show possession. "The horse's hooves" is the same as saying "the hooves of the horse." If you can rearrange the words using "of," you know you're dealing with the possessive and may need an apostrophe!

5.3.1 Apostrophe Rules

I remember eating ice-cold watermelon on my <u>neighbors</u> swing; their backyard was my favorite spot in the whole town.

1. **A.** NO CHANGE
   B. neighbors'
   C. neighbor's
   D. neighbors's

He left the building and came out into the large, empty parking lot at the <u>sidewalks</u> end.

2. **F.** NO CHANGE
   G. sidewalk's
   H. sidewalks'
   J. sidewalks's

<u>Explanation's</u> were put forth by some of the reporters who had gathered, but the evidence at the crime scene didn't support any of their ideas. "Something is missing," Detective Peralta thought, and he was determined to find out what it was.

3. **A.** NO CHANGE
   B. Explanations
   C. Explanations'
   D. Explanation

5.3.2 Irregular Nouns and Apostrophes

1. ____

____

2. ____

____

3. ____

____

1. The __________ homes were all destroyed in the tornado.
2. The __________ most prized possession was stolen during the break-in.
3. All the __________ are joining us for the awards ceremony.
4. We have the highest scoring school district among all the ________ found south of the Mason-Dixon line.
5. There are good places for our __________ children to play.
6. The finish line was situated under the __________ famous monument.
7. Her __________ first steps were caught on tape.
8. The store sold the __________ shoes in the back.
9. With all the __________ napping at the same time, it was a quiet and peaceful afternoon.

5.4.1 Set One

I exited the trolley and walked up the steep, winding incline to the tourist shop at the boulevards end.

1. **A.** NO CHANGE
   B. boulevard's
   C. boulevards'
   D. boulevards's

The contract's terms states that the singer, escorted by a jazz band, must wear a Mardi Gras-inspired costume and carry a purple-frilled parasol along the two-mile parade.

2. **F.** NO CHANGE
   G. contracts terms
   H. contracts's terms
   J. contracts' terms

When Kevin was thirteen, he purchased both Tony Aliva's and Steve Ruffing's skateboard's for his birthday, using the money his Aunt Silvia sent to him for his birthday.

3. **A.** NO CHANGE
   B. skateboards
   C. skateboards'
   D. skateboards,

END OF SET ONE
STOP! DO NOT GO ON TO THE NEXT PAGE
UNTIL TOLD TO DO SO.

1 ■ ■ ■ ■ ■ ■ ■ ■ ■ 1

5.4.2 Set Two

A childhood nickname can cast a shadow over a persons family name.

4. **F.** NO CHANGE
   G. a person's
   H. an individuals
   J. an individuals'

After school, Susan helped Shaun change the tire of his parents car before he dropped her off at home.

5. **A.** NO CHANGE
   B. his parents'
   C. Shaun's parents
   D. Shauns parents'

Samara said that at the fair this weekend, there will definitely be, pig's squealing, cows mooing, and geese honking.

6. **F.** NO CHANGE
   G. be pig's
   H. be, pigs
   J. be pigs

END OF SET TWO
STOP! DO NOT GO ON TO THE NEXT PAGE
UNTIL TOLD TO DO SO.

5.4.3 Set Three

Upon hearing the news of the mayor's choice for city dog catcher, the citys residents took up a petition to show their disapproval.

7. A. NO CHANGE
   B. cities
   C. cities'
   D. city's

I was convinced that people today would not appreciate the conservation of the old structures, barns, gas stations, and homes that one finds on a lazy Sunday afternoon when driving around the county's dusty, backroads.

8. F. NO CHANGE
   G. counties dusty,
   H. counties dusty
   J. county's dusty

Torch lights near the actors' feet, lit up the stage such that we could see their expressions of pain, anger, and joy.

9. A. NO CHANGE
   B. actors' feet
   C. actors feet,
   D. actors feet

END OF SET THREE

STOP! DO NOT GO ON TO THE NEXT PAGE UNTIL TOLD TO DO SO.

5.4.4 Set Four

She had even drawn several sketches that depicted the butterflies, some making lazy circles amongst the flowers, some flitting in front of the <u>boy's faces</u>.

10. **F.** NO CHANGE
G. boys' faces
H. boys faces
J. boys face's

<u>Puppies</u> first attempts at navigating stairs produce excited responses from owners, who stimulate and assist the animals by placing them two steps from the bottom to make the journey seem less daunting.

11. **A.** NO CHANGE
B. Puppy's
C. Puppys
D. Puppies'

We design the frosting pattern on the <u>cake's tiers</u> layer by layer.

12. **F.** NO CHANGE
G. cakes tiers,
H. cakes tiers
J. tier's for the cake,

END OF SET FOUR
STOP! DO NOT GO ON TO THE NEXT PAGE
UNTIL TOLD TO DO SO.

5.4.5 Set Five

When Jennae's sister turned sixteen, Jennae gave her both Led Zeppelin's and The Smiths' <u>album's</u> for her birthday, and the sisters listened to them for hours on end.

13. **A.** NO CHANGE
B. albums
C. albums'
D. albums,

By the end of the day, <u>Jacksonville's students</u> had collected only seventy-five signatures on their petition.

14. **F.** NO CHANGE
G. Jacksonville's student's
H. Jacksonvilles student's
J. Jacksonvilles students

To save time and still meet their <u>customer's needs,</u> butchers began trimming the fat and removing bones from cuts of meat.

15. **A.** NO CHANGE
B. needs' of the customers,
C. customers' needs,
D. customers needs,

END OF SET FIVE
STOP! DO NOT GO ON TO THE NEXT PAGE
UNTIL TOLD TO DO SO.

Sum It Up

Apostrophes

A singular common noun with no *s* on the end – add *'s*

A singular common noun with an *s* on the end – add *'s*

A plural common noun with no *s* on the end – add *'s*

A plural common noun with an *s* on the end – only add *'*

Tips and Techniques

The "Of Test": Many times you can use the "of test" to determine if an apostrophe is needed to show possession. If you can rerrange the words using "of," you know you're dealing with the possessive and may need an apostrophe!

Lesson 6

Confusing Pairs

CAPTION:

6.1 Entrance Ticket

Choose the correct words to use in the sentences below.

1. Every laptop comes equipped with its / it's own username and password.

2. I'll make the invitations, but who's / whose going to mail them?

3. Elephants stay with their / there young for almost 16 years.

4. Its / It's so hot out there / their, so I vote we stay home and watch Netflix.

6.2 Learning Targets

1. Correctly identify confusing pairs in various contexts

2. Recognize proper pronouns used for possession

Self-Assessment

Circle the number that corresponds to your confidence level in your knowledge of this subject before beginning the lesson. A score of 1 means you are completely lost, and a score of 4 means you have mastered the skills. After you finish the lesson, return to the bottom of this page and circle your new confidence level to show your improvement.

Before Lesson

1 2 3 4

After Lesson

1 2 3 4

6.3.1 It's vs. Its

1. The butterfly fluttered it's / its wings and flew away.

2. The weather is returning to it's / its pattern of raining all day long.

3. It's / Its my lifelong dream to fly.

4. It's / Its raining again.

5. It's / Its only on Fridays that the cafeteria serves pizza.

6. It's / Its mangy fur was so dirty, I didn't want to touch the dog.

7. It's / Its likely the dog doesn't want it's / its owner to know it was digging in my flowerbed.

English Tip

Its' doesn't mean anything. It's not a real word. ***Its' is always wrong!*** If you see ***its'*** as an answer choice, cross it off right away. This narrows down your options and might make the right answer more obvious.

6.3.2 Their, There, Who's, and Whose

1. Without a president, ________ isn't a way the club can continue.

2. I told the unruly boys that if they can't stay out of detention, it's ________ own fault and not the teacher's.

3. That red barn over ________ has been standing for at least a century.

4. Because my boutique hasn't sold many clothes, ________ suggestion was that I close.

5. Hank threw his books here and his jacket over ________, and he tracked mud everywhere.

6. All of my teachers think that ________ classes are more important than my leisure time.

7. From the hotel balcony, Molly and Nicole watched ________ car get towed.

English Tip

If you are not sure what is being tested by an English question, make a habit of reviewing the answer choices. If the choices change between *their* and *there*, ask yourself, "Could this be about a possession or a place?" If it is about an object or a thing that is owned, choose *their*. If it is about a place or location, choose *there*.

6.4.1 Set One

Its not easy growing up in a world where perspectives shift constantly and information bombards the senses; one hardly knows what to think of as right or wrong.

1. **A.** NO CHANGE
   B. It's
   C. Its'
   D. That's

In actuality, the association could not defend it's inane argument that the puppy compromised the child's safety.

2. **F.** NO CHANGE
   G. they are
   H. it is
   J. its

Selma High School simultaneously gives back to the community and raises funds for its field trips by organizing community activities throughout the year in exchange for small donations.

3. **A.** NO CHANGE
   B. it's
   C. its'
   D. its's

END OF SET ONE
STOP! DO NOT GO ON TO THE NEXT PAGE
UNTIL TOLD TO DO SO.

1 ■ ■ ■ ■ ■ ■ ■ ■ ■ 1

6.4.2 Set Two

The snake now has a freshly grown skin. Each month, it will <u>shed it's old, worn</u> skin and regrow a new one, protecting it from parasites and injuries.

4. **F.** NO CHANGE
   G. sheds its' old, worn
   H. have shed it's old, worn
   J. shed its old, worn

This all changed in the late 1960s, when Apollo 11 succeeded in <u>it's</u> mission of landing the first humans on the moon.

5. **A.** NO CHANGE
   B. there
   C. its
   D. its'

At times, the wind blew through the trees, carrying on <u>its' chilling</u> gusts the scents of the nearby ocean.

6. **F.** NO CHANGE
   G. it's chillier
   H. its chilling
   J. it's chilling

END OF SET TWO

STOP! DO NOT GO ON TO THE NEXT PAGE
UNTIL TOLD TO DO SO.

6.4.3 Set Three

Despite the fact that he had clearly requested an iced coffee earlier, they're was no convincing the barista that his order was correct.

7. **A.** NO CHANGE
   B. there
   C. but there
   D. their

A girl thats waiting for the bus to arrive finds herself continuously looking down at her watch to check the time. The bus is incredibly late, and she cannot fathom why.

8. **F.** NO CHANGE
   G. is
   H. whose
   J. who's

A young boy, whose holding an empty bronze shell casing, watches somberly as a massive train lurches off into the distant plains.

9. **A.** NO CHANGE
   B. thats
   C. is
   D. who's

END OF SET THREE
STOP! DO NOT GO ON TO THE NEXT PAGE
UNTIL TOLD TO DO SO.

6.4.4 Set Four

Now that twenty-first century identity has had time to develop, we notice a distinct lack of a one-size-fits-all look—the hipsters might like there pants tight-fitting and brightly toned, while the preps prefer a muted, straight cut.

10. **F.** NO CHANGE
    G. his or her
    H. their
    J. they're

The bond between two good friends are strengthened by there similarities, differences, and all of the idiosyncrasies that make them both individuals and companions.

11. **A.** NO CHANGE
    B. are strengthened by their
    C. is strengthened by there
    D. is strengthened by their

This is a town that's main attraction is a giant statue of Albert Einstein peacefully relaxing on a set of stone steps, his most recognizable equation displayed prominently on a pad of paper.

12. **F.** NO CHANGE
    G. who's
    H. whose
    J. that has a

END OF SET FOUR

STOP! DO NOT GO ON TO THE NEXT PAGE UNTIL TOLD TO DO SO.

6.4.5 Set Five

The primary philosophy among professors of law <u>involves their</u> utilization of the Socratic Method, teaching by asking questions rather than giving detailed lectures.

13. **A.** NO CHANGE
    B. involves they're
    C. involves there
    D. involves its

It is important to recognize the amiability of an organization <u>who's</u> only pursuit is making the lives of the downtrodden just a little bit better. Each movement toward making our world a better place, no matter how small, is a move worth making.

14. **F.** NO CHANGE
    G. whose
    H. that's
    J. that the

These days, our world is full of diversity. People have developed <u>their</u> own unique sense of identity, style, and fashion instead of attempting to conform into a single cultural norm.

15. **A.** NO CHANGE
    B. one's
    C. there
    D. they're

END OF SET FIVE

STOP! DO NOT GO ON TO THE NEXT PAGE
UNTIL TOLD TO DO SO.

Sum It Up

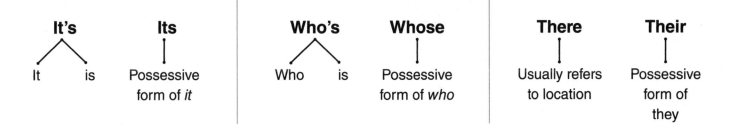

Confusing Pairs

It's	**Its**	**Who's**	**Whose**	**There**	**Their**
It + is	Possessive form of *it*	Who + is	Possessive form of *who*	Usually refers to location	Possessive form of they

Remember *there* has **here** in it, which refers to location. *Their* has **heir** in it, which refers to possessions.

Break the contraction into *it is* or *who is* to see if *it's* or *who's* is correct.

Subject–Verb Agreement

CAPTION:

7.1 Entrance Ticket

Select the best alternative to the underlined portion in each section below. If no change is necessary, select NO CHANGE.

What happens to a memory when <u>it isn't</u> actively being thought about?

1. **A.** NO CHANGE
   B. they're not
   C. they aren't
   D. its not

In the field of transportation, aerodynamics <u>may</u> had a large effect on future developments.

2. **F.** NO CHANGE
   G. could of
   H. have
   J. has

Not one of the many furry animals at the zoo with stripes <u>were a</u> tiger.

3. **A.** NO CHANGE
   B. was a
   C. were an actual
   D. would have been an actual

7.2 Learning Target

1. Ensure a variety of subject–verb agreement, whether it's straightforward or in more challenging situations

Self-Assessment

Circle the number that corresponds to your confidence level in your knowledge of this subject before beginning the lesson. A score of 1 means you are completely lost, and a score of 4 means you have mastered the skills. After you finish the lesson, return to the bottom of this page and circle your new confidence level to show your improvement.

Before Lesson

1 2 3 4

After Lesson

1 2 3 4

7.3.1 Hidden Subjects

1. The moon is shining brightly.

2. After the meeting finished, the lawyer went to lunch.

3. One of my cats, stuck in the tree, is really in need of my help.

4. The answers, given in Spanish and pronounced carefully, failed to impress the teacher.

5. Since they had left the camp, the scouts, under great stress and forced to find food in the woods, looked for a place to spend the night.

Subject–Verb Agreement Rule 1:

Subject–Verb Agreement Rule 2:

7.3.1 Hidden Subjects

The musicians at our club is kept busy throughout the day with all sorts of responsibilities.

1. **A.** NO CHANGE
   B. keeps
   C. are kept
   D. has been keeping

Last Friday, a book of poems were delivered to my house as an early birthday gift from my mother.

2. **F.** NO CHANGE
   G. were being
   H. was
   J. are

Medications are available that searches for and then destroys cancer cells.

3. **A.** NO CHANGE
   B. searches for and destroys
   C. search for and destroys
   D. search for and destroy

7.3.1 Hidden Subjects

<u>One of the liveliest</u> forms of entertainment to develop in recent years is the flash mob.

4. **F.** NO CHANGE
   G. One of the most liveliest
   H. The most lively
   J. The most liveliest

In the middle of the room <u>sits</u> toy bins filled with dolls, trucks, and dinosaurs.

5. **A.** NO CHANGE
   B. is sitting
   C. sets
   D. sit

What was once hidden away in the shadows <u>are</u> now seen in the light of day.

6. **F.** NO CHANGE
   G. is
   H. were
   J. have been

English Tip

Too Much Information: Most sentences have more information than you actually need to correct subject-verb agreement. Scratch through modifiers (like adjectives, adverbs, and prepositional phrases) to rid yourself of TMI.

7.3.2 Difficult Nouns

1. The team is practicing / are practicing this afternoon.

2. None of the students turn / turns in their assignments late.

3. Everybody tries / try the new food.

4. Our staff works / work hard to meet deadlines.

5. Everything is / are okay in the end.

6. All of the girls wants / want to make the squad.

7. The audience cheers / cheer for the speaker.

8. Most businesses is / are customer friendly.

English Tip

Consistent, Clear, and Concise: The most important rule to remember for subjects and verbs is that they have to be consistent with each other. Remember to be careful when you are facing collective nouns or other tricky nouns such as *each* and *all*.

1 ■ ■ ■ ■ ■ ■ ■ ■ ■ 1

7.4.1 Set One

The color scheme of the various canvases create a harmonious blend of light and dark landscapes.

1. **A.** NO CHANGE
   B. have the effect of creating
   C. are intended to create
   D. creates

A flowing waterfall crashes against the rocks, shimmering stones rustle on the river bottom, and the sun glisten off the sparkling water.

2. **F.** NO CHANGE
   G. glistening
   H. has glistened
   J. glistens

His efforts to boost sales have been praised by upper management, who admired his strong work ethic and determination.

3. **A.** NO CHANGE
   B. has been
   C. was
   D. would have been

END OF SET ONE

STOP! DO NOT GO ON TO THE NEXT PAGE UNTIL TOLD TO DO SO.

---

1 ■ ■ ■ ■ ■ ■ ■ ■ ■ 1

7.4.2 Set Two

What was once found only in science fiction <u>are</u> now part of our everyday lives.

4. F. NO CHANGE
   G. have been
   H. were
   J. is

These days, with people traveling all over the world in mere weeks, it's easy to forget that at one point traveling the world <u>were</u> rare.

5. A. NO CHANGE
   B. have been
   C. are
   D. was

Barking, the sound most often associated with dogs, <u>by themselves tell</u> us much about the state of mind of an animal.

6. F. NO CHANGE
   G. on themselves tell
   H. on itself tells
   J. by itself tells

END OF SET TWO

STOP! DO NOT GO ON TO THE NEXT PAGE UNTIL TOLD TO DO SO.

7.4.3 Set Three

Some Japanese women having viewed the binding of feet as symbolic of their history of limited human rights.

7. A. NO CHANGE
   B. view
   C. views
   D. has viewed

Nearly every piece of music that is played at the club include someone singing loudly.

8. F. NO CHANGE
   G. include somebody
   H. includes someone
   J. includes them

Not one of the children running around the brightly colored slides and ropes were a friend of my sister.

9. A. NO CHANGE
   B. was a
   C. was an actual
   D. would have been an actual

END OF SET THREE
STOP! DO NOT GO ON TO THE NEXT PAGE
UNTIL TOLD TO DO SO.

7.4.4 Set Four

Almost every ski shop in Colorado <u>have skis designed</u> for deep powder and back country skiing.

10. **F.** NO CHANGE
    G. have skis and designed
    H. has skis designed
    J. have skis that designed

<u>One of the slowest</u> methods of cooking that still results in deep flavors and satisfying tastes is roasting.

11. **A.** NO CHANGE
    B. One of the most slowest
    C. The most slow
    D. The slowest

Such endorsement of women's contributions <u>were to be</u> the turning point in scientific and technological advances.

12. **F.** NO CHANGE
    G. if it were
    H. was
    J. if it was

END OF SET FOUR

STOP! DO NOT GO ON TO THE NEXT PAGE UNTIL TOLD TO DO SO.

1 ■ ■ ■ ■ ■ ■ ■ ■ ■ 1

7.4.5 Set Five

His photos of famous landmarks <u>includes</u> Yellowstone, the Grand Canyon, and the Rocky Mountains.

13. **A.** NO CHANGE
B. does include
C. including
D. include

When sweat from an increase in heart rate and blood pressure <u>occur</u>, the body is able to cool down.

14. **F.** NO CHANGE
G. occurs
H. are occurring
J. happen

When I visited the beach the next year, I noticed for the first time what a <u>massive variety of shells was</u> on the shore.

15. **A.** NO CHANGE
B. massive variety of shells were
C. massive variety, of shells was
D. massive variety of shells

END OF SET FIVE
STOP! DO NOT GO ON TO THE NEXT PAGE
UNTIL TOLD TO DO SO.

Sum It Up

Subject–Verb Agreement

Subject
A person, place, or thing

Verb
Describes an action, state, or occurrence

Linking Verb
Connects the subject with information about the subject, such as a condition or relationship; does not show any action but links the subject with the rest of the sentence

---

Action Verb
Specifically describes what the subject of the sentence is doing; expresses physical or mental action

Tips and Techniques

Process of Elimination: Once you know whether the subject is singular or plural, eliminate any verbs that don't match it.

Consistent, Clear, and Concise: Keep the subject and verb consistent in number.

Lesson 8

Identify Purpose

CAPTION:

8.1 Entrance Ticket

Answer the following questions.

1. What is pronounced as a single letter, written with three letters, and most animals have two of them?

---

2. A man builds a rectangular house. All sides of the house are exposed to the south. A huge bear walks by. What color is the bear? Why?

---

3. What is not inside or outside a house, yet no house would be complete without it?

---

4. A woman gives a beggar fifty cents. The woman is the beggar's sister, but the beggar is not the woman's brother. How can this be?

8.2 Learning Targets

1. Discern the main idea of a paragraph

2. Examine how each sentence functions in a good paragraph

3. Determine the best addition or deletion to a paragraph

Self-Assessment

Circle the number that corresponds to your confidence level in your knowledge of this subject before beginning the lesson. A score of 1 means you are completely lost, and a score of 4 means you have mastered the skills. After you finish the lesson, return to the bottom of this page and circle your new confidence level to show your improvement.

Before Lesson

1 2 3 4

After Lesson

1 2 3 4

8.3.1 Getting the Gist

"You always carry a football," my daughter casually mentions. "Just put it down."

I have this conversation fairly regularly—embarrassedly laying down a football or similar object. I am the sort of person who cradles a throw pillow like a football, even at a neighbor's home. This is not a purposeful habit, just an unconscious tendency to treat things like a football.

Possibly this is because I'm a football player, and I've always felt the most comfortable with a football in my hands. I usually have a football in my gym bag or backpack. I am just more relaxed knowing I have a football nearby. Who knows if a pickup game will suddenly start?

Maybe I'm afraid an old fan will come by, desiring an autograph, and I'll be unable to please them. You can always sign a scrap of paper, a random article of clothing, or even their arm, but without a true memento to give them, I feel ill-prepared to meet my fans.

Unsurprisingly, footballs are also seen scattered throughout my home. It's as though each winning ball gathered of its own volition on my shelves. Although I don't believe I have yet lost my will to play the game at every chance I get, the existence of these footballs represents my enduring concern that I someday will.

My collecting habit, like many habits, comes with some undesirable side effects. The embarrassment at being mocked for continually cradling objects isn't the only problem. There's the deeper problem that keeping in prime physical form has consumed my life. Where I used to dream of taking up hobbies, my everyday life is now absorbed by maintaining a strict diet and exercising three times a day.

I know that attempting to cling to the athleticism of my twenties as I enter my fifties is guaranteed to lead to heartache and disappointment. After a recent injury while exercising, my wife convinced me to try to move past football. Personally, it feels like I've let go as much as I possibly can. Regardless of the inevitable displeasures, I still carry my championship ring, tucked away but on my person.

With your group, write a bullet point for your assigned paragraph. Write the outline for the passage with the rest of the class.

8.3.1 Getting the Gist

In order to answer questions about adding/deleting information:

1. Get the ____________or main idea of a ____________or essay.

2. Determine whether a piece of ____________is ___________ to what's already been ___________.

8.3.1 Getting the Gist

Passage I

When violinist Roger Pennifort plays, everyone listens. Wearing a dark suit, a bright green bowtie, and a gold pocket watch, the sixty-seven-year-old Pennifort seems to disappear into the pieces that he performs. The gold pocket watch that he wears costs $250. His body moves in time with the music as he plays his instrument. And though the pieces are haunting and sometimes melancholy, Pennifort knows that music has many different purposes. Indeed, in an interview he once said that he believed music's purpose was to uplift the soul, and that this could be accomplished through a pop song just as easily as through a concert.

1. When violinist Roger Pennifort plays, everyone listens. **Wearing a dark suit, a bright green bowtie, and a gold pocket watch,** the sixty-seven-year-old Pennifort seems to disappear into the pieces that he performs. The gold pocket watch that he wears costs $250. His body moves in time with the music as he plays his instrument. And though the pieces are haunting and sometimes melancholy, Pennifort knows that music has many different purposes. Indeed, in an interview he once said that he believed music's purpose was to uplift the soul, and that this could be accomplished through a pop song just as easily as through a concert.

2. When violinist Roger Pennifort plays, everyone listens. Wearing a dark suit, a bright green bowtie, and a gold pocket watch, the sixty-seven-year-old Pennifort seems to disappear into the pieces that he performs. **The gold pocket watch that he wears costs $250.** His body moves in time with the music as he plays his instrument. And though the pieces are haunting and sometimes melancholy, Pennifort knows that music has many different purposes. Indeed, in an interview he once said that he believed music's purpose was to uplift the soul, and that this could be accomplished through a pop song just as easily as through a concert.

3. When violinist Roger Pennifort plays, everyone listens. Wearing a dark suit, a bright green bowtie, and a gold pocket watch, the sixty-seven-year-old Pennifort seems to disappear into the pieces that he performs. The gold pocket watch that he wears costs $250. **His body moves in time with the music as he plays his instrument.** And though the pieces are haunting and sometimes melancholy, Pennifort knows that music has many different purposes. Indeed, in an interview he once said that he believed music's purpose was to uplift the soul, and that this could be accomplished through a pop song just as easily as through a concert.

4. When violinist Roger Pennifort plays, everyone listens. Wearing a dark suit, a bright green bowtie, and a gold pocket watch, the sixty-seven-year-old Pennifort seems to disappear into the pieces that he performs. The gold pocket watch that he wears costs $250. His body moves in time with the music as he plays his instrument. And though the pieces are haunting and sometimes melancholy, Pennifort knows that music has many different purposes. **Indeed, in an interview he once said that he believed music's purpose was to uplift the soul, and that this could be accomplished through a pop song just as easily as through a concert.**

8.3.1 Getting the Gist

Passage II

If we were going downtown, we would try to find a parking spot on the street. But if this wasn't possible, we could look for one of the public lots and pay for a space. Then, our wallets a bit lighter, we would walk into town. Unfortunately, even in public lots, parking spaces are few. My friends and I typically drive a sedan. The lots become full early in the day, after which it becomes very difficult to find a place at all.

1. **If we were going downtown,** we would try to find a parking spot on the street. But if this wasn't possible, we could look for one of the public lots and pay for a space. Then, our wallets a bit lighter, we would walk into town. Unfortunately, even in public lots, parking spaces are few. My friends and I typically drive a sedan. The lots become full early in the day, after which it becomes very difficult to find a place at all.

2. If we were going downtown, we would try to find a parking spot on the street. But if this wasn't possible, **we could look for one of the public lots and pay for a space.** Then, our wallets a bit lighter, we would walk into town. Unfortunately, even in public lots, parking spaces are few. My friends and I typically drive a sedan. The lots become full early in the day, after which it becomes very difficult to find a place at all.

3. If we were going downtown, we would try to find a parking spot on the street. But if this wasn't possible, we could look for one of the public lots and pay for a space. Then, our wallets a bit lighter, we would walk into town. Unfortunately, even in public lots, parking spaces are few. **My friends and I typically drive a sedan.** The lots become full early in the day, after which it becomes very difficult to find a place at all.

4. If we were going downtown, we would try to find a parking spot on the street. But if this wasn't possible, we could look for one of the public lots and pay for a space. Then, our wallets a bit lighter, we would walk into town. Unfortunately, even in public lots, parking spaces are few. My friends and I typically drive a sedan. The lots become full early in the day, **after which it becomes very difficult to find a place at all.**

English Tip

Keep It: If you aren't sure whether a part of a sentence should be kept or deleted, your best guess will be to keep it because, more often than not, it is the correct answer. Always try to find the right answer first, but choose to keep it if you're completely stuck.

8.3.2 Relevant, Emphasize, Explain

- Italian instrument-maker Antonio Stradivari (1646–1737) made 1,116 string instruments during his lifetime, but only 540 violins, fifty cellos, and twelve violas survive today.
- Stradivari instruments are considered superior, though experts often don't agree on why—some cite the wood, others say it's the varnish, etc.
- No one has yet been able to reproduce the sound of a Strad (the nickname for this type of instrument).
- Strads have been stolen throughout history.
- The Art Loss Register lists eighteen missing Stradivarius violins, including two stolen in New York.
- On February 28, 1936, Polish virtuoso violinist Bronislaw Huberman performed a Carnegie recital and left his other violin, a Strad called the Gibson Stradivarius, in his dressing room.
- Julian Altman, who worked in New York as a journeyman violinist, stole the Strad from Huberman.
- Altman spent his career playing in clubs, churches, and pickup orchestras.
- Altman used shoe polish to disguise the Gibson Strad, which he played for the next five decades.
- On his deathbed, Altman confessed to the theft and blamed his mother for concocting the plan to steal the famous violin.
- In the summer of 2001, American virtuoso Joshua Bell bought the violin.
- In October, Sony released "Romance of the Violin," Bell's first recording with the long-missing Gibson Strad.

Source: New York Daily News, "A Fiddle Found" by David J. Krajicek, January 4th 2004.

Write a short paragraph about the topic, using the bullet points above.

____

____

____

____

____

____

____

____

English Tip

REE: A phrase or sentence is a good addition to a paragraph if it is **relevant** to the rest of the paragraph and **emphasizes** or **explains** information related to the focus of the paragraph.

8.3.2 Relevant, Emphasize, Explain

Passage I

The search for the pharaoh's tomb began in the desert. Signs of the tomb had been detected for years by numerous archaeologists excavating in the area. The archaeologists had discovered artifacts that seemed to indicate the pharaoh was buried nearby. After examining such artifacts—including what appeared to be an ancient map of the region—archaeologists finally set up their excavation.

Potential addition	Add	Don't add
They chose the coordinates for the dig based on clues from the map, which indicated a more western burial site than previously thought.		
Archaeologists excavate in numerous regions, including Egypt, Iceland, Australia, and many more.		
In the 1970s, archaeologists excavated the remains of a dinosaur in the same region.		
The year before, a museum put on an exhibit about King Tut that generated increased interest in mummies.		

8.3.2 Relevant, Emphasize, Explain

Passage II

My garden in Pinewood, Washington, was enclosed by a long wooden gate. Large trees gave the small but elegant garden ample shade and even shielded it from heavy rainstorms. Red roses grew along the eastern-facing side, and an herb garden sprawled near the house. Pests could be a problem; surprisingly, rabbits were the worst offenders. A few hungry rabbits would all but destroy months of careful cultivating.

Potential addition	Add	Don't add
Pinewood is a little town about twenty miles out from Seattle.		
Sometimes storms would be accompanied by thunder and lightning.		
Other pests included mice, deer, and a variety of bugs.		
Many people prefer red roses, but white roses are my favorite.		

8.3.2 Relevant, Emphasize, Explain

Passage III

Not all guests, however, have been so well-behaved. A few years ago, a class came to the museum and knocked over a series of expensive statues from the Renaissance era. A few of these priceless pieces shattered on the marble floor. Luckily, the museum's insurance covered the cost of most of the damages, though that particular school was not invited back to visit.

Potential addition	Add	Don't add
The museum had many exhibits: some of sculptures, others of paintings, and still others of historical artifacts.		
Insurance is always highly advisable for businesses, especially those open to the public.		
Michelangelo was a famous sculptor from that time.		
A few of the students scrambled to try to put the pieces back together, but to no avail.		

8.3.2 Relevant, Emphasize, Explain

Passage IV

The Garcia family always took a long road trip during the summer, driving from Texas to the Denver mountains or the California coast. Their father loved to go hiking and spend time outdoors. Their mother preferred snapping photos and visiting small, quaint towns along the way. The Garcias were adventurous and good-natured, and they always ended a road trip with a picnic on a hill, watching the sunset as they talked about their experiences.

Potential addition:	Add	Don't add
Picnics generally attract ants, so it is important to bring bug spray.		
Beaches are generally crowded at this time of year.		
Sometimes they would take backroads and admire the natural beauty of the landscape.		
The Garcias also took vacations in winter, either to ski or to visit family.		

This page is intentionally left blank.

8.4.1 Set One

As the road lengthened behind me, the brilliant sun gave way to an inky night. Memories from my youth rapidly occupied the darkening emptiness. I saw my brother grinning before a cake at our parents' house when I graduated high school. We feasted on brisket, latkes, and dozens of fresh figs. I can still see the two grinning faces next to my brother—Dad with his laughing eyes and Mom with her big white teeth showing as she smiled—both congratulating me on my success at beginning college in New York. [1]

1. At this point, the author is considering adding the following true statement:

In Hebrew, *mazel tov* means "congratulations."

Should the author make this addition here?

A. Yes, because it clarifies what the narrator believes were his parents' true emotions.
B. Yes, because it supports the rest of the paragraph by explaining a Jewish tradition.
C. No, because it distracts readers from the main focus of this paragraph.
D. No, because it creates confusion between the narrator's culture and his college choice.

The University of Notre Dame was established in 1842, but football didn't come to the school until 1887. That year, University of Michigan paid a visit and taught students there how to play the game. Since then, Notre Dame has established itself as a premier athletic team, despite remaining outside any athletic conferences. The team claims eleven consensus national championships and has the highest winning percentage in NCAA history. Unsurprisingly, many great football players began their careers at the University of Notre Dame. [2]

2. The author is considering adding the following true information at the end of the previous sentence:

including Heisman winners Paul Hornung and Tim Brown

Should the writer add this phrase, assuming a comma would be placed after the word *Dame*?

F. Yes, because it helps explain why Notre Dame eliminated its football program.
G. Yes, because it adds evidence that supports the sentence's claim.
H. No, because the addition diverts the sentence's focus on the university.
J. No, because the level of detail added isn't consistent with the detail provided in the rest of the paragraph.

GO ON TO THE NEXT PAGE.

Joel Embiid was born and raised in Cameroon. The son of a military officer, he first held ambitions to be a professional volleyball player. However, at sixteen, Joel was discovered by Luc Mbah a Moute, a fellow Cameroonian, who encouraged him to try out for the National Basketball Association. Later, Joel moved to the United States to attend the University of Kansas. He left the university after only one year to become the third pick in the 2014 NBA draft, despite having been raised as a volleyball player. [3]

3. The writer is considering deleting "in the 2014 NBA draft" from the preceding sentence. Should the phrase be kept or deleted?

   A. Kept, because it specifies where the player was raised.
   B. Kept, because it provides important details to clarify Joel's successes.
   C. Deleted, because it provides redundant information.
   D. Deleted, because it distracts the reader from Joel's athleticism.

END OF SET ONE

STOP! DO NOT GO ON TO THE NEXT PAGE UNTIL TOLD TO DO SO.

8.4.2 Set Two

Sperm whales are the largest toothed predator in the world. Male whales can reach up to sixty-seven feet, although they average fifty-two feet. They are found throughout the world but typically only in areas more than 3,300 feet deep that are also free of ice. In the Gulf of Mexico, at the mouth of the Mississippi River, sperm whales are able to survive because the river deepens the ocean floor. [10] Here, shrimpers, cargo ships, and oil rigs stake a working space in the waters for their business operations.

4. The author is considering deleting this phrase from the preceding sentence (and correcting capitalization as needed):

    In the Gulf of Mexico, at the mouth of the Mississippi River,

    Should the phrase be kept or deleted?

    F. Kept, because it explains that sperm whales live only at the mouth of the river inside of the Gulf of Mexico.
    G. Kept, because it provides details referred to by "here" in the following sentence.
    H. Deleted, because it opposes the previous sentence, which makes it clear that whales live throughout the Gulf of Mexico.
    J. Deleted, because the information is stated later in the paragraph.

Harry Caray was a baseball announcer for the St. Louis Cardinals, Oakland Athletics, Chicago White Sox, and most famously, the Chicago Cubs. His unique broadcasting style distinguished him from other sports commentators. Expressions like "Holy cow!" became synonymous with his name because he used them so frequently. Caray's play-by-play brought color and life to the players and their teams by using clever turns of phrase. For example, he liked saying a player's name backwards: Mota became Atom. [8]

5. The author is considering changing "Mota became Atom" to:

    Mota became Atom so that Caray could announce, "Atom hit that right at 'em."

    Assuming the new phrase is accurate, should the author make the revision or keep the phrase as it appears?

    A. Make the revision, because the change contributes to the information about key players Caray discussed.
    B. Make the revision, because it illustrates how saying names backwards enhanced Caray's broadcasts.
    C. Keep the phrase as is, because the unchanged phrase illustrates how to say a name backwards.
    D. Keep the phrase as is, because the focus is on Caray, not on his broadcast techniques.

GO ON TO THE NEXT PAGE.

Longboards are becoming increasingly popular in today's society. They are useful modes of transportation as well as enjoyable recreational vehicles. People especially enjoy using longboards on downhill trails. Most longboards have decks constructed of varying types of wood, bamboo, or fiberglass. The decks are cut into shapes similar to skateboards but are always greater in length. [6]

6. The author is considering deleting the preceding sentence. Should the sentence be kept or deleted?

F. Kept, because it's important that the reader understands the various longboard types.
G. Kept, because it aids the reader in visualizing a longboard.
H. Deleted, because it distracts from the focus in the previous sentence.
J. Deleted, because it is overly wordy.

END OF SET TWO

STOP! DO NOT GO ON TO THE NEXT PAGE
UNTIL TOLD TO DO SO.

8.4.3 Set Three

As a leader in the field of archaeology, Heinrich Schliemann made tremendous steps in clearing up our past. Before he discovered Troy in the 1870s, archaeologists doubted the existence of the fabled site, dismissing it as an invention of the Greek poet Homer (850–780 B.C.). [7] Schliemann was a bit of an amateur in the field of archaeology. He made a fortune during the gold rush in America, which he used to fund his passion: locating the setting of Homer's epics. With his money and knowledge of *The Odyssey* and *The Iliad*, Schliemann discovered that a mythological place was once a reality.

7. The author is considering removing the parenthetical information from the previous sentence. If the writer does delete this information, the paragraph would lose:

A. information explaining Schliemann's motivation to research sites present in Homer's works.
B. information that puts Homer's life into an appropriate historical perspective.
C. the suspected time at which Homer began writing.
D. the era during which the existence of Troy was not doubted.

Once considered a novelty only found on expensive technologies like the early MP3 players, a touch-based input device—or touchscreen—has materialized as a useful, ubiquitous, and good-looking feature. It is hard to find a device that doesn't have a touchscreen option. Many laptops have them, and every tablet uses a touchscreen as its only input system. It's more surprising to find a cellphone that does not have a touchscreen than it is to find a cellphone that does. [4]

8. The writer is considering adding the following after the preceding sentence:

> Touchscreens are still found on MP3 players, however.

Should the writer add this true statement?

F. Yes, because it supports the point made in the previous sentence.
G. Yes, because it is a good introduction to the essay's main idea.
H. No, because it interrupts the paragraph to restate implied information.
J. No, because it contradicts the assertion that touchscreens are ubiquitous.

GO ON TO THE NEXT PAGE.

In 1906, Bradbury Robinson, a quarterback for St. Louis University, completed the first legal forward pass in American football history. [9] Today, the forward pass is an integral part of football. Imagining the game without passing is difficult for many fans. Over the last decade, we have seen nearly every passing record in NFL history broken. Drew Brees, quarterback for the New Orleans Saints, set many such records when he led the Saints to their only championship.

9. At this point, the writer considers whether to include the following sentence:

> Football teams commonly utilized mass plays in which all the players crowded together and initiated violent collisions.

Should this addition be made?

A. Yes, because the essay is about the introduction of the forward pass.
B. Yes, because the rules had to be changed against mass plays to encourage the risk of a forward pass.
C. No, because the essay focuses on the forward pass, not on mass plays.
D. No, because the essay focuses on the prevalence of the forward pass today, not on its creation.

END OF SET THREE
STOP! DO NOT GO ON TO THE NEXT PAGE UNTIL TOLD TO DO SO.

8.4.4 Set Four

Pollution is an ever-growing issue. In response to the threat pollution poses, many leading scientists and environmentalists are proposing innovative solutions for saving the environment. Researchers are investigating promising alternative forms of energy, such as wind and water power. Scientists also encourage people to use hybrid and electric cars, but those aren't the only vehicular-based pollution reduction options. Carpooling isn't just environmentally friendly, it's sociable. [5]

10. The writer wants to add the following true statement here:

> Some highways have created carpool-only lanes to diffuse traffic for these drivers.

Should the writer add this statement?

F. Yes, because it supports the writer's claim that carpooling is faster than driving alone.
G. Yes, because it explains how carpooling is better for the environment.
H. No, because it portrays carpooling benefits as unfair to other drivers.
J. No, because it distracts from the writer's purpose of displaying the environmental benefits of carpooling.

F. Scott Fitzgerald's *The Great Gatsby*, published in 1925, has become widely recognized as one of the great American novels. The story centers on the character Jay Gatsby and his love for Daisy Buchanan. Jay often contemplates a green light at the end of Daisy's boat dock. This green light comes to represent both hope and unrealistic expectations as Fitzgerald weaves the symbol into both optimistic and depressing situations. [11]

11. The writer is considering adding the following statement here:

> Many of the green lights in the world come from light-emitting diodes.

Should the writer include this sentence?

A. Yes, because it helps explain how Fitzgerald's green light can be simultaneously optimistic and depressing.
B. Yes, because it provides further details about the uses of green light.
C. No, because it doesn't relate to Fitzgerald's main idea of the green light as a symbol.
D. No, because it only mentions one producer of green light.

GO ON TO THE NEXT PAGE.

Much art regarding life in Louisiana is on display at the museum. Photographs depict everyday life on the streets of New Orleans. Large painted canvases realistically portray bayous and landscapes. Smaller canvases portray laborers in an assortment of Louisiana industries. [12]

12. The writer is considering adding the following phrase at the end of the previous sentence:

> such as culinary arts, maritime trade, and health care.

Assuming the period after *industries* is changed to a comma, should this addition be made?

F. Yes, because it further defines a general term.
G. Yes, because it allows readers to understand how the canvases were made.
H. No, because it gives only a selection of industries rather than a complete listing.
J. No, because it distracts the reader from the main idea of the sentence.

END OF SET FOUR
STOP! DO NOT GO ON TO THE NEXT PAGE
UNTIL TOLD TO DO SO.

8.4.5 Set Five

Meryl Streep has portrayed different characters on the stage and screen for over forty years. Growing up in the Northeast United States, Streep quickly became a highly decorated actress over the course of four decades. [13] She holds the record for the most Academy Award nominations: she has nineteen. Even though she has only won three Oscars, these awards were in the most competitive acting categories.

13. The writer is considering deleting the phrase "over the course of four decades" from the sentence. Should the phrase be kept or deleted?

A. Kept, because it helps readers understand the duration of Streep's success.
B. Kept, because it allows readers to calculate when Streep began her career.
C. Deleted, because it restates information previously mentioned in the paragraph.
D. Deleted, because Streep's longevity is irrelevant to the focus of this writing.

Philadelphia International Airport is tough to get to. It's also crowded; the thousands of travelers who pass through often wait hours to get through security. One redeeming feature of the airport is that you never go hungry. Around every turn, you can find a delicious eatery to ease your wait. Some even say the best cheesesteak in the whole city can be found at Terminal D. [14]

14. The writer is considering adding the following statement after the previous sentence:

> Chicago and Los Angeles also have large and crowded airports.

Should the writer add this statement?

F. Yes, because it shows that the airport in Philadelphia is not unique.
G. Yes, because it helps the reader picture the airport.
H. No, because it distracts the reader from the paragraph's main idea.
J. No, because the tone and style don't match the paragraph.

GO ON TO THE NEXT PAGE.

By his early twenties, Pete Davidson was already featured in a number of comedies throughout popular media. He regularly appeared in popular cable TV shows, acting both as himself and as other characters. In 2014, he joined the storied cast of *Saturday Night Live*, which began airing in 1975. From there, he was set to rise to national fame. [15]

15. The writer is considering adding the following statement here:

> *Saturday Night Live* began several decades previous.

Should the writer make the addition?

A. Yes, because it tells which show Davidson joined.
B. Yes, because the essay's main idea is on examining the differences in the cast of *Saturday Night Live* over the years.
C. No, because the essay focuses on the recent success of *Saturday Night Live*, making its history unrelated.
D. No, because it repeats information already given in the paragraph.

END OF SET FIVE
STOP! DO NOT GO ON TO THE NEXT PAGE
UNTIL TOLD TO DO SO.

Sum It Up

Tips and Techniques

REE: A phrase or sentence is a good addition to a paragraph if it is **relevant** to the rest of the paragraph and **emphasizes** or **explains** information related to the focus of the paragraph.

Keep It: If you must guess, choose to keep the sentence.

Text Deletion

CAPTION:

9.1 Entrance Ticket

Unscramble the five anagrams below and determine what they all have in common.

1. TUTOR: ______________________________

2. RAHKS: ______________________________

3. CASH FIT: ____________________________

4. HOLD PIN: ____________________________

5. ROUND ELF: __________________________

9.2 Learning Targets

1. Identify the main idea in a passage quickly
2. Analyze how a main idea loses detail when deleting specific phrases or sentences
3. Create strategies to find the correct answers and to eliminate wrong ones efficiently

Self-Assessment

Circle the number that corresponds to your confidence level in your knowledge of this subject before beginning the lesson. A score of 1 means you are completely lost, and a score of 4 means you have mastered the skills. After you finish the lesson, return to the bottom of this page and circle your new confidence level to show your improvement.

Before Lesson

1 2 3 4

After Lesson

1 2 3 4

9.3.1 Identify What Is Lost

What's missing in these pictures?

Andrew Denton was just a small boy when his father played as the quarterback for the Lions, a team that would go on to win the national championship. But Andrew himself unwittingly played an important role for the team. The team's photographer traveled with the athletes, capturing images of fans, families, and the players in action. Photos of Andrew—held in his mother's arms—depicted the most enthusiastic fan one could imagine. He mimicked signs for plays and pointed to where his dad needed to pass the ball. When the team won the Super Bowl, Andrew was there, and his excitement was captured on camera. The next day, the local newspaper published a picture of him with a caption that read "Most Valuable Player." [1]

1. If the writer were to delete the phrase "Most Valuable Player" in the last sentence and replace it with "Lions are cheered on to victory," the paragraph would primarily lose:
   - **A.** a specific detail that adds humor.
   - **B.** a prediction of events that occur later in the story.
   - **C.** an element of suspense that increases the reader's curiosity.
   - **D.** a distinction between the father and son mentioned in this paragraph.

9.3.1 Identify What Is Lost

The movie industry was wowed by the performance of the astounding young talent. In 1934, <u>Temple, only six at the time</u>, won a miniature Academy Award for her contribution to film in both *Bright Eyes* and *Little Miss Marker*. Temple would go on to be the recipient of countless awards and the subject of many statues. With a filmography of over thirty feature-length films before her sixteenth birthday, Shirley Temple remains one of Hollywood's most prolific child stars.

2. If the writer were to delete the underlined portion (adjusting the punctuation as needed), the paragraph would primarily lose information that:

F. helps establish a detail about a milestone in the young actress's career.

G. disrupts the flow of the paragraph and introduces extra information that detracts from the actress's filmography.

H. implies that the actress was too new to the industry to appreciate such an award.

J. supports the paragraph's claim that the best actors demonstrate a natural talent at a young age.

When the popularity of the music industry was in decline and record sales had begun plummeting, one band seemed able to stand the test of time. Crowds of over thirty thousand people attended its shows in arenas across the United States to watch the best musicians of their generation perform. [3]

3. If the writer were to delete the phrases "of over thirty thousand people" and "in arenas across the United States" from the preceding sentence, the paragraph would primarily lose details that:

A. describe a particularly well-attended concert that was talked about for decades.

B. indicate the widespread popularity of a band's live performances.

C. explain why people have enjoyed watching live music for hundreds of years.

D. provide information about the benefits of arenas as music venues.

9.3.1 Identify What Is Lost

On the morning of the spelling bee, the trophies still hadn't been delivered to the school. The winners, however, were given cupcakes and an extra fifteen minutes at recess for their hard work. [4] The trophies came in that Thursday, and the winners were finally given something to take home and show off.

4. If the writer were to delete the preceding sentence, the paragraph would primarily lose:

F. an illustration that specifies how the winners were compensated when the trophies came in late.
G. the suggestion that the teachers rewarded some winners with cupcakes and some with trophies.
H. the suggestion that the school had stopped allowing teachers to reward with costly prizes.
J. a list of sweets and extracurricular activities that the winning students enjoyed.

Very few musicians can claim to have as much talent as Brian Wilson. Wilson's ear as a musician—his sense of pitch and chord structures—led him to develop a unique approach as a producer. [5] He integrated the use of unusual harmonies, sound effects, and odd instrumentation to arrange some of the most innovative records of the 1960s.

5. The writer is considering deleting the preceding sentence from the essay. The sentence should NOT be deleted because it:

A. indicates that Wilson's role as a producer came before his talent as a musician.
B. describes Wilson's ability as a musician, which is essential to the structure of this essay.
C. begins to explain the methods of perfecting one's pitch and choosing the right chord structures to create a pop hit.
D. provides a transition that illustrates a connection between Wilson the musician and Wilson the producer.

9.3.1 Identify What Is Lost

In Herzog's *Fitzcarraldo*, the main character has a dream of building an opera house in the middle of the Amazon. To accomplish this, he must somehow move a large boat over the top of a mountain. The impossible nature of this task seems to symbolize the director's own insurmountable challenge—creating the film. [6]

6. If the writer were to delete the preceding sentence, the paragraph would primarily lose:

F. a reflection of Herzog's talent as a director that places him in a historical context.

G. an evaluation of the main character that compares him to Herzog

H. an explanation of a directing technique that refers back to the essay's introduction

J. an interpretation of the film which serves to summarize the passage.

English Tip

Your Own Words: What do you think this sentence or phrase adds to the essay? Put it in your own words. You might find an answer choice that says the same thing, and you will likely be able to eliminate a few that contradict your version.

9.3.2 Eliminating Answer Choices

Following your teacher's example, create a strategy to eliminate the wrong answers in this question.

Notepads are a staple in my life. They rest in almost every room, as if they live there. [1] Although I usually end up making a to-do list and leaving it behind, the notepads' presence symbolizes my desire to get organized.

1. At this point, the writer is considering adding the following true statement:

   I'll even find them in my glove compartment.

   Should the writer make this addition here?

   A. Yes, because it helps clarify the preceding information.
   B. Yes, because it provides a detail that is relevant to this paragraph.
   C. No, because the information is vague and unnecessary.
   D. No, because it detracts from the main idea of this paragraph.

9.3.2 Eliminating Answer Choices

Many people are convinced that the government oversees controversial operations that the public knows nothing about. This leaves a void that many fill with speculations and theories. To some, the suspicion that the U.S. Air Force intended to conduct top-secret experimental aircraft operations in remote areas was confirmed by the government's acquisition of Area 51. [2]

2. The writer is considering adding the following phrase to the end of the preceding sentence (replacing the period after Area 51 with a comma):

an area of restricted airspace where experimental aircraft could be tested.

Should the writer add this phrase here?

F. Yes, because it helps the reader understand the paragraph's primary focus.

G. Yes, because it provides a definition of Area 51.

H. No, because Area 51 has already been described.

J. No, because it refers to topics not mentioned in the paragraph.

9.3.2 Eliminating Answer Choices

Audiences were stunned by the film *Apocalypse Now,* one of the most impressive undertakings in cinematic history. When the producers decided to create original wartime footage for the movie, their original budget of two million dollars skyrocketed. [3] One can only imagine the response of audiences to this blockbuster at the time.

3. The writer is considering adding the following true information to the end of the preceding sentence:

to 31.5 million dollars.

Should the writer add this phrase here?

A. Yes, because it supports the theme of rising cost of ticket prices for moviegoers.

B. Yes, because it adds detail that illustrates the assertion made in the sentence.

C. No, because it strays from the paragraph's focus on the declining movie industry.

D. No, because it weakens the assertion made in the paragraph about the high cost of production.

9.3.2 Eliminating Answer Choices

Luckily, there are affordable options for travel. People can save their money and also have a unique traveling experience. Overnight trains are not glamorous, [4] but passengers have a bed and a window.

4. At this point the writer is considering adding the following true statement (deleting the comma):

—the compartments are small, and the ride is bumpy—

Should the writer make this addition here?

F. Yes, because it adds an example that supports the claim that overnight trains are not extravagant.

G. Yes, because it explains the dimensions of the sleeping compartments.

H. No, because it provides information that counters details from the passage's introduction.

J. No, because it changes the essay's focus from airline to train transportation.

9.4.1 Set One

There have been many people who have made significant contributions to the field of aviation. These pioneers helped give birth to modern aviation; out of this group, one stands out above all the others. Charles Lindbergh, at the age of twenty-five, piloted the first nonstop flight from New York to Paris in over thirty-three hours. [1]

1. The writer is thinking of revising the preceding sentence to read:

Charles Lindbergh piloted the first nonstop flight from New York to Paris.

If this revision was made, the sentence would primarily lose:

A. unnecessary details that disrupt the flow of the narrative.
B. specific details that enrich the narrative.
C. additional details that make the paragraph confusing.
D. repetitive information that is given earlier in the narrative.

Stuart considered himself a man of mystery and was greatly amused by his own talent as a performer. He looked at his whole life as an act carried out for the benefit of the world around him. He regularly assumed the names of legendary illusionists, registering at hotels as Harry Houdini or Mandrake the Magician.

2. The writer is considering deleting the phrase "registering at hotels as Harry Houdini or Mandrake the Magician" (adjusting the punctuation as needed). If the writer were to make this deletion, the sentence would primarily lose:

F. an explanation of why Stuart chose to assume these particular names.
G. an indication of the many different places where Stuart used these names.
H. details about the way hotel guests react to Stuart's use of pseudonyms.
J. examples of illusionists whom Stuart considered worthy of emulation.

GO ON TO THE NEXT PAGE.

Someone tapped me on the shoulder as I waited in line for ski equipment in Vail, Colorado. "You're going to need warmer clothing than what you have on," said a woman I had never met. She got the attention of an assistant. "He needs an insulated jacket and snow pants if he's going to hit the slopes," she told him. "His luggage tag says 'Hawaii.'"

3. If the writer deletes the phrase "in Vail, Colorado" from the first sentence and also deletes the final sentence of this paragraph, the essay would lose details that are:
   - **A.** illogical because of the great geographical distance between the two locales.
   - **B.** vivid but unnecessary to understanding the interaction described in the paragraph.
   - **C.** helpful to understanding the stranger's behavior, which would otherwise be unclear.
   - **D.** amusing and thought-provoking, since they indicate the narrator's probable preference for light clothing.

END OF SET ONE

STOP! DO NOT GO ON TO THE NEXT PAGE UNTIL TOLD TO DO SO.

9.4.2 Set Two

My grandparents' estate has been in our family for generations. When we arrived, the sun was beginning to set, adding an ephemeral quality to the landscape. At the entrance to the home, the last of the daylight bounced off the smooth surface of the front door's dark brown, mahogany frame.

4. If the writer were to delete the words *smooth*, *dark brown*, and *mahogany* from the preceding sentence, the paragraph would lose descriptive details that primarily:
   F. reveal the narrator's emotions upon approaching the estate.
   G. support the narrator's case for keeping family heirlooms intact.
   H. help depict what the narrator saw when arriving at the estate.
   J. describe the craftsmanship required to build such a home.

Francis couldn't wait for P.E. because he got to play dodgeball. His strategy was to stay on the fringe for the first half of the game, appearing to be unfocused while quietly observing the players' movements. [5] In the second half of the game, Francis would catch his opponents off guard and lead his team to victory.

5. If the writer were to delete the preceding sentence, the paragraph would primarily lose a statement that:
   A. describes a specific instance in which Francis outwitted his opponents.
   B. adds an amusing tone to an otherwise formal paragraph.
   C. sets up the reader for the contrast described in the next sentence.
   D. helps explain a point about Francis's technique that is made earlier in the paragraph.

GO ON TO THE NEXT PAGE.

My company's headquarters are located in Chicago, but I'm still not used to the Illinois winters. I've managed to adapt to being away from home for the most part—building a small circle of friends and dating a girl from the area—but it's still difficult sometimes. Luckily, I'm doing well at my job, and they're steadily promoting me, but the downside is that I have less time to go back home.

Of course I miss the love and support from my friends and family back home. I go to a lot of gatherings with my girlfriend and her family. And although I'm grateful for their hospitality, it makes me miss my own family even more. The friends I've made at work are great, and we share some laughs, but it's nothing like the shorthand I have with friends in my hometown.

I was born and raised in Southern California with the beach as my backyard. In the coldest months of the year in Chicago, I long to smell the briny air of the ocean. I know it's ridiculous, but every January my mother sends me a box of seashells to remind me of home. When I open the package, memories of bonfires on the beach come flooding back to me. Somehow, missing the place I was raised feels just like missing another person. [6]

6. If the writer were to delete this final paragraph, the essay would primarily lose:

F. details that illustrate an aspect of his hometown that the narrator especially misses.
G. images that reveal how the narrator is slowly forgetting the beaches of his youth.
H. a sense that the narrator is planning to move back to California as soon as possible.
J. information about the narrator's youth that is irrelevant to the passage's focus on the narrator's career.

END OF SET TWO
STOP! DO NOT GO ON TO THE NEXT PAGE
UNTIL TOLD TO DO SO.

9.4.3 Set Three

There is some upsetting news about deer in our area: their habitats are being destroyed for other uses. For example, fields on which deer graze are being cleared for the construction of shopping centers and condominiums. [7] As a result, the deer population is diminishing every year.

7. The writer is considering deleting the preceding sentence from the paragraph. If the writer makes this deletion, the paragraph would primarily lose:

A. an example of ways residents can help stop the destruction of deer habitats.
B. information that strays from the main idea about the endangered deer population.
C. an example that supports the claim that deer habitats are destroyed.
D. scientific evidence that proves the deer population is being diminished.

A firefighter was given an award for bravery in our town. Having helped rescue a family from their burning home, he was highlighted in the newspaper. The article commended him for his heroic feat, noting that few people were capable of such bravery. The article describes him as strong and agile, with a wet nose and four legs.

A wet nose? Four legs? Of course, this firefighter was actually man's best friend. For seven years, Rusty has been living in the fire station alongside his human colleagues and accompanying them to each emergency. Rusty's loyalty and bravery have earned him much acclaim throughout our state and have made him the most-loved dog since Lassie.

8. If the firefighter were to delete the questions "A wet nose? Four legs?" from the paragraph, the essay would primarily lose:

F. an emphasis on the surprising twist in the paragraph.
G. nothing, since this is an unnecessary detail.
H. an assertion of the paragraph's main idea.
J. a solemn tone that contradicts the rest of the paragraph.

GO ON TO THE NEXT PAGE.

I had worked harder on this book report than anything else in my life. Thanks to this assignment, I ate, drank, and dreamed *The Odyssey*. I knew it would be devastating if Mrs. Daniels gave me anything less than a perfect grade. I was prepared to see a typical letter grade of A, B, C, D, or even F, but instead she had written, "See me after class." [9]

9. The writer is considering deleting the first part of the preceding sentence, so that the sentence would read:

She had written, "See me after class."

If the writer were to make this change, the essay would primarily lose:

A. examples of the grades the narrator typically receives on book reports.
B. a contrast between what Mrs. Daniels wrote and what the narrator was anticipating.
C. details that suggest that the narrator knew the grade before the book report was returned to her.
D. an indication that the narrator deeply respected Mrs. Daniels.

END OF SET THREE

STOP! DO NOT GO ON TO THE NEXT PAGE UNTIL TOLD TO DO SO.

9.4.4 Set Four

Sometimes the hardest part of writing a book is putting that very first word down onto the page. Staring at a blank page in August of 1998 was the most terrifying feeling Chang had ever experienced. By December, he was celebrating with his friends and family: Chang had just completed the first chapter of what would become his best-selling masterpiece. [10]

10. The writer is concerned about the level of detail in the preceding sentence and is considering deleting the phrase "the first chapter of" from it. If the writer were to make this deletion, the paragraph would primarily lose information that:
    - **F.** clarifies that only one chapter of the novel had been written by December of 1998.
    - **G.** makes clear that by December of 1998, Chang had already begun writing the second chapter of his novel.
    - **H.** provides evidence that Chang's loved ones believed the entire novel was completed at this time.
    - **J.** reveals how much time and effort would go into writing a novel the length of Chang's.

In the late twentieth century, sculpture was making an enormous comeback. A new generation of artists had found their passion within the medium, and they took to it in innovative and modern ways. In the mid-1980s, the Metropolitan Museum of Modern Art commissioned three local artists to sculpt a <u>seventeen-foot</u> statue in the museum's lobby.

11. If the underlined phrase were deleted, the sentence would primarily lose a detail that:
    - **A.** provides new and relevant information to the sentence.
    - **B.** is vague and unnecessary to the sentence.
    - **C.** repeats details that have already been mentioned in the paragraph.
    - **D.** must be included for the sentence to be grammatically correct.

GO ON TO THE NEXT PAGE.

On August 8, 1914, the Imperial Trans-Antarctic Expedition was underway. Sir Ernest Shackleton, famed polar explorer, left Plymouth, England, to lead what he intended to be the first land crossing of the Antarctic continent. A team of twenty-eight men were dispatched for the voyage. Their destination would be Deception Island in the Ross Sea, north of the tip of the Antarctic Peninsula. Shackleton's plan was to first sail his ship, *The Endurance*, to the Vahsel Bay area. From there, he and his men would undertake an 1,800-mile journey across land to Deception Island using dogs, sledges, and other equipment.

Months into the trip, *The Endurance* sank after it became trapped in ice and was crushed. Stranded, Shackleton and his crew were forced to make encampments on the drifting ice until it melted and disintegrated. They then launched their lifeboats and headed for the closest land mass, Elephant Island. It was uninhabited and devoid of any usable resources.

Shackleton left his men on Elephant Island and made an open-boat journey of 800 miles to the closest island of South Georgia. There, he was able to mount a rescue mission of his crew, who had been left on Elephant Island for months. The island of South Georgia would be the crew's final destination.

12. If the writer were to delete the final paragraph of this essay, the essay would primarily lose information that:

F. explains how Shackleton was able to rescue his stranded crew and bring them to South Georgia.
G. explains why journeying to Elephant Island was not part of Shackleton's initial plan.
H. describes the conditions Shackleton faced during his solo journey to South Georgia.
J. indicates Shackleton's disappointment at having to mount a rescue mission rather than continue with the intended plan.

END OF SET FOUR
STOP! DO NOT GO ON TO THE NEXT PAGE
UNTIL TOLD TO DO SO.

9.4.5 Set Five

I grew up with a Christmas tree farm in my backyard and loved examining the trees. Each new sapling had its own distinct shape that I found captivating. [13] I quickly became an expert arborist and worked my way up to managing the family business.

13. The writer is considering revising "Each new sapling had its own distinct shape that I found captivating" to read "Each new sapling had its own unique shape." That revision would cause the sentence to lose primarily:
    - **A.** variation on the writer's theme of his career as an arborist.
    - **B.** fascination with the writer's own use of descriptive language.
    - **C.** emphasis on the narrator's enthusiasm for the trees.
    - **D.** details describing the various characteristics of the trees.

Industry outsiders are always surprised by how many recorded songs musicians have in their repertoire. Record producers will typically have an artist record as many songs as possible so they can edit them and pick out the best songs. Generally, an album will only include about twenty percent of what was originally recorded in the studio. [14] Why don't we ever hear the other songs?

14. If the writer were to delete the preceding sentence, the essay would primarily lose:
    - **F.** a detail about the volume of songs an artist records when making an album.
    - **G.** a factual detail about how song selection increases an artist's fan base.
    - **H.** information that helps put record production into a broader context.
    - **J.** a potential answer to the question asked next in the paragraph.

As a brilliant inventor, Alexander Graham Bell laid the foundations for many of the technologies we still use today. Bell's experimentation with electrical currents and sound waves led to his invention of the telephone in 1874. Many of his theories were challenged, but Bell's invention was financially backed in part by someone else. [15]

15. The writer is deciding whether to add the following true statement (replacing the period with a comma after else):

    who had faced doubt over his inventions—Thomas Edison.

    Should the writer make this addition?
    - **A.** Yes, because it demonstrates that most inventions are made through collaboration.
    - **B.** Yes, because it adds interesting and relevant information to the paragraph.
    - **C.** No, because it weakens the claim that most of Bell's theories faced opposition.
    - **D.** No, because it shifts the paragraph's focus away from Bell's biography.

END OF SET FIVE

STOP! DO NOT GO ON TO THE NEXT PAGE UNTIL TOLD TO DO SO.

Sum It Up

Text Deletion

Main Idea
The central topic of a paragraph or essay

Purpose
The reason why an author writes a sentence, paragraph, or essay

Tips and Techniques

Your Own Words: What do you think this sentence or phrase adds to the essay? Put it in your own words. You might find an answer choice that says the same thing, and you will likely be able to eliminate a few that contradict your version.

Lesson 10

Redundancy Part 1

CAPTION:

10.1 Entrance Ticket

Select the best alternative to the underlined portion in each section below. If no change is necessary, select NO CHANGE.

These helmets protect a construction worker's brain from damaging harm if there is ever an unforeseen breach in safety protocol.

1. **A.** NO CHANGE
   B. harmful damage
   C. damage
   D. damage that could harm it

The psychiatrist asked her questions in an effort to help her recall places that were once familiar that she would remember.

2. **F.** NO CHANGE
   G. to remember
   H. to recall
   J. DELETE the underlined portion and end the sentence with a period.

The congressmen worried that more lobbying efforts would postpone and delay the legislation they hoped to pass before the start of the winter holidays.

3. **A.** NO CHANGE
   B. to a later time
   C. by delaying
   D. DELETE the underlined portion.

10.2 Learning Target

1. Recognize and delete repetitive and wordy components in written material

Self-Assessment

Circle the number that corresponds to your confidence level in your knowledge of this subject before beginning the lesson. A score of 1 means you are completely lost, and a score of 4 means you have mastered the skills. After you finish the lesson, return to the bottom of this page and circle your new confidence level to show your improvement.

Before Lesson

1 2 3 4

After Lesson

1 2 3 4

10.3.1 Determining Redundancy

Mark whether each sentence is redundant or not. If it is redundant, rewrite the sentence without the redundant word(s).

1. The police put out a notice for the wanted criminal who had broken the law.

______________________________ ☐ **yes** ☐ **no**

____

2. There are many parts to this puzzle that need to be looked over.

______________________________ ☐ **yes** ☐ **no**

____

3. However, on the other hand, I have no desire to watch the movie.

______________________________ ☐ **yes** ☐ **no**

____

4. His car needed expensive repairs that cost a lot of money.

______________________________ ☐ **yes** ☐ **no**

____

5. Initially, Thomas was offered a job as a clerk, but he eventually became a manager.

______________________________ ☐ **yes** ☐ **no**

____

6. Ellen celebrated her team's successful victory over the other soccer team.

______________________________ ☐ **yes** ☐ **no**

____

10.3.2 Revising Redundancy

The Uninvited Intruders
By Michael Prince

For a number of days, the two armed gunmen waited outside the Harris property. Their boss who employed them, Big Daddy Denny, wanted them to acquire a particular artifact that Mrs. Lenore Harris found at a recent auction last week. She wasn't supposed to buy it, but she did. Hooper and Marco decided that they would wait for the old lady to leave before snooping and looking for the artifact. They weren't sure or very clear about what they were supposed to be scrupulously looking for. All they were told was that they wouldn't miss it.

"I heard she's a witch," Hooper said.

"How do you know?" Marco questioned his partner.

"During the course of my research of this place, I heard rumors."

"When did you become so intelligent and smart?"

"When I decided that from now on, each and every time I rob someone, I find out everything I can about them. It seems fair. We should always be ready and prepared."

"Is she home?" Marco said impatiently. It was 6 a.m. in the morning.

"No. She should be out for her usual customary walk around the town now. It takes about three hours because she stops and talks to just about everyone," Hooper said.

"Some wicked witch."

They ascended up the stairs to the front door at the entrance of the house. In an emergency situation and as unwanted intruders, they would break down the door quickly, but this morning they had time. Hooper carefully picked the lock and opened the door of the grand old house. It looked like the exact same door that belonged to the boarding school he went to as a child.

Marco, a former veteran of big crime, brought a gun.

"Just in case," he said.

"I don't think witches can be hurt by guns."

"I don't think she's a witch."

Suddenly, a noise was heard across the house. It was dark, and neither Marco nor Hooper could see in the darkness. They waited a moment of a few minutes to see if they heard anything else, and when they were both relieved with full satisfaction, they continued. If there was a future recurrence, Hooper decided he would run for it, and Marco decided he would stay in one place. You don't upset Big Daddy Denny. Even the local residents knew that.

10.3.3 Expanding Vocabulary

Troubled	Mirthful	Chirpy	Miserable
Elated	Upbeat	Pained	Gleeful
Exultant	Sunny	Forsaken	Thrilled
Down	Overjoyed	Jolly	Depressed
Peppy	Morose	Delighted	Perky
Melancholy	Grave	Jubilant	Ecstatic
Sorrowful	Pleased	Gratified	Discouraged

She created a <u>photographically</u> companion to the watercolor portrait by framing a photograph of the painting's subject and hanging it directly next to the painting.

1. **A.** NO CHANGE
B. visually photographically
C. photographic
D. DELETE the underlined portion.

First, we used a seam ripper and a needle to remove the crooked stitches and re-sew <u>the seams in straight lines.</u> We then began to piece the garment together.

2. **F.** NO CHANGE
G. the seams in straight lines where the stitches had previously been removed by us.
H. the seams in very straight lines since it is necessary for garments to have straight seams.
J. DELETE the underlined portion and end the sentence with a period.

10.3.3 Expanding Vocabulary

The ferry takes approximately fifteen minutes to complete the crossing, which runs from Ellis Island to the Battery Park ferry terminal <u>in under twenty minutes.</u>

3. A. NO CHANGE
   B. in order to complete the crossing.
   C. in about fifteen minutes.
   D. DELETE the underlined portion and end the sentence with a period.

Every Sunday morning, <u>as she walks to the church down the street,</u> she stops at the café on the corner to buy a pastry on her way to church.

4. F. NO CHANGE
   G. after commencing her walk to the church down the street,
   H. needing to buy a pastry,
   J. DELETE the underlined portion.

Mature great white sharks may <u>attain</u> a length of twenty-one feet and weigh over 7,000 pounds.

5. A. NO CHANGE
   B. in terms of length attain
   C. strive to attain
   D. attain and reach

Margaret works at a bookstore now, but last year she was unemployed and repeatedly filled out job applications <u>over and over again</u> to find work.

6. F. NO CHANGE
   G. in order to seek out and
   H. and sought them out
   J. DELETE the underlined portion.

English Tip

If It Sounds Wrong, It Probably Is Wrong: Read the sentence in your head. If you know a word sounds wrong or a sentence sounds too wordy and weird, go with your gut!

English Tip

Plug It In: Read the sentence with each answer option. Sometimes "hearing" it will help you eliminate wrong answers. Go with the one that sounds best!

10.4.1 Set One

It occurred to me that <u>my rushed manner of speeding</u> through my chapter reading was not the most effective way to study for my history test.

1. **A.** NO CHANGE
   B. my hurried way of rushing
   C. my rush in haste
   D. rushing

Underwater explorer Jaques <u>Cousteau, exploring under the sea,</u> would go on to develop the first open-circuit underwater breathing regulator tank called the "aqua-lung."

2. **F.** NO CHANGE
   G. Cousteau
   H. Cousteau—who was exploring under the sea—
   J. Cousteau, explorer of the sea,

Even in his youth, Ming's parents knew his art was extraordinary and destined for <u>prestigious acclaim.</u>

3. **A.** NO CHANGE
   B. renowned fame.
   C. prestigious recognition.
   D. acclaim.

END OF SET ONE
STOP! DO NOT GO ON TO THE NEXT PAGE
UNTIL TOLD TO DO SO.

1 1

10.4.2 Set Two

Initially, he <u>first</u> thought the berries were poisonous and avoided eating them.

4. **F.** NO CHANGE
   G. at first
   H. originally
   J. DELETE the underlined portion.

We were flabbergasted that the hibiscus plant can <u>reach</u> a height of up to fifteen feet tall.

5. **A.** NO CHANGE
   B. achieve to reach
   C. attain and reach
   D. in terms of height reach

Owners of the new building hired security guards to deter potential <u>trespassers who might wrongfully enter their property.</u>

6. **F.** NO CHANGE
   G. people who might trespass by walking on to the private property.
   H. trespassers who sneak into the building where they are not allowed.
   J. trespassers.

END OF SET TWO
STOP! DO NOT GO ON TO THE NEXT PAGE
UNTIL TOLD TO DO SO.

10.4.3 Set Three

The results of the local election showed that Buddy Primeaux won the popular vote, with people choosing him to be in office.

7. **A.** NO CHANGE
   B. with voters picking who they wanted to be in office.
   C. as the people's choice for who should be in office.
   D. DELETE the underlined portion and end the sentence with a period.

Angela was terribly concerned about the potential side effects of her new medicine, but the doctor insisted there was only a minimal and extremely small chance they would affect her.

8. **F.** NO CHANGE
   G. minimal in that it was extremely small
   H. minimally small
   J. minimal

James had told me he was studying to prepare for his medical licensing exam, but when I looked at the materials on his desk, I found only comic books.

9. **A.** NO CHANGE
   B. to get himself ready
   C. like someone who is planning to be ready
   D. DELETE the underlined portion.

END OF SET THREE
STOP! DO NOT GO ON TO THE NEXT PAGE
UNTIL TOLD TO DO SO.

10.4.4 Set Four

As a military man, one of General Dwight Eisenhower's greatest achievements was his role in the preparation and planning of the Allied D-Day invasion at Normandy.

10. **F.** NO CHANGE
    G. preparation, which was the planning
    H. preparation, that is, the planning
    J. preparation

We worked together to find a realistic solution that we could achieve.

11. **A.** NO CHANGE
    B. to achieve.
    C. to solve.
    D. DELETE the underlined portion and end the sentence with a period.

The Sahara Desert is harsh and prohibitive to those who are not familiar with it, but the adventurous tourist can have an amazing experience in the desert with an experienced guide leading the way.

12. **F.** NO CHANGE
    G. whose job it is to lead him or her.
    H. who goes along as the guide.
    J. guiding the tourist, as a leader.

END OF SET FOUR

STOP! DO NOT GO ON TO THE NEXT PAGE UNTIL TOLD TO DO SO.

1 ■ ■ ■ ■ ■ ■ ■ ■ ■ 1

10.4.5 Set Five

At first I was repulsed by the idea of enrolling in an entry-level class, but <u>before long, enough time had passed, that</u> as I mused over it longer, I gradually came around and decided to attend.

13. **A.** NO CHANGE
B. soon, not much time had passed
C. after awhile, not long after,
D. after awhile,

My sister, however, can finish the <u>crossword, completing it</u> in less than fifteen minutes.

14. **F.** NO CHANGE
G. crossword
H. crossword's end
J. crossword by working on it

At first glance, the cryptic directions <u>(you couldn't figure them out) seemed impossible</u> to understand.

15. **A.** NO CHANGE
B. seemed impossible
C. seemed impossible so you couldn't figure them out
D. seemed so impossible you almost couldn't figure them out

END OF SET FIVE
STOP! DO NOT GO ON TO THE NEXT PAGE
UNTIL TOLD TO DO SO.

Sum It Up

Tips and Techniques

If It Sounds Wrong, It Probably Is Wrong: Read the sentence in your head. If you know a word sounds wrong or a sentence sounds too wordy, go with your gut!

Plug It In: Read the sentence with each answer option. Sometimes "hearing" it will help you eliminate wrong answers. Go with the one that sounds best!

Conciseness Is Key: ACT questions usually get right to the point. Other times, you have to help them get there.

Knowing Is Half the Battle: Words may look like they add detail, but they may in fact be redundant. Remember the "happy" activity.

Lesson 11

Redundancy Part 2

CAPTION:

11.1 Entrance Ticket

Write a few sentences about what you had for your most recent lunch in the most flowery, wordy, poetic, over-explanatory way that you possibly can. Then trade with a partner. Both of you will rewrite each other's sentences in the most basic and plain way possible without losing any meaning or information.

Redundant/Rambling

Concise

11.2 Learning Targets

1. Effectively remove material in writing that is not concise

2. Appropriately add needed information and clarity to writing

Self-Assessment

Circle the number that corresponds to your confidence level in your knowledge of this subject before beginning the lesson. A score of 1 means you are completely lost, and a score of 4 means you have mastered the skills. After you finish the lesson, return to the bottom of this page and circle your new confidence level to show your improvement.

Before Lesson

1 2 3 4

After Lesson

1 2 3 4

11.3.1 Concise vs. Wordy

Conciseness Rule 1: ______________________________

____

____

Leather jackets, at once stylish and wild, edgy and refined, can be worn anywhere for various purposes, which makes them a perfect gift for anyone.

1. **A.** NO CHANGE
   B. which are edgy and they're refined,
   C. as something refined can also come across as edgy,
   D. having edgy also being refined,

Because what is inside the courtyard reflects the style outside, the architect was praised for his subtle, refined choices and the continuity throughout his work.

2. **F.** NO CHANGE
   G. at the exterior,
   H. on the opposite side,
   J. far out and beyond,

The enormous luxury apartment complex with which the small office faces will soon create traffic and parking issues.

3. **A.** NO CHANGE
   B. that faces the small office
   C. toward the small office faces
   D. which the small office facing

11.3.1 Concise vs. Wordy

Conciseness Rule 2: ______________________________

____

____

In many cases, the footage from the film can enhance the <u>music that a viewer can hear.</u>

1. **A.** NO CHANGE
   B. qualities that are musical in everyday life.
   C. music heard.
   D. music.

The bed was spacious enough for him to stretch out as he <u>slowly drifted</u> off to sleep.

2. **F.** NO CHANGE
   G. reached, slowly drifting
   H. spread his arms, beginning to slowly drift
   J. slowly spread out to drift

11.3.1 Concise vs. Wordy

Conciseness Rule 3: ______________________________

____

____

During the <u>afternoon after that lunch,</u> on a walk through the park, we had finally calmed down about the terrible service we'd received at the restaurant during lunch.

1. **A.** NO CHANGE
   B. afternoon after that lunch before,
   C. afternoon as we left the restaurant,
   D. afternoon,

As I listened to my music, all the problems I was facing began to fade <u>away.</u>

2. **F.** NO CHANGE
   G. away, like a wall between the past and the present.
   H. away, like a vessel heading towards the unknown.
   J. away, like a barrier that blocks the outside world.

Watson knew that any unresolved arguments—and there were plenty—would be forgotten in time, and their friendship would <u>remain the same.</u>

3. **A.** NO CHANGE
   B. remain the same as it had in the past.
   C. in any case, remain the same.
   D. also stay the same.

English Tip

Plug It In: If you aren't sure whether something is too wordy, try to read the sentence with each of the given answer choices. This will help you understand how the choices relate to the sentence as a whole. You'll be better able to notice if something is repeated or made unclear.

11.3.2 Concise vs. Unclear

1. You DO NOT want sentences that sound unnatural or clumsy, but you DO add words that:

____

2. You DO NOT want sentences that are repetitive, but you DO add words that:

____

3. You DO NOT want sentences that are unclear or lacking necessary information, but you DO add words that:

____

---

1. Some musicians mail albums to our office with a tagline saying that their music will be the future of rock and roll; others <u>may have been recorded badly.</u> The record executives only care if they have a hit record on their hands.

   Given that all are true, which of the choices creates the most logical and appropriate contrast to the first part of this sentence?

   A. NO CHANGE
   B. don't seem to understand how many albums our staff have to listen to.
   C. only ask us to acknowledge that their music has some potential.
   D. come to us on a cheap CD-R.

English Tip

Consistent, Clear, and Concise: You should only choose a longer answer on a conciseness question when it makes the sentence clearer. If you need to guess, choose the shortest option. It is almost always correct.

11.4.1 Set One

During his freshman year of high school, Jack Murano, Cougar High School's band director, took an interest in David's drumming on the line and thought he might perhaps be good enough to be in the drum core maybe to become a first-chair drummer.

1. A. NO CHANGE
   B. thought David had the capacity
   C. noticed that he displayed some type of possible potential talent
   D. saw David's potential gifts that he could utilize

Like so many sophomores, he no longer felt the fear and excitement that came with starting high school, nor was the maturity and responsibility bestowed on him as it was on the seniors.

2. F. NO CHANGE
   G. was he as mature and responsible as
   H. was he bestowed and granted the maturity and responsibility like
   J. the maturity and responsibility bestowed on

When the star quarterback ran onto the field, I wasn't anticipating the mayhem.

3. A. NO CHANGE
   B. ready for the unforeseen mayhem.
   C. anticipating, in terms of the mayhem, what would eventually happen.
   D. prepared for the mayhem, which I did not expect to happen.

END OF SET ONE
STOP! DO NOT GO ON TO THE NEXT PAGE
UNTIL TOLD TO DO SO.

11.4.2 Set Two

After rock music became popular in the 1970s, the leather jacket became a fashion statement among people who wanted their personal style to express two distinct character traits that rock musicians had of going against the norm and not being afraid to show it.

4. **F.** NO CHANGE
   G. this.
   H. edginess and confidence.
   J. aspirations or hopes to exhibit a certain coolness everywhere they went, as well as self-assurance.

It can be seen that these pants are stylish, comfortable, and (along with many of the jackets in the same collection) water-repellent.

5. **A.** NO CHANGE
   B. incapable of having water soak through the fabric.
   C. have the ability to repel water.
   D. resist water damage.

One of the highlights of his career was the time he volunteered aid through the supervision of the construction of the new park downtown.

6. **F.** NO CHANGE
   G. for the supervision of
   H. to aid by supervising
   J. to supervise

END OF SET TWO
STOP! DO NOT GO ON TO THE NEXT PAGE
UNTIL TOLD TO DO SO.

1 ■ ■ ■ ■ ■ ■ ■ ■ ■ 1

11.4.3 Set Three

She also loved abbreviations typically formed from parts of words, such as NATO, Scuba, Radar, or Interpol.

7. A. NO CHANGE
   B. words that stood in place of more words or phrases,
   C. abbreviated phrases or words,
   D. acronyms,

Over time, Alice learned that any mishaps on Thanksgiving—and there were always unforeseen problems—were possible to overcome.

8. F. NO CHANGE
   G. to be handled in a successful way.
   H. to overcome, more or less.
   J. to overcome and handle well.

The director's odd style didn't fit the techniques of filmmaking I had learned in college.

9. A. NO CHANGE
   B. that was learned while being instructed
   C. I watched learning
   D. I saw when I was learning

END OF SET THREE

STOP! DO NOT GO ON TO THE NEXT PAGE UNTIL TOLD TO DO SO.

11.4.4 Set Four

Sandra knew she could get extra fries out of the waitress. She just had to inspire some pity and appeal to the compassionate feelings of the waitress's sympathy.

10. **F.** NO CHANGE
    G. the emotional attributes of
    H. the sensitive qualities pertaining to
    J. DELETE the underlined portion

After years of arguing, I found it my responsibility as a homeowner to take action; no longer would my neighbors' leaves fall all over my driveway.

11. Which of the following alternatives to the underlined portion would be LEAST acceptable in terms of the context of this sentence?
    A. resolve this issue
    B. create a plan to fix the problem and issue at hand
    C. conclude this matter
    D. end this dispute

In only a couple of years, she would become the person who leads the marketing division.

12. **F.** NO CHANGE
    G. be the person who leads
    H. receive her duty to lead
    J. lead

END OF SET FOUR
STOP! DO NOT GO ON TO THE NEXT PAGE UNTIL TOLD TO DO SO.

11.4.5 Set Five

Pulling the piping-hot cake out of the oven, Stefan realized that his finished creation did not match the <u>anticipation of the expected result.</u>

13. **A.** NO CHANGE
B. picture in the recipe book.
C. shape that all of his other cakes had previously.
D. pictorial representation of the cake that he had seen in the recipe book.

The men admired his compassion, his strong resolve, and <u>they had an admiration for his sense of responsibility for those close to him.</u>

14. **F.** NO CHANGE
G. an admiration for his sense of responsibility for those close to him.
H. his sense of responsibility for those close to him.
J. the sense of responsibility for those close to oneself.

Lately, the emotional power behind her <u>music</u> began to inspire my own art.

15. **A.** NO CHANGE
B. arrangement of melodical sounds
C. composition of notes and melody
D. harmonious combination of sounds

END OF SET FIVE
STOP! DO NOT GO ON TO THE NEXT PAGE
UNTIL TOLD TO DO SO.

Sum It Up

Redundancy Part 2

Concise

Providing necessary and accurate information in as few words as possible

Tips and Techniques

Consistent, Clear, and Concise: Choose the shortest answer unless you think you need to keep additional words for clarity or meaning.

Plug It In: Try plugging in the answer choices if you can't tell if they are wordy. Sounding them out in context will help you.

Lesson 12

Transitions Part 1

CAPTION:

12.1 Entrance Ticket

Write a paragraph (at least five sentences) about a time of transition in your life or a significant change you once experienced. Use five transition words in your paragraph.

12.2 Learning Targets

1. Understand the role transition words play in writing

2. Understand and use the different categories of transition words

Self-Assessment

Circle the number that corresponds to your confidence level in your knowledge of this subject before beginning the lesson. A score of 1 means you are completely lost, and a score of 4 means you have mastered the skills. After you finish the lesson, return to the bottom of this page and circle your new confidence level to show your improvement.

Before Lesson

1 2 3 4

After Lesson

1 2 3 4

12.3.1 Sentence Transitions

Choose the best transition word for each sentence using the word bank provided by your teacher.

I set my alarm last night; ____________, I didn't hear it and overslept.
1 2

I barely had any time to get ready ____________ I saw the bus flying by my house.
3 4

I was late for school this morning ____________ I missed the bus.
5 6

I normally take the bus. ____________, my mom had to bring me today.
7 8

I did manage to eat breakfast before I left, ____________ I wasn't hungry in first hour.
9 10

My mom told me to make sure not to oversleep again. ____________, I'll be in trouble if this happens again!
11 12

English Tip

Sounds Best: Even if you don't know the exact grammar rules, it's okay to guess based on what sounds best. You can often trust your instincts to know if something sounds right or wrong.

12.3.2 Transition Categories

Sort the transition words your teacher provides into the correct category and write an example sentence for each word.

Time	Cause and Effect	Contrast
Exemplification/Clarification	**Intensification**	**Addition**

12.4.1 Set One

For the poorest of settlements, wasting money on food that soon spoiled was worse than having a shortage. Many decreed, <u>consequently,</u> that no trade for food should be carried out before the fishermen returned with either their catch or their empty nets.

1. **A.** NO CHANGE
   B. otherwise,
   C. however,
   D. frequently,

She forgot her homework in her locker, <u>for</u> her mother, more than a little annoyed, had to drive her back to school.

2. **F.** NO CHANGE
   G. so
   H. but
   J. because

The sound of a whistle pierced the thin night air of the woods, and the gate flung open without warning. <u>Immediately,</u> the dogs ran through the opening and into the forest.

3. Which of the following would be the best alternative to the underlined portion of the sentence?
   A. Again,
   B. Now and then,
   C. At the same time,
   D. Occasionally,

END OF SET ONE
STOP! DO NOT GO ON TO THE NEXT PAGE
UNTIL TOLD TO DO SO.

12.4.2 Set Two

She campaigned ceaselessly all year. Accordingly, the voters remained skeptical of her carefully arranged words and empty promises.

4. F. NO CHANGE
   G. Therefore,
   H. Nevertheless,
   J. Furthermore,

The captain's wretched crew was forced to row blindly through the driving sheets of rain, or else the ship would be pushed too far off course.

5. A. NO CHANGE
   B. and so
   C. then
   D. as well as

The remote Rainbow Waterfall is an arduous three-mile hike into the heart of the rainforest. Also, once you reach the timeworn *Cachoeira do Arco-iris* sign, the site is only a quarter of a mile away.

6. F. NO CHANGE
   G. Once
   H. Additionally, once
   J. However, once

END OF SET TWO

STOP! DO NOT GO ON TO THE NEXT PAGE UNTIL TOLD TO DO SO.

12.4.3 Set Three

Most of the frontiersmen carried enough supplies to last them the entire westward journey. Others, likewise, relied more heavily on fellow travelers to barter with or sell them supplies.

7. **A.** NO CHANGE
   B. however,
   C. also,
   D. too,

Our mother's first apartment was the height of luxury, filled with wonderful conveniences she had never had before. Otherwise, mother could wash her dishes in a dishwasher, heat the house with an electric heater, and dry her clothes in a machine instead of on a line of string through the kitchen.

8. **F.** NO CHANGE
   G. Likewise, our mother
   H. Regardless, Mother
   J. Mother

At the concert last night, the band played all of Jermaine's favorite songs from its very first album. To be sure, it was surprising to hear all of those old hits from five albums ago.

9. **A.** NO CHANGE
   B. Furthermore,
   C. Likewise,
   D. For example,

END OF SET THREE
STOP! DO NOT GO ON TO THE NEXT PAGE
UNTIL TOLD TO DO SO.

12.4.4 Set Four

We ensured, with a keen eye, that all sweets were dispersed evenly because the older children often caused disputes and hurt the little ones' feelings.

10. Which of the following would NOT be an appropriate alternative to the underlined section of this sentence?

F. even though
G. knowing that
H. given that
J. since

When my father drives, he actually enjoys being stuck in heavy traffic, surrounded by other cars, even though most people consider traffic jams to be among the worst of life's inevitable annoyances.

11. Which of the following would NOT be an appropriate alternative to the underlined section of this sentence?

A. since
B. although
C. but
D. even if

Almost constantly, each vivid color of North American Azalea can be seen in the Nestors' back garden.

12. Which of the following would NOT be an appropriate alternative to the underlined section of this sentence?

F. Most of the time,
G. Continuously,
H. Nearly always,
J. Infrequently,

END OF SET FOUR

STOP! DO NOT GO ON TO THE NEXT PAGE UNTIL TOLD TO DO SO.

12.4.5 Set Five

Because fledgling birds do not always willingly leap from the nest, the mother bird sometimes has to give her offspring their first gentle push into the air.

13. **A.** NO CHANGE
    B. Even if
    C. While
    D. Except that

Some say it is impossible to discover buried treasure with a metal detector. However, it has happened in the past, so it is not a completely futile venture.

14. **F.** NO CHANGE
    G. Likewise,
    H. Therefore,
    J. Accordingly,

The encyclopedia set I bought my grandparents last year has been handy in more ways than I could ever have anticipated. My grandpa, therefore, uses the fourth and fifth volumes to balance his wobbly kitchen table.

15. **A.** NO CHANGE
    B. on the contrary,
    C. for instance,
    D. consequently,

END OF SET FIVE
STOP! DO NOT GO ON TO THE NEXT PAGE
UNTIL TOLD TO DO SO.

Sum It Up

Transitions Part 1

A **transition** is a word or phrase used to link two ideas together.

Common Transitions:

Instead
So
Otherwise
In other words
Before
Meanwhile
However
Indeed
Because
For example
Also

Tips and Techniques

Sounds Best: Remember to check how an answer sounds if you don't know the rules.

Lesson 13

Transitions Part 2

CAPTION:

13.1 Entrance Ticket

Rewrite the following paragraph. Add transition words and rearrange the sentences to clarify the meaning and information in the paragraph.

One of my favorite pastimes is swimming. I compete as a short-distance swimmer. I wanted to find a summer job. My mother recommended that I try to do what I love for work. I decided to get a job that paid me to swim. I trained to become a lifeguard. I worked at the local fitness club. I learned that being a lifeguard doesn't involve much swimming. I sat in the lifeguard chair. I made sure people stayed safe. I got a tan. I got very bored. After work, I did get to swim in the pool. The pool closed soon after my shift was over. The job would have been fun if anyone had needed saving. Every person at the fitness club was a good, safe swimmer. I won't be working as a lifeguard again at that fitness club's pool.

13.2 Learning Targets

1. Determine if transition words need to be added to a sentence or passage

2. Determine if transitional sentences need to be added between paragraphs

Self-Assessment

Circle the number that corresponds to your confidence level in your knowledge of this subject before beginning the lesson. A score of 1 means you are completely lost, and a score of 4 means you have mastered the skills. After you finish the lesson, return to the bottom of this page and circle your new confidence level to show your improvement.

Before Lesson

1 2 3 4

After Lesson

1 2 3 4

13.3.1 Transition Direction

Brainstorm some transition words that fit in each category below.

Backward

Stays the Same

Forward

13.3.1 Transition Direction

Move forward and backward along the path based on the type of transition word your teacher provides.

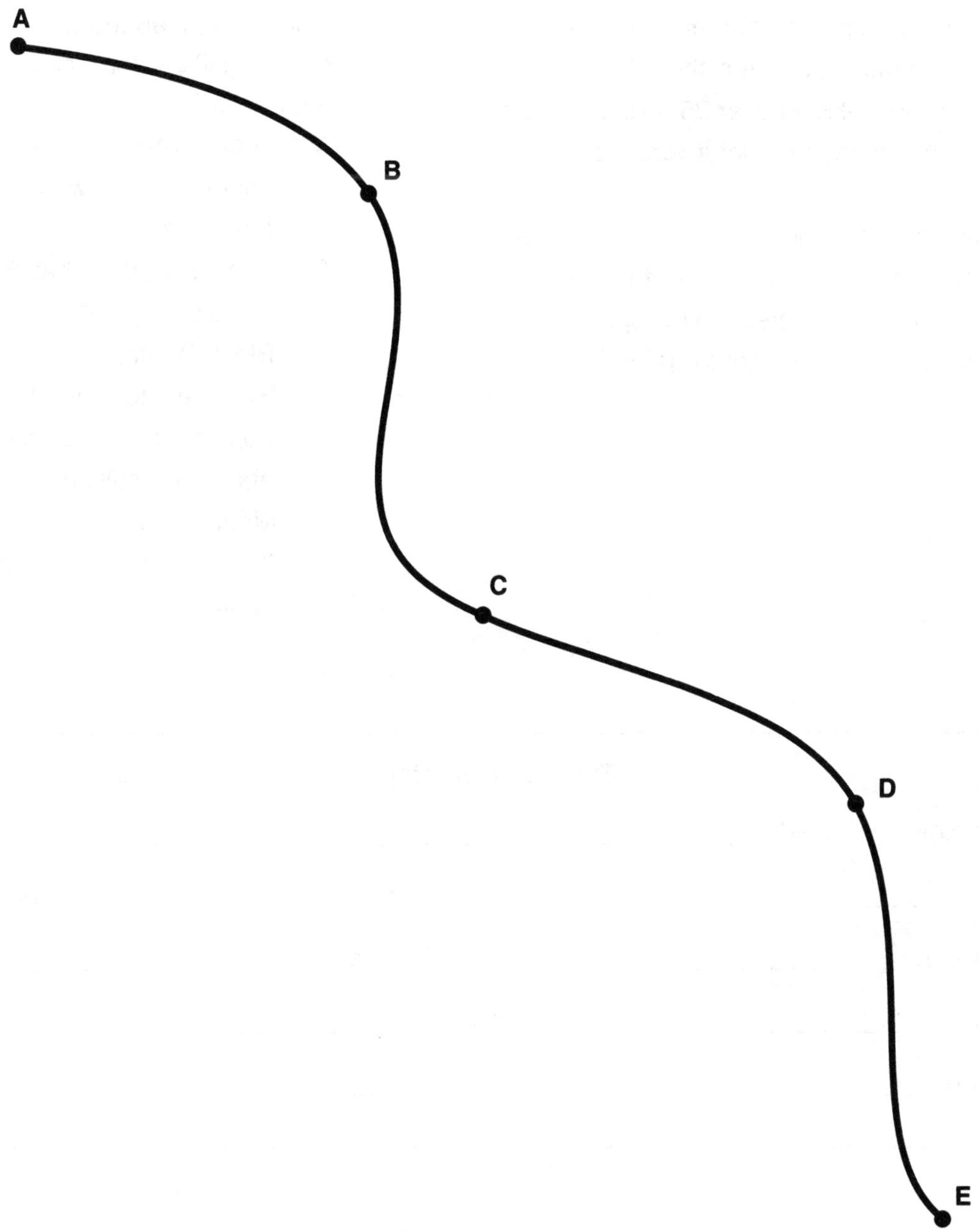

English Tip

Look Around: If the answers are all transition words, look at the phrases that surround the underlined portion. Are they negative, positive, or just restating the same things? Choose a transition word based on the relationship you see. If you are not sure, eliminate any transitions that are synonyms of one another.

13.3.2 Paragraph Transitions

The Middle Ages boasted no scientific investigation to speak of; good and bad occurrences were simply providence. So when the Black Death spread across Europe—killing over 25 million people in under five years—many thought it was the end of the world. [1]

Modern medicine and forensics have shown that, in fact, the pandemic was caused by the bacteria *Yersinia pestis*. The disease spread to Europe through merchant ships fleeing the Mongol siege of Caffa.

1. Given that all of the following are true, which one, if added here, would offer the best transition from the first paragraph to the second?

A. There were not many doctors who understood how the body actually functions.

B. It is estimated that 30–60% of the world's population perished in the Black Death.

C. By the fourteenth century, the population of Europe was down to about 360 million.

D. Medieval society did not know that this pestilence came from a peculiar source.

Transition Strategy

1. Determine what needs __________ __________ __________.

2. __________ the __________ of each __________ or sentence.

3. Choose the __________ __________ that includes __________ relating to the __________ of both paragraphs or __________.

4. Use the __________ of __________.

1 ■ ■ ■ ■ ■ ■ ■ ■ ■ 1

13.4.1 Set One

The bubble gum was stuck too deep in his hair to get it out completely. Therefore, his mother had to grab the scissors and cut it out.

1. A. NO CHANGE
   B. Additionally,
   C. On the other hand,
   D. Furthermore,

Her father's train was overdue, and Maria could hardly control her worry. However, time seemed to be passing as slowly as cold molasses pouring out of a jar.

2. F. NO CHANGE
   G. Time, although,
   H. Besides, time
   J. Time

Since tar may take many hours to completely solidify, it is exceptionally strong and durable when dry. They are required to keep their work area properly illuminated for the safety of both the crew and anyone who may drive by.

3. Given that all of the choices are true, which replacement to the underlined portion would provide an essential link to the sentence that follows?

   A. NO CHANGE
   B. many road crews work throughout the night.
   C. law requires that caution signs be put up around the area.
   D. this does not stop cars from driving over wet tar.

END OF SET ONE

STOP! DO NOT GO ON TO THE NEXT PAGE UNTIL TOLD TO DO SO.

13.4.2 Set Two

Tensions in Europe were coming to a head, with the French, Spanish, and English all ready to go to war over land and riches. Although the English queen, Elizabeth I, had many foreign suitors who promised peace treaties, she rebuffed their advances and kept them at a distance. This refusal to marry led to many egos being injured.

4. Given that all of the following are true, which choice would provide the most effective link between sentences?

   F. NO CHANGE
   G. they never followed through with signing them.
   H. she intended to conquer her enemies on the battlefield.
   J. England was ill-prepared for such a momentous war.

Expressing one's style was difficult in the hospital, where everyone was required to dress in scrubs and lab coats. With exceptional taste in fashion, Dr. Blytheson's socks were unfailingly unique—always patterned, colorful, or matched to his shirt.

5. Given that all of the following are true, which choice would provide the most effective link between sentences?

   A. NO CHANGE
   B. Unlike most surgeons,
   C. Regardless of this dress code,
   D. Rather than be a slob,

We will attend the orientation meeting first, and in the last, final step we will be put into groups for discussions, tours of the campus, and an introduction to our department head—fretting all the while about the impending placement tests that could drop several hours off our course loads freshman year.

6. **F.** NO CHANGE
   G. instead
   H. then
   J. therefore

END OF SET TWO
STOP! DO NOT GO ON TO THE NEXT PAGE
UNTIL TOLD TO DO SO.

13.4.3 Set Three

Sonia's mother used to tell her the story of Chandira, a princess who was captured by pirates. While the pirates were negotiating with her father over the ransom price, cunning Chandira discovered a means of escape. She returned to her father just as he was about to pay for her release. [4]

In South Asian tradition, a bindi is either a red dot or a piece of jewelry worn on the forehead between the eyebrows. A bindi can signify love and prosperity, concentration in meditation, or can simply be an ornamental beauty mark. Chandira wore hers as a means of strengthening her intellect and maintaining her courage. And that, went the story, was the secret of crafty Chandira's escape from danger.

7. Which of the following sentences, if added here, would most effectively lead the reader from the first paragraph to the discussion of the bindi in the second paragraph?

A. Chandira kept just one thing as a memento from her adventure upon the seas.
B. Because she was not wearing her bindi when she was captured, her father was furious.
C. Chandira attributed her escape to one thing—her bindi.
D. After returning home, Chandira's tenacious spirit was weakened by the ordeal.

Mike had never eaten at Anwar's family's house, so he was confused when he bit into his slice of birthday cake and tasted <u>a different flavor.</u>

Anwar told Mike that what he was tasting was saffron, a spice his parents had grown up with in Turkey, and that his mother only used it for special occasions. It had gotten so expensive in this part of the world that Mrs. Demir had precious little of it left in her spice cupboard.

8. Which of the following provides the most specific transition to the next paragraph?

F. NO CHANGE
G. something really good.
H. a strange, exotic flavor.
J. something.

GO ON TO THE NEXT PAGE.

I became interested in archery after a class trip to an archery range. We were learning about ancient field sports in gym class, so Mr. Bellamy took us to visit the Fell Oak Range. Although we were each able to try shooting at least twenty arrows, only one person hit the target. Still, I was hooked.

[5] I checked out a few archery books from the library, browsed archery magazines in the bookstore, and even built a makeshift bow and arrow out of things I found in the park. Once I've saved up enough money, I'll buy a real bow and a quiver of arrows and practice at the Fell Oak Range until I can hit the bullseye.

9. Which of the following statements, if added here, would provide the most effective transition between the two paragraphs?

A. I've done everything in my power to learn about archery.
B. Practicing would make us better at aiming for the target.
C. Although many field sports are very old, they can still be fun.
D. I'd never even seen a bow before, much less used one.

END OF SET THREE
STOP! DO NOT GO ON TO THE NEXT PAGE
UNTIL TOLD TO DO SO.

1 1

13.4.4 Set Four

Watching movies isn't as fulfilling to me as it seems to be for most people. A movie is over in under three hours, and then you're left wondering what happens to the characters you grew to care for. You watched their lives play out on your screen, and then—suddenly—it's over.

Although television shows are shorter, they take longer to watch. You're connected to them; you watch them grow and develop at a slower rate. If you're following along episode by episode, season by season, those characters—those people—could be in your life for years.

10. Which choice would most effectively and appropriately lead the reader from the topic of the first paragraph to that of the second?

F. NO CHANGE
G. Watching a television show, however, gives you a more complex relationship with the characters.
H. Television shows do share some similarities with movies, but not in the ways you might expect.
J. Sometimes, filmmakers make sequels to popular movies to answer those questions.

In reading through our itinerary, I noticed that we were to visit the Colosseum while we were in Rome. I pictured crowds of spectators dressed in togas, speaking Latin and eating grapes. I imagined watching epic gladiator fights, horse races, and battle reenactments. [13]

When we walked up to the gigantic amphitheatre, however, it was nothing if not 2015. Somehow, it seemed perfectly ordinary for the ancient structure to be in the middle of the city over 2,000 years after its completion. People—dressed in pants and speaking a myriad of modern languages—were waiting in line to tour the Colosseum; others were talking on cellphones, hailing taxis. It was not the step back into the past I had so hoped for.

11. Which of the following, if added here, would best reinforce the preceding sentence and set up the contrast with the Colosseum's description in the next paragraph?

A. I wanted to see history come alive before my eyes.
B. I was hoping to watch a fighting demonstration.
C. Ancient Rome is one of my favorite historical periods.
D. At first, I was not very interested in visiting the Colosseum.

END OF SET FOUR
STOP! DO NOT GO ON TO THE NEXT PAGE
UNTIL TOLD TO DO SO.

Finally, winter turns into spring, and the end of the semester quickly approaches. During April and May, we review and grade the progress of each student.

Students are graded on various criteria, such as attendance, participation, accuracy, critical thinking, and overall academic performance.

12. Which of the following should the author use to create the clearest and most logical transition between paragraphs?

F. NO CHANGE
G. we hardly have time to smell the new flowers.
H. you probably know it's different than August.
J. they grade hundreds of tests and papers.

GO ON TO THE NEXT PAGE.

1 ■ ■ ■ ■ ■ ■ ■ ■ ■ 1

13.4.5 Set Five

Although Robin Hood had a price on his head, he was impossible to arrest. The many renditions of Robin Hood's story all have in common the idea that he was a hero, not simply a petty thief. By stealing from the rich to give to the poor, Robin Hood and his merry band provided their fellow peasants with money crucial to their very existence.

13. Given that all of the following are true, which choice most effectively leads the reader from the first sentence of this paragraph to the description that follows in the next two sentences?

A. NO CHANGE
B. The tale of Robin Hood depicts the triumphs of an underdog on a quest for justice.
C. The romance of Robin Hood and Maid Marian is one of the most charming of all legends.
D. Robin Hood's negligence of the codes of chivalry has cast him as a criminal throughout all of history.

Rather than wearing their baseball gloves, many students tucked them under their arms to better engage their phones' touchscreens. It upset the gym coach to see her students so distracted instead of enjoying the scrimmage, so she came up with an unconventional game plan.

She called a time-out, gathered everyone around, and collected the students' cellphones into two buckets, one for each team. "If you must play on your phones during the game," she said, "do it when your team is at bat." Thus, she eliminated the distraction in the outfield, and the students noticed for the first time that they were having fun.

14. Given that all of the following are true, which choice most logically follows the preceding sentence and leads into the next paragraph?

F. NO CHANGE
G. talked to the umpire about her frustration.
H. continued to watch the game, becoming more irate.
J. considered how distractions affect students' education.

GO ON TO THE NEXT PAGE.

Leung suddenly realized that nearly every person in the class, apart from himself, had grown up in suburbia. They came from a common history of upper-class wealth and luxury. They actually *had* travel experiences to write about in this assignment. He had never felt so out of place. [15]

He decided that—since this was a creative writing class, after all—he would approach the writing prompt in a more imaginative way. Since he had never in his life traveled outside the city limits, he decided to write his short story about what would happen if he did just that.

Here's the catch: the reason his character is forced to leave the city is because it has become overrun with a virus that turns people into werewolves. He is the only person to make it to the city line and across the bridge, but after that, he is clueless as to where to go next. His adventure leads him to meet many new and fascinating characters. And so *The Rising Moon* was born.

Once he began writing, Leung couldn't stop. By the end of the week, he had written over fifteen pages. By the end of the semester, he'd produced a ninety-eight-page novella and had gotten it printed by the university press. His story was an overnight sensation, and Leung was finally able to travel to New York City to co-author a screenplay based on *The Rising Moon* and then to Hollywood to film the movie.

15. Which of the following true statements, if added here, would best serve as a transition between the challenges Leung faced while in school and his success in meeting those challenges?

A. Then he had an idea that would become his greatest accomplishment.
B. He wondered whether he should have taken the class at all.
C. He had no idea what to say to his classmates with whom he had nothing in common.
D. At that point, Leung nearly gave up on college altogether.

END OF SET FIVE
STOP! DO NOT GO ON TO THE NEXT PAGE
UNTIL TOLD TO DO SO.

Sum It Up

Transitions Part 2

Transition

A word or phrase used to link two ideas together

Common *Backward* Transitions:

However
Though
Otherwise
Nevertheless
Instead

Common *Stays the Same* Transitions:

In other words
Still

Common *Forward* Transitions:

Because
Therefore
So
Since
Thus

Tips and Techniques

Sounds Best: Check how an answer sounds if you do not know the rules.

Verb Tense

CAPTION:

14.1 Entrance Ticket

Select the best alternative to the underlined portion in each section below. If no change is necessary, select NO CHANGE.

Flowers hang from the cast-iron railing, and water droplets had dripped off the petals.

1. **A.** NO CHANGE
   B. drip
   C. dripped
   D. could have dripped

By the time I learned that use of the term for my favorite coffee drink, the *Americano*, had begun during World War II in Italy, I was already studying Italian in school.

2. **F.** NO CHANGE
   G. begun
   H. had began
   J. have begun

Efforts to conserve natural resources in the United States are increasing, and this encourages activists everywhere. America's wetlands were the beneficiaries of the conservation movement's fundraising, awareness campaigns, and volunteer service days.

3. **A.** NO CHANGE
   B. had been
   C. would have been
   D. are

14.2 Learning Targets

1. Recognize and correct inappropriate shifts in verb tense
2. Maintain consistent and logical verb tense in sentences, paragraphs, and passages

Self-Assessment

Circle the number that corresponds to your confidence level in your knowledge of this subject before beginning the lesson. A score of 1 means you are completely lost, and a score of 4 means you have mastered the skills. After you finish the lesson, return to the bottom of this page and circle your new confidence level to show your improvement.

Before Lesson

1 2 3 4

After Lesson

1 2 3 4

14.3.1 Understanding Verb Tense

past	specific point in the past	present	specific point in the future	future

---

look

He _________ tired.

She _____________ out the window, wishing it would stop raining.

We ____________________ everywhere for her keys.

drip

The water _________ from the faucet incessantly.

The sticky syrup _____________ onto the book I was reading.

The rain ____________________ off the roof into that flower pot for years.

14.3.1 Understanding Verb Tense

begin

past tense: ______________ past perfect tense: ______________

______________ We have begun to sing. I had begun to forget until you reminded me.

______________ We have began to sing. I begun to forget until you reminded me.

Similar verbs: ____

____

take

past tense: ______________ past perfect tense: ______________

______________ We have took the bus every day. They taken all the tests by then.

______________ We have taken the bus every day. They will have taken all the tests by then.

Similar verbs: ____

____

throw

past tense: ______________ past perfect tense: ______________

______________ We have threw the football for an hour. You thrown away so much trash.

______________ We have thrown the football for an hour. You will have thrown away so much trash.

Similar verbs: ____

____

14.3.2 Using the Passage to Identify Tense

1. ____

2. ____

____

Clue Word or Phrase	Verb Tense

English Tip

Process of Elimination: It is always wrong to say *would of* or *could of*. The correct forms are *would have* and *could have*. If you see one of those incorrect verb forms or something similar to them, eliminate it immediately.

14.3.2 Using the Passage to Identify Tense

But we <u>had agreed</u> beforehand to take the train to the shore.

1. **A.** NO CHANGE
   B. had to of agreed
   C. have agree
   D. agreed that

By the time I learned that scuba diving had begun in the 1600s with deep underwater exploration, I <u>am developing</u> a habit of looking for a place to dive in every costal town.

2. **F.** NO CHANGE
   G. have developed
   H. had developed
   J. have been developing

I <u>was</u> on a boat across the harbor from Rhode Island last weekend, sitting on a hard bench between my parents.

3. **A.** NO CHANGE
   B. is
   C. will be
   D. would of been sitting

The drapes and curtains are bright pink, and the tile on the walls <u>has been</u> painted to match, although later it was covered with a more neutral varnish.

4. **F.** NO CHANGE
   G. have been
   H. were
   J. are

14.3.2 Using the Passage to Identify Tense

Flowers hang on the walls, and ivy vines <u>had sprawled</u> everywhere.

5. A. NO CHANGE
   B. sprawl
   C. sprawled
   D. could have sprawled

After the last monologue performance, constructive criticism <u>had been</u> given to the actors in private, highlighting areas that need improvement and praising what was done well. Each actor then has another two days to perfect his or her final audition piece.

6. F. NO CHANGE
   G. has been
   H. was
   J. is

When her friends found her two hours later—still reading on the couch—Jill <u>was prepared</u> to remind them that she often loses track of time.

7. A. NO CHANGE
   B. has been preparing
   C. will be prepared
   D. is prepared

English Tip

Context Clues: Every verb tense question can be answered by looking at the context of the entire sentence or paragraph. Look around and make sure the verb either matches other verbs in the context or connects to a clue word or phrase.

1 ■ ■ ■ ■ ■ ■ ■ ■ ■ 1

14.4.1 Set One

By 2075, the United States Census Bureau predicts the population <u>will of doubled</u>.

1. A. NO CHANGE
   B. had doubled
   C. doubled
   D. will have doubled

The imprisonment and eventual release of those early protestors transformed what people thought of privileged rights for the few. It <u>had made</u> a strong case for the settlers' right to freedom of assembly.

2. F. NO CHANGE
   G. made
   H. makes for
   J. makes

Before they created a simpler code language, Russian spies <u>had</u> been using complicated cryptographs to send messages to one another for decades.

3. A. NO CHANGE
   B. have
   C. are
   D. will have

END OF SET ONE

STOP! DO NOT GO ON TO THE NEXT PAGE UNTIL TOLD TO DO SO.

1 ■ ■ ■ ■ ■ ■ ■ ■ ■ 1

14.4.2 Set Two

My mother said she <u>would have checked</u> with my father, who agreed that if I wanted to earn money, I should get a paper route.

4. **F.** NO CHANGE
   G. would check
   H. have checked
   J. must checked

As the ground shifted, the street <u>have given</u> way to a massive sinkhole.

5. **A.** NO CHANGE
   B. had gave
   C. gave
   D. give

On a beautiful blue day when I was ten years old, I <u>will go</u> sailing with my mother.

6. **F.** NO CHANGE
   G. gone
   H. went
   J. had did some

END OF SET TWO
STOP! DO NOT GO ON TO THE NEXT PAGE
UNTIL TOLD TO DO SO.

14.4.3 Set Three

The result of his careful brush strokes is a painting that enriches the culture of the natives and took on a life of its own.

7. **A.** NO CHANGE
   B. takes
   C. taking
   D. had took

When winter comes, the town will look virtually the same except for a few feet of snow covering the roads. The miners can, however, have sixteen tons of coal and a sore back to show for their efforts.

8. **F.** NO CHANGE
   G. miners did,
   H. miners will,
   J. miners,

Although the drug that begun to produce results, the doctors advised caution before declaring that the disease had been completely cured.

9. **A.** NO CHANGE
   B. that had began producing
   C. that begun producing
   D. began producing

END OF SET THREE
STOP! DO NOT GO ON TO THE NEXT PAGE UNTIL TOLD TO DO SO.

14.4.4 Set Four

These archeologists excavating delicate burial sites and using special tools to unearth ancient objects that could be the key to understanding this civilization.

10. **F.** NO CHANGE
    G. excavating delicate burial sites and use
    H. excavated delicate burial sites to use
    J. excavate delicate burial sites and use

Writing would of long been thought of as a private act, a solitary deed of putting pen to paper and crafting a story.

11. **A.** NO CHANGE
    B. If writing had been long
    C. Writing has long been
    D. Supposing writing were long

The Texas craze for the cowboy hat began when cattle drivers from Mexico first drove their herds across the Rio Grande.

12. **F.** NO CHANGE
    G. begins
    H. begun
    J. had begin

END OF SET FOUR

STOP! DO NOT GO ON TO THE NEXT PAGE
UNTIL TOLD TO DO SO.

1 ■ ■ ■ ■ ■ ■ ■ ■ ■ 1

14.4.5 Set Five

The house was abandoned, but we managed to find our way in through an unlocked window in the back. Everything smelled like chicory and looked like an artist lived among the mess.

13. **A.** NO CHANGE
    B. had smelled like chicory and looked
    C. will smell like chicory and look
    D. smells like chicory and looks

As musicians tap to the music, they were also tapping in time to a rich history of artistry and beauty that moves the souls of all those privileged to hear it.

14. **F.** NO CHANGE
    G. are also tapping
    H. have also tapped
    J. also will tap

The book inspired artists, so they having created a statue in honor of the author who had so dramatically altered public perception of mental illness.

15. **A.** NO CHANGE
    B. creating
    C. to have created
    D. created

END OF SET FIVE
STOP! DO NOT GO ON TO THE NEXT PAGE
UNTIL TOLD TO DO SO.

Sum It Up

Verb Tense

Verb
A word that expresses an action or a state of being

Verb Tense
The form a verb takes that indicates when the action took place; the verb's place in time

Tips and Techniques

Process of Elimination: Eliminate any unacceptable verb forms, such as *would of* or *could of*. Those answers are always wrong.

Context Clues: Make sure your answer choice always matches the context. Keep in mind the tenses of the other verbs and the clue words or phrases that suggest when something happened.

Lesson 15

Accomplish Purpose Part 1

CAPTION:

15.1 Entrance Ticket

Write a paragraph about one of your goals. It can be for something you need to do today, want to achieve by the end of the year, or some other goal for the future. Write the steps you will take to accomplish this goal, examples of what you will do, how you will know you have accomplished the goal, and how you will feel after accomplishing it.

15.2 Learning Targets

1. Determine a purpose and identify its necessary context

2. Determine a context and identify the purpose it is supporting

Self-Assessment

Circle the number that corresponds to your confidence level in your knowledge of this subject before beginning the lesson. A score of 1 means you are completely lost, and a score of 4 means you have mastered the skills. After you finish the lesson, return to the bottom of this page and circle your new confidence level to show your improvement.

Before Lesson

1 2 3 4

After Lesson

1 2 3 4

15.3.1 Accomplish Straightforward Purpose

1. While many cultures have had their own version of basketball, the game we play today can be linked to a similar game that was played by the Olmec, Aztec, and Mayan civilizations, where a basketball-like sport <u>had been a popular activity for hundreds of years.</u>

   Given that all the choices are true, which one provides the most effective evidence of the long and revered history of basketball in these ancient civilizations?

   A. NO CHANGE
   B. had been a pastime for many years.
   C. was a game that was played with skulls or coconuts rather than rubber balls.
   D. resembled the enthusiasm that ancient China and Greece had for early versions of soccer.

   Essential Phrase: ______________________________

2. One doesn't need any prior experience in painting to <u>take part in an activity that is fun for everyone.</u>

   Which of the choices best helps the writer emphasize that painting is an activity in which anyone can participate and not reserved for trained professionals only?

   F. NO CHANGE
   G. get the idea.
   H. go to art school.
   J. know how to create artistic masterpieces.

   Essential Phrase: ______________________________

3. <u>Although Malcolm had never coached kids, he reluctantly</u> agreed to coach the small middle school boxing team.

   At this point in the essay, the writer wants to show that Coach Malcolm did not feel prepared to coach boxing at the middle school level. Given that all the choices are true, which one best conveys the message?

   A. NO CHANGE
   B. In general, students in his program were usually well into their twenties, and he
   C. Given the fact that most of his guys were a lot older, he deliberately
   D. After a healthy dialogue with the boys' parents, he

   Essential Phrase: ______________________________

15.3.1 Accomplish Straightforward Purpose

4. When Rodney settled down in Los Angeles, he planned to become a solo recording artist with the help of Taylor MacArthur, a record producer and band manager who <u>had seen Rodney play</u>.

Given that all the choices are true, which one most clearly and effectively establishes the personal and business relationship between MacArthur and Rodney?

F. NO CHANGE
G. had become Rodney's close friend and musical mentor.
H. had produced records for years up to that point.
J. was positive Rodney had potential.

Essential Phrase: ______________________________

5. By midday, <u>there is more water being pumped into</u> the city.

The writer would like to indicate that at this point, the water from the flood was extremely powerful. Given that all the choices are true, which one best accomplishes the writer's goal?

A. NO CHANGE
B. the water current is more intense throughout
C. a concentrated deluge of water invades
D. a sort of barrier of water descends into

Essential Phrase: ______________________________

English Tip

Most Valuable Phrases: The most important thing to identify in purpose questions is the essential phrase in the question. Your answer will follow that phrase very closely. In fact, you can ignore the grammar on these questions and focus entirely on the essential phrase.

15.3.2 Adding Specific Details

1. Roger Ebert died in 2013, but his accomplishments—as film critic and Pulitzer Prize winner—live on, as a remarkable career in the world of cinema.

   Which choice would most effectively guide readers to understand the global impact of Roger Ebert's career on cinema?

   A. NO CHANGE
   B. as a successful TV personality.
   C. spreading his knowledge of film criticism to more than 200 newspapers around the world.
   D. showing that others will continue the work of film criticism in the future.

2. My fascination with stamp collecting began when my grandfather let me look at all the things he brought back home from the war. I was looking at the old French and German money, thinking about how many hands had touched the bills. I took out the satchel of letters my grandfather had sent to my grandma, and I asked if I could read them. That's when I noticed the still-bright green stamp on one of the old, yellowed envelopes. I asked my grandfather where it had come from.

   "Lithuania," he said, almost admiringly. "It was the first stop on my European tour."

   At ten years old, I had never even heard of the place. When I went back home at the end of the summer, I took out my trusty encyclopedia set and got to work researching countries that fought in World War II. I can say with absolute certainty that this little green square is what sparked my obsession with history—not to mention stamps!

   Twenty years later, the memory came back to me in the middle of a philatelic—stamp collecting—exposition. I thought about all those old stamps: Polish, Italian, Austrian, even German. It occurred to me that my grandfather's war story could be told by tracing those stamps, beginning with that first one and ending when he got back to my grandma's waiting arms.

   Given that all the choices are true, which one would help clarify the logic of this sentence by making the most vivid reference back to the scene described earlier in the passage?

   F. NO CHANGE
   G. stamp worth collecting
   H. little green stamp
   J. valuable stamp

15.3.2 Adding Specific Details

In this kind of question, use this method:

1. Find the ________________ phrases.
2. Get the ________________ .
3. Choose the answer that ________________ the ________________ and the ________________ .

3. The development of the new capitol building took a look at past cultures and different architectural styles to influence its design. The architects on this project researched various styles throughout the centuries so as to inspire their team to push the boundaries of what a capitol could look like. The people in the city were excited to see the final project—a blend of ancient and modern. The <u>standard-width</u> columns, which stood in the front of the state capitol, served to reflect the structure's Greek and Roman influences.

   Given that all the choices are true, which description of the columns best supports the architects' intent in creating this design, as described in this paragraph?

   A. NO CHANGE
   B. soundly built
   C. stately, classical
   D. expensive

4. Located in the Kelabit Highlands of Central Borneo, the Cultured Rainforest Project brings together a team of anthropologists, archaeologists, and paleoecologists to investigate the long-term and everyday interactions between the people and the rainforest in order to understand how societies functioned in the past. [4]

   Which of the following true statements, if added here, would best point out the organizations from which the Cultured Rainforest Project receives its orders?

   F. Anthropology professors from the University of Leicester contributed to the Cultured Rainforest Project.
   G. Anthropologists and archaeologists often disagreed with one another during the Cultured Rainforest Project's planning.
   H. Many administrative offices and dedicated scholars have shown interest in the Cultured Rainforest Project's promise.
   J. The Cultured Rainforest Project is managed jointly by the University of Leicester and the State Planning Unit of Sarawak.

15.3.2 Adding Specific Details

5. The *Avanti* project is a series of massive plans carried out at London Stansted Airport and the BAA Heathrow Express. The project was developed by a group of transportation specialists who assessed the issues faced by modern travel and devised solutions that would alleviate the worst difficulties. [5]

Which of the following true statements, if added here, would best point out the governing bodies from which the *Avanti* project receives its orders?

A. *Avanti* is run by the U.K. Department of Trade and Industry with the International Alliance for Interoperability (IAI), Loughborough University and Co-Construct.
B. Many construction companies provided information and labor to the *Avanti* project.
C. Various information agencies proposed different strategies for fixing the problems faced by the *Avanti* project.
D. Many companies and commuters were eager to see the results of the *Avanti* project.

English Tip

Process of Elimination: Most of the time you can eliminate several answers based on the essential phrase in the question. If you are running out of time or get stuck, eliminate any choice that seems to contradict the question, then mark and move.

15.3.2 Adding Specific Details

6. Typically, the procedure on the field of battle, especially during intense periods of fighting, relies on each soldier's experience; in order for the company to reunite, the officers must communicate through long-distance signals, such as flags, messengers, and gunshots.

Given that all the choices are true, which one provides the most logical cause for the action described in the statement immediately following the underlined portion?

F. NO CHANGE
G. disperses multiple bands across large areas of land;
H. involves the regiment covering long distances;
J. requires the full capabilities of every officer and personnel member;

15.4.1 Set One

Toward evening, <u>a sort of light from the storm was visible through</u> the whole of New England.

1. The writer would like to indicate that at this point, the thunderstorm is incredibly powerful. Given that all the choices are true, which one best accomplishes the writer's goal?
   A. NO CHANGE
   B. the storm was loud across
   C. there was a larger electrical storm throughout
   D. a raging thunderstorm dominated

When Matthew moved to New Jersey to be a pro at the Pine Valley Golf Club, he met with Ellis—ex-pro golfer and former coach—who <u>had seen Matthew beat the competition.</u>

2. Given that all of the choices are true, which one most clearly and efficiently establishes the personal and business relationship between Ellis and Matthew?
   F. NO CHANGE
   G. would become Matthew's role model.
   H. had been playing the circuit for years.
   J. believed Matthew had the talent to compete at a professional level.

Carlos knew he had to seriously commit to this new job if he expected his mom to let him move out of the dorms the next semester. He'd been saving up pocket change, but now that he had a job, he could put his nose to the grindstone. Every day he woke up at the crack of dawn, biked to the coffee shop to work his five-hour shift, went to class, studied in the library, went home, and then slept. <u>Meanwhile, his classes were getting more difficult as the semester progressed.</u> Carlos lived this hectic schedule for three months when, finally, his mom came to town and cosigned the lease of his first apartment. Then he slept for a solid week.

3. At this point, the writer wants to provide a specific example of the efforts made by Carlos to reach his goal. Given that all the choices are true, which one would best accomplish this purpose?
   A. NO CHANGE
   B. Carlos understood that this job was a means to an end, and he'd soon have his own place.
   C. He saved his future rent money in the metal box he kept in his sock drawer.
   D. His mom had no idea that he was planning to show her all the money he had saved.

END OF SET ONE
STOP! DO NOT GO ON TO THE NEXT PAGE UNTIL TOLD TO DO SO.

15.4.2 Set Two

While juggling has taken on many variations and styles over the years, the most common juggling we see today can be linked to ancient Egyptian culture, where juggling was always popular.

4. Given that all the choices are true, which one provides the most effective evidence of the long history of enthusiasm for juggling in Egyptian culture?
   - **F.** NO CHANGE
   - **G.** represented the circle of life, death, and rebirth.
   - **H.** was revered even above sword-swallowing.
   - **J.** had been a religious and royal pastime for centuries.

It struck David that his fascination with exploration, naval battles, and the sea came from C.S. Forester's series about Horatio Hornblower, a fictional Royal Navy officer. With the aid of Hornblower, David had read about historical situations in the world.

5. Given that all the choices are true, which one best illustrates the variety of settings for the Horatio Hornblower series and also expresses David's interest in these books?
   - **A.** NO CHANGE
   - **B.** Along with Hornblower, David explored the jungles and the high seas with a whole cast of characters from other novels.
   - **C.** With Hornblower at the helm, David fought in the Napoleonic Wars and traveled on secret missions to Central America.
   - **D.** Through his discovery of Hornblower, David learned about geography and traveled to new places around the world.

One cricket player, Lenny Dawson, a young man from Sydney, was a fan favorite.

6. Given that all of the choices are true, which one makes clear that Dawson was unmatched in his ability to draw spectators to a cricket match in which he was playing?
   - **F.** NO CHANGE
   - **G.** attracted more fans to the cricket fields than did any other player.
   - **H.** would enthrall the audience with his nimble skills and quick moves.
   - **J.** was an athlete who could also play other sports.

END OF SET TWO

STOP! DO NOT GO ON TO THE NEXT PAGE UNTIL TOLD TO DO SO.

15.4.3 Set Three

You don't even need to have a formal lesson to pick up an instrument and join in the fun.

7. Which of the choices best helps the writer stress that playing music is an activity in which all can participate rather than just an elitist art form?
   - **A.** NO CHANGE
   - **B.** understand the theory.
   - **C.** go to a conservatory.
   - **D.** know how to create sound.

Although Diego Rivera passed away in 1957, his legacy—the Mexican Mural Movement—still remains a remarkable period of expression in Mexican art.

8. Which choice would most effectively guide readers to understand the remarkable influence that the Mexican Mural Movement has on the world?
   - **F.** NO CHANGE
   - **G.** a vehicle for sharing the passion and struggle of his Mexican culture with the rest of the world.
   - **H.** an established movement in art history.
   - **J.** a fountain of inspiration for a new generation of Mexican artists.

Beginning with the success of his first blockbuster feature in 1975, Spielberg has been a recipient of many awards and accolades for the movies he has written, produced, and directed.

9. Given that all the choices are true, which one most effectively helps the sentence establish a sense of how long director Steven Spielberg has been a driving force in the movie industry?
   - **A.** NO CHANGE
   - **B.** Sometimes teaming up with his friend George Lucas to work on the *Indiana Jones* films,
   - **C.** Winning his first Academy Award with the drama *Schindler's List*,
   - **D.** Examining such diverse political subjects as the Holocaust, war, and terrorism,

---

END OF SET THREE

STOP! DO NOT GO ON TO THE NEXT PAGE UNTIL TOLD TO DO SO.

15.4.4 Set Four

Briana scored at least ten points higher than her classmates on every Latin test. Her parents reached out to the university and found Cynthia Henderson, a well-known and respected student tutor. Cynthia wanted to be sure of Briana's vocabulary level and asked whether she had any experience speaking the ancient language. Although Cynthia had never tutored so young a student, she reluctantly agreed to teach the young girl Latin.

10. At this point in the essay, the writer wants to show that Cynthia felt it necessary to inquire about Briana's Latin background. Given that all the choices are true, which one best conveys the message?

F. NO CHANGE
G. Generally, her students were high school students, so she
H. Given that the girl's parents had sought her out personally, she
J. After talking to the girl's previous Latin teachers, Cynthia

---

One of Coach Gregg's signature practice drills calls upon the players' experience and speed; in order for their teammates to hit their marks, the players subtly signal one another mid-play.

11. Given that all the choices are true, which one provides the most logical cause for the action described in the statement immediately following the underlined portion?

A. NO CHANGE
B. disperses players throughout the field;
C. requires the players to pay close attention;
D. involves the entire team;

When he was lecturing in the classroom, whether it was the Peloponnesian War or the Battle of the Bulge, he refused to leave any area uncovered.

12. At this point, the writer would like to provide a glimpse into the specific topics of his teacher's lectures. Given that all the choices are true, which one best accomplishes this purpose?

F. NO CHANGE
G. fulfilling his role as a history teacher,
H. things I hoped I would be able to memorize,
J. ancient wars or battles from modern times,

END OF SET FOUR
STOP! DO NOT GO ON TO THE NEXT PAGE
UNTIL TOLD TO DO SO.

15.4.5 Set Five

Academy Award-winning filmmaker John Carpenter is most widely known for the box-office hit *Halloween*, released in 1978. His filmography of over forty productions shows him as a filmmaking jack-of-all-trades. Horror movies still draw a lot of people to the theater.

13. Given that all the choices are true, which one would most effectively express the writer's viewpoint about John Carpenter's role in the horror movie genre?
    - **A.** NO CHANGE
    - **B.** Since the silent era, audiences have been enthralled by horror movies such as *Nosferatu* and *Frankenstein.*
    - **C.** John Carpenter actually never watched his own films once they were completed.
    - **D.** On top of writing and directing horrific storylines, Carpenter also composed musical scores that were even more frightening.

The best way to avoid car trouble is regular maintenance. Experts suggest getting check-ups on your engine, oil, brakes, and tires. They warn that after a certain amount of miles, you should get your brakes and oil checked.

14. In this paragraph, the writer intends to recommend a number of specific actions to take in order to keep a car in the safest working order. This is to be the second recommendation. Given that all the choices are true, which one would best accomplish the writer's intention?
    - **F.** NO CHANGE
    - **G.** propose that you wash your car frequently to keep it looking new.
    - **H.** advise you to contact a professional if you have any questions or notice anything out of the ordinary.
    - **J.** suggest that you be aware of the ways in which malfunctions may occur.

The cast included a lead actress I knew from comedies, a supporting actor who won an Oscar for drama, and the remarkable actor who terrified audiences with his film last year. I knew I was in for something different the moment I sat down.

15. Given that all the choices are true, which one most clearly adds new information about the mixture of talent in the film the narrator was about to watch?
    - **A.** NO CHANGE
    - **B.** famous man
    - **C.** versatile comedian
    - **D.** horror villain

END OF SET FIVE

STOP! DO NOT GO ON TO THE NEXT PAGE UNTIL TOLD TO DO SO.

Sum It Up

Tips and Techniques

Most Valuable Phrases: Look for the essential phrases in each author's purpose question and ignore the grammar. These phrases indicate exactly what content you should look for in the answer choices.

Process of Elimination: Eliminate any answer that contradicts the question, even before you look at the passage.

Lesson 16

Accomplish Purpose Part 2

CAPTION:

16.1 Entrance Ticket

Read each sentence and answer the question given.

The polar bear's paws are short and stocky compared to its brown bear cousin, and its claws are a scoop-shaped in order to assist in its natural terrain.

1. Given that all the choices are true, which one provides the most specific information about the function of the polar bear's claws?
   - **A.** NO CHANGE
   - **B.** in the functions for which is it adapted.
   - **C.** in digging into hard ice.
   - **D.** in accessing materials that could be difficult for the bear to reach.

Americans of modest means could now bypass weeks of bumpy stagecoach travel by traveling from coast to coast on a locomotive in under ten days.

2. Which choice would most effectively conclude the sentence by indicating clearly how the locomotive could address the problem described in the first part of the sentence?
   - **F.** NO CHANGE
   - **G.** traveling more effectively on a locomotive.
   - **H.** trying a different mode of transportation.
   - **J.** staying free of dust on a locomotive.

Over an eight-year period, Pavarotti canceled multiple scheduled appearances, earning himself the reputation of "King of Cancellations."

3. Which choice most precisely identifies how many appearances were canceled by Pavarotti?
   - **A.** NO CHANGE
   - **B.** 26 out of 41
   - **C.** a large number of
   - **D.** the majority of his

16.2 Learning Targets

1. Analyze purpose questions and understand what details support or clarify this purpose

2. Use basic essay structure to quickly scan for content

Self-Assessment

Circle the number that corresponds to your confidence level in your knowledge of this subject before beginning the lesson. A score of 1 means you are completely lost, and a score of 4 means you have mastered the skills. After you finish the lesson, return to the bottom of this page and circle your new confidence level to show your improvement.

Before Lesson

1 2 3 4

After Lesson

1 2 3 4

16.3.1 Specific Purpose

Following your teacher's instructions, write a short story with your group.

A prime example of a hardy water plant is the gray mangrove—a tolerant shrub with a system of pencil-sized roots that protrude from the water.

1. Given that all the choices are true, which one most specifically describes the appearance of a gray mangrove for readers who have never seen one?
   A. NO CHANGE
   B. an odd and interesting tree
   C. a member of the plant family *Acanthaceae*
   D. a short, grayish-white shrub

English Tip

Most Valuable Phrases: When you are attempting to find the answer to an accomplish purpose question, focus on the specific details in the question. The goal is to find an answer choice that matches the question. Your answer will have nothing to do with grammar.

16.3.1 Specific Purpose

What my nephew loves best about these Boy Scout outings is the hike itself: an opportunity to stretch his legs and burn off some energy.

2. Which choice most effectively supports the point being made in the first part of this sentence?
   - **F.** NO CHANGE
   - **G.** overcome obstacles.
   - **H.** learn about nature and survival techniques.
   - **J.** build teamwork and learn about leadership.

The skunk possesses two scent glands capable of releasing a powerful odor, which helps protect the skunk when necessary.

3. Given that all the choices are true, which one provides the most specific information about the skunk's behavior?
   - **A.** NO CHANGE
   - **B.** as it goes about its daily life.
   - **C.** from life-threatening predators.
   - **D.** as it hunts for insects, rodents, and eggs.

Biologists in North Carolina have recently recorded 192 bald eagle nests, encouraging the theory that the once-endangered species is returning. [4]

4. Which of the following true statements, if added here, would best strengthen the assertion that bald eagles are making a comeback in North Carolina?
   - **F.** Many other bald eagle sightings have no doubt gone unreported.
   - **G.** Some farmers have reported finding feathers around their barns and a marked decrease in the mouse population.
   - **H.** One hiker reported seeing a bird that looked like a bald eagle as she was trekking through a densely-wooded area.
   - **J.** In 1983, there were no bald eagle nests throughout the entire state.

16.3.2 Identifying the Main Idea

Introduction Paragraph:

Main Idea of the Essay: ______________________________

____

____

Body Paragraph #1:

Main Idea of the Paragraph: ______________________________

____

Topic Sentence: ______________________________

____

Supporting Idea: ______________________________

____

Body Paragraph #2:

Main Idea of the Paragraph: ______________________________

____

Topic Sentence: ______________________________

____

Supporting Idea: ______________________________

____

Body Paragraph #3:

Main Idea of the Paragraph: ______________________________

____

Topic Sentence: ______________________________

____

Supporting Idea: ______________________________

____

Conclusion Paragraph:

Main Idea of the Conclusion: ______________________________

____

English Tip

Mark and Move: These questions typically come at the end of the essay. If after quickly looking over the essay, you still feel lost about what is being described, it is probably best to mark and move. Do not worry about these questions until the end of the passage.

1 ■ ■ ■ ■ ■ ■ ■ ■ ■ 1

16.4.1 Set One

For the most part, though, piloting an aircraft requires <u>two particular traits.</u>

1. Given that all the choices are true, which one provides the most specific information?
   A. NO CHANGE
   B. demonstrating two qualities.
   C. a level head and a knowledge of physics.
   D. expertise in this career field.

Conversely, the Victorian era—<u>the period when Queen Victoria reigned over the British Empire</u>—was an age of relative peace and prosperity in Britain.

2. Given that all the choices are true, which one most effectively describes the definition of the Victorian Era?
   F. NO CHANGE
   G. which coincided with the Gilded Age in the United States
   H. famous for its straitlaced morality and attitudes
   J. familiar to those who have read the fiction of Sir Arthur Conan Doyle

---

Some of the sites that the U.S. National Park Service oversees are not only places of natural beauty but are also readily recognizable symbols of America, <u>many of which are familiar from books and movies.</u>

3. Given that all of the choices are true, which one would conclude this sentence by providing the clearest example of some readily recognizable symbols of America?
   A. NO CHANGE
   B. including both national parks and national monuments.
   C. including Mount Rushmore National Memorial and Grand Canyon National Park.
   D. places that visitors from other countries want to visit when they tour the United States.

END OF SET ONE
STOP! DO NOT GO ON TO THE NEXT PAGE
UNTIL TOLD TO DO SO.

16.4.2 Set Two

What Jake loved most was the driving itself: the chance to get out of the city and immerse himself in the surrounding countryside.

4. Which choice most effectively supports the point being made in the first part of this sentence?
   F. NO CHANGE
   G. the feeling of freedom on the open road and the ability to determine his next destination.
   H. the feel of the steering wheel under his hands and the response of the car underneath him.
   J. the vibrant colors of the scenery whizzing by and the strains of his favorite song on the radio.

Fortunately, the rain let up during the final two hours of hiking, and for the final 300 meters, they were able to pick their way carefully up to the crater formed by the dormant volcano. [5]

5. Which of the following true statements, if added here, would most effectively and specifically emphasize the hikers' main accomplishment as described in this paragraph?
   A. The hike had been long and arduous.
   B. They had reached the summit of Mt. Fuji.
   C. They were relieved to have safely ascended the mountain.
   D. The final ascent over the wet rocks was painstaking.

In the midst of the chaotic market, my sister honed in on the fishmonger in the third stall.

6. Given that all the choices are true, which one adds new information about the physical appearance of the fishmonger?
   F. NO CHANGE
   G. as she scanned the crowd.
   H. during our shopping excursion.
   J. in the yellow apron.

END OF SET TWO
STOP! DO NOT GO ON TO THE NEXT PAGE
UNTIL TOLD TO DO SO.

---

1 1

16.4.3 Set Three

Shoppers can browse the selection of merchandise at any time of the day or night; the most popular categories for online retail include home goods, children's clothing, and kitchen appliances.

7. Given that all the choices are true, which one best emphasizes a main benefit of online shopping?
   A. NO CHANGE
   B. The department store chain has recently started to sell some items online;
   C. The department store's new online retail department has performed exceedingly well in its first three months;
   D. Female customers do more online shopping than male customers;

Five years ago, the fate of another crumbling historic home was featured in the local newspaper and was widely discussed.

8. Given that all the choices are true, which one best indicates that an effort to save the home was successful?
   F. NO CHANGE
   G. was researched by local historians.
   H. has received considerable media coverage.
   J. was later spared from demolition.

On a street that used to buzz with the noise of construction workers and haggling street vendors, we heard only birds singing and the occasional passing car.

9. Which choice best sets up a contrast within the sentence?
   A. NO CHANGE
   B. On a crumbling residential street on the neighborhood's eastern edge,
   C. While strolling down the street and listening for signs of life,
   D. It is not surprising, then, that

END OF SET THREE

STOP! DO NOT GO ON TO THE NEXT PAGE UNTIL TOLD TO DO SO.

16.4.4 Set Four

In December 1903, the Wright brothers tested their carefully designed engine and successfully completed the first powered aircraft flight on record. [10]

10. Given that all of the following sentences are true, which one should be placed here to offer an explanation for why the Wright brothers continued to work on creating a practical aircraft?
- **F.** Five people witnessed the flight, including the photographer who snapped the famous "first flight" photograph with a pre-positioned camera.
- **G.** Unfortunately, the aircraft did not stay airborne for more than 60 seconds during any of the test flights.
- **H.** Modern analysis has shown that the 1903 Wright Flyer was probably unmanageable to anyone other than the Wrights, who had trained in it.
- **J.** In Paris, members of the Aero Club of France took notice of the flight and made efforts to contact the Wrights.

The old storefront had such a wonderful sense of history about it that we consulted with <u>a team of experts who agreed to paint it, refurbish the original awning, and help restore its former appearance.</u>

11. Given that all the choices are true, which one provides the most specific information?
- **A.** NO CHANGE
- **B.** a group people who valued its historical significance as much as we did.
- **C.** a team of workers who had knowledge in restoring historic buildings.
- **D.** a group of professional experts who were highly qualified in a range of subjects.

In October 1879, Thomas Edison used a carbon filament to conduct the first successful test of a commercially practical incandescent light. [12]

12. Given that all of the following sentences are true, which one should be placed here to offer a logical explanation for why Edison continued to experiment with other types of filament materials?
- **F.** Several earlier inventors had already devised other less practical types of incandescent lamps
- **G.** Edison was driven by a sense of competition and wanted to prove his worth with this particular invention.
- **H.** Unfortunately, the light did not burn for as long as Edison had hoped.
- **J.** Edison filed for a U.S. patent for his invention the following month.

END OF SET FOUR

STOP! DO NOT GO ON TO THE NEXT PAGE
UNTIL TOLD TO DO SO.

16.4.5 Set Five

Although I had never set foot in my father's hometown, I had never intentionally avoided visiting.

13. The writer wants to balance the statement made in the earlier part of the sentence with a related detail that suggests a sense of familiarity. Given that all of the choices are true, which one best accomplishes this goal?
    A. NO CHANGE
    B. I had personal reasons for visiting it for the first time.
    C. I hoped I could get to know it.
    D. I instinctively recognized it.

He spent many hours gazing at that crack in the floorboard when he was grounded during those rough years. [14]

14. At this point, the writer wants to add a sentence that would further describe the crack in the floorboard. Which of the following sentences would best accomplish this?
    F. To him, the crack's triangular shape resembled a slice of pie.
    G. Sometimes he would see a line of ants marching out of the crack in a quest for food.
    H. The surrounding floorboards had attained a high gloss from his mother's weekly polishing.
    J. He often wondered what had caused the crack in the first place.

Sharks have formidable jaws that allow them to quickly and efficiently crush their prey. The powerful force that allows them to clamp down on prey, however, causes sharks to lose large numbers of teeth while hunting. Therefore, over millions of years of evolution, sharks have developed the ability to replace teeth rapidly, sometimes losing and regrowing over 30,000 teeth in a lifetime.

15. The writer wants to describe the way sharks lose and replace teeth. Which choice would be most consistent with the way the process of losing and replacing teeth has been described up to this point?
    A. NO CHANGE
    B. through a painstakingly slow process
    C. often only losing one or two teeth over a period of several years
    D. leaving their jaws weak and their ability to hunt diminished

---

END OF SET FIVE

STOP! DO NOT GO ON TO THE NEXT PAGE UNTIL TOLD TO DO SO.

Sum It Up

Tips and Techniques

Most Valuable Phrases: When you are attempting to find the answer to an accomplish purpose question, focus on the specific details in the question. The goal is to find an answer choice that matches the question. Your answer will have nothing to do with grammar.

Mark and Move: These questions typically come at the end of the essay. If after quickly looking over the essay, you still feel lost about what is being described, it is probably best to mark and move. Do not worry about these questions until the end of the passage.

Lesson 17

Adjectives and Adverbs

Eat at Frank's Burgers for the most delicious, exciting, gourmet, scrumptious, amazing, spectacular meal of your life!
Eat at Johnny's and eagerly, happily, hungrily, hurriedly, madly, accidentally spend all your money on the world's best hamburgers!

CAPTION:

17.1 Entrance Ticket

Select the best alternative to the underlined portion in each sentence below. If no change is necessary, select NO CHANGE.

I'm going to be a judge in the Beta Club's annual T-shirt design project.

1. **A.** NO CHANGE
   B. annually T-shirt design
   C. annual T-shirt designed
   D. annually T-shirt designing

The musician will be honored for his success orchestrated composition.

2. **F.** NO CHANGE
   G. successfully orchestrating
   H. successfully orchestra
   J. successful orchestra

Even though I trained more than Chelsea, I still ran slowest than she did.

3. **A.** NO CHANGE
   B. most slowly
   C. more slowly
   D. slow

17.2 Learning Targets

1. Correctly combine multiple adjectives

2. Correctly combine adverbs with adjectives and nouns

3. Correctly form comparatives and superlatives

Self-Assessment

Circle the number that corresponds to your confidence level in your knowledge of this subject before beginning the lesson. A score of 1 means you are completely lost, and a score of 4 means you have mastered the skills. After you finish the lesson, return to the bottom of this page and circle your new confidence level to show your improvement.

Before Lesson

1 2 3 4

After Lesson

1 2 3 4

17.3.1 Adjectives and Adverbs

The storm was brutal and spared no one, destroying the park benches, the picnic tables, and a broadly expanse of oak trees.

1. **A.** NO CHANGE
   B. broad expanse
   C. expanding broad
   D. broad expansive

17.3.1 Adjectives and Adverbs

1. Megan _________ ran a few laps around the gym before practicing her _________ layups.

2. Megan _________ ran a few laps around the gym before practicing her _________ layups.

3. _________, Megan _________ ran a few laps around the gym before _________ practicing her layups.

4. Carrying his _________ backpack, Steve walked __________ from his car to his house.

5. Carrying his backpack, _________ Steve walked from his _________ car to the house.

6. Carrying his _________ backpack, Steve _________ walked from his car to the _________ house.

English Tip

When figuring out adjectives versus adverbs:

1. Skim the answer choices.
2. If you see an adverb or an adjective, find the word it modifies.
3. If it modifies a verb, choose an adverb answer choice. If it modifies a noun, choose an adjective answer choice.

17.3.2 Adverbs, Comparatives, and Superlatives

The French exam, which was my most easiest passed final, unfortunately did not count toward my grade point average

1. **A.** NO CHANGE
   B. most easily
   C. most easy
   D. easiest

If I lived closer to work, my busy schedule might be a bit more easily managed.

2. **F.** NO CHANGE
   G. more easy to
   H. more easy
   J. more easier

English Tip

Do Not Rush: If you see an adjective or adverb in the underlined portion, do not choose the first option that looks good. Take some time to analyze the sentence, find all of the verbs and nouns, and see how everything relates. Then choose the best answer available.

17.3.2 Adverbs, Comparatives, and Superlatives

_____ The easiliest accommodated

_____ The easiest accommodated

_____ The most easily accommodated

_____ The easiest accommodation

_____ The quicklier moving train

_____ The quicker moving train

_____ The more quickly moving train

_____ The quicker move

17.3.2 Adverbs, Comparatives, and Superlatives

Kim tiptoed into the house quietly.

Her parents waited even more quietly in the dark living room for her.

Kim's little sister hid most quietly on the stairs to see what would happen next.

17.4.1 Set One

Smith determined that the best possible course of action would be to implement a comprehend tiered solution to the infrastructure problem at hand.

1. **A.** NO CHANGE
   B. comprehend tier
   C. comprehensive tiered
   D. comprehensive tier

But coming from a damp and chilly climate, the English tourists take a much different approach than the locals, eagerly sprawling themselves on the beach to absorb the warmly magnificence of the sun.

2. **F.** NO CHANGE
   G. magnificently warm
   H. warm magnificent
   J. warm magnificence

Far too many laborers suffer torn shoulder labra as a result of the destruction chopping technique required by the work.

3. **A.** NO CHANGE
   B. destructive chopping
   C. destroy chopping
   D. destroy chopper

END OF SET ONE
STOP! DO NOT GO ON TO THE NEXT PAGE
UNTIL TOLD TO DO SO.

17.4.2 Set Two

The report established that the community was in need of a <u>dynamic, ambition</u> plan that would meet the needs of the entire population.

4. **F.** NO CHANGE
   G. dynamically, ambition
   H. dynamically, ambitiously
   J. dynamic, ambitious

Retirement brings to him a new placidity, and he spends his days observing his natural surroundings and enjoying the <u>calmly elegant</u> of the still lake.

5. **A.** NO CHANGE
   B. calmly elegance
   C. calm elegance
   D. calm elegantly

The candidate demonstrates <u>the technical</u> prowess, extensive experience, and unwavering confidence necessary in an effective leader.

6. **F.** NO CHANGE
   G. how technical
   H. how technically
   J. the technically

END OF SET TWO
STOP! DO NOT GO ON TO THE NEXT PAGE
UNTIL TOLD TO DO SO.

17.4.3 Set Three

The majestic bird is <u>most quickest</u> recognized by its brilliant array of colors and dominant stature.

7. **A.** NO CHANGE
   B. more quicker
   C. most quickly
   D. mostly quick

If we were to cut certain corners, such luxuries would be <u>more easily</u> acquired.

8. **F.** NO CHANGE
   G. more easy
   H. more easier
   J. most easy

When the food finally arrived, those who had been waiting the longest were the <u>most quickliest</u> served in the crowded gymnasium.

9. **A.** NO CHANGE
   B. most quick
   C. most quickly
   D. most quickest

END OF SET THREE
STOP! DO NOT GO ON TO THE NEXT PAGE
UNTIL TOLD TO DO SO.

17.4.4 Set Four

Jackie Robinson, who broke Major League Baseball's color line in 1947, is an example of how many athletic ability, moral fortitude, and superhuman patience combined to alter America's perception of race.

10. **F.** NO CHANGE
    G. how much athletically
    H. how athletic
    J. the athletic

Although spaghetti carbonara is likely to impress your guests, spaghetti marinara is more easily prepared.

11. **A.** NO CHANGE
    B. more easy
    C. more easier
    D. more easy to

The runt of the litter, an adorable brown and white flop-ear, was the most gentlest handled and fussed over of all the animals on the farm.

12. **F.** NO CHANGE
    G. most gentle
    H. gentlest
    J. most gently

END OF SET FOUR
STOP! DO NOT GO ON TO THE NEXT PAGE
UNTIL TOLD TO DO SO.

17.4.5 Set Five

However, none of their taunts made me any less enthralled by Hamlet, Beowulf, or the fate pride of Oedipus Rex.

13. **A.** NO CHANGE
B. fatally prideful
C. fatal pride
D. pridefully fatal

Her personal wealth is unimaginable larger, yet she still displays a genuine passion for helping underprivileged children, as well as for championing environmental causes.

14. **F.** NO CHANGE
G. unimaginable large
H. unimaginably larger
J. unimaginably large

The ship's hull was fundamentally sounder, made of thick cypress planks that seemed to have grown together along a single, powerful arc.

15. **A.** NO CHANGE
B. fundamentally sound
C. fundamental sound
D. fundamental sounder

END OF SET FIVE
STOP! DO NOT GO ON TO THE NEXT PAGE
UNTIL TOLD TO DO SO.

Sum It Up

Adjectives and Adverbs

With nearly all adverbs ending in *-ly*, use *more* to form the comparative, not *-er*.

With nearly all adverbs ending in *-ly*, use *most* to form the superlative, not *-est*.

Tips and Techniques

Do Not Rush: If you see an adjective or adverb in the underlined portion, do not choose the first option that looks good. Take some time to analyze the sentence, find all of the verbs and nouns, and see how everything relates. Then choose the best answer available.

Lesson 18

Word Choice Part 1

CAPTION:

18.1 Entrance Ticket

Fill in the blanks to the story using words from the word bank. Not all of the words will be used.

Word Bank

into	rival	and	company
celebrated	grandfathers	specialized	cooperating
he	Two	the	while
competing	that	for	Ebenezer
They	they	brothers	teams
or	out	competed	striving
Louisa	clans	named	
in	reveled	One	
strangers	by	be	

_______________ and Malcolm were two _______________ who grew up always _______________ against each other. They _______________ in school, striving for _______________ best grades and to _______________ top of their class. _______________ competed in sports, always _______________ to make the best _______________ or become captain. When _______________ were older, they started _______________ pie companies. Ebenezer's company _______________ in cherry almond pie, _______________ Malcolm's company became famous _______________ its chocolate marshmallow pies. _______________ day, though, a man _______________ Gilbert came to town _______________ started a pecan pie _______________, and the brothers found _______________ their businesses were suddenly _______________ trouble.

18.2 Learning Targets

1. Choose the most appropriate word or phrase to include in a given sentence

2. Analyze the wording in different questions to determine the most suitable answer choice

Self-Assessment

Circle the number that corresponds to your confidence level in your knowledge of this subject before beginning the lesson. A score of 1 means you are completely lost, and a score of 4 means you have mastered the skills. After you finish the lesson, return to the bottom of this page and circle your new confidence level to show your improvement.

Before Lesson

1 2 3 4

After Lesson

1 2 3 4

18.3.1 Plugging In

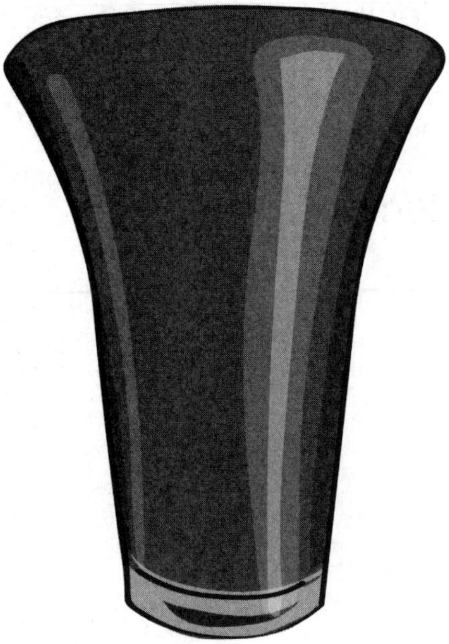

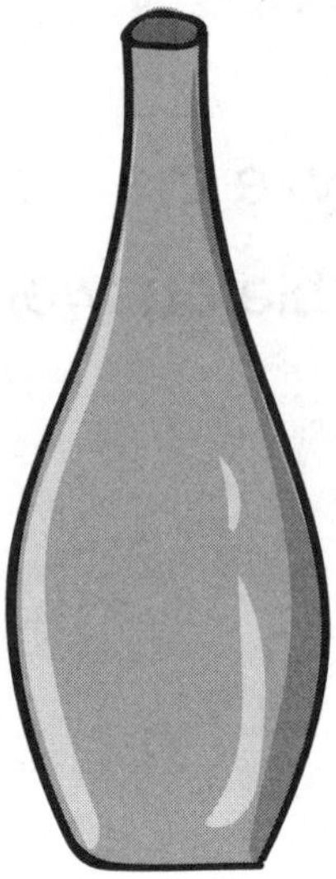

______________________ ______________________ ______________________

lacked **missed** **neglected** **overlooked**

Movie critics felt that the film ______________ a clear focus and relied too much on extensive car chases and battle scenes to move its plot along.

18.3.1 Plugging In

Searching the bags of incoming guests is a <u>specific</u> procedure at most large arenas.

1. **A.** NO CHANGE
   B. medium
   C. routine
   D. limited

The bride and groom were <u>following</u> the Indian tradition of performing skits at weddings.

2. **F.** NO CHANGE
   G. allocating
   H. coming after
   J. pursuing

The party planner worried that the heat of the day would cause the helium balloons to <u>expand.</u>

3. **A.** NO CHANGE
   B. increase.
   C. evaporate.
   D. multiply.

English Tip

Plug It In: Try plugging in the answer choices to see which word best fits the sentence. If you don't know the meaning of one of the words, don't eliminate it. You might be able to narrow down the answers by eliminating other choices.

18.3.2 Decoding Standards

Kendra bowed her head to the group when they shot down her proposal for the science project.

1. Which choice most effectively expresses Kendra's anger with the group?
   - **A.** NO CHANGE
   - **B.** shrugged her shoulders at
   - **C.** was fine with
   - **D.** fiercely turned her back to

Giveaway: ______________________

Rule: ______________________

Leslie did not enroll in a formal French class, but she worked quickly to grasp the language prior to her trip to Provence.

2. The writer wants to emphasize the characterization that Leslie spent much time learning a new language. Given this purpose, which choice would work best?
   - **F.** NO CHANGE
   - **G.** day and night
   - **H.** against the clock
   - **J.** DELETE the underlined portion

Giveaway: ______________________

Rule: ______________________

18.3.2 Decoding Standards

The name for the <u>bundle</u> of islands southeast of the state of Florida is derived from the Spanish word for "shallow sea."

3. Which choice would best help the reader visualize a collection of islands stretching across the Atlantic Ocean for hundreds of miles?

   A. NO CHANGE
   B. chain
   C. cluster
   D. block

Giveaway: ______________________________

Rule: ______________________________

On many days, the crystal clear, topaz waters shimmer in the sunlight until the glowing <u>lunar</u> moon rises into the dark, sapphire sky.

4. Which choice would be most consistent with the figurative description provided elsewhere in this sentence?

   F. NO CHANGE
   G. full
   H. radiant
   J. ivory

Giveaway: ______________________________

Rule: ______________________________

18.3.2 Decoding Standards

During the summer months, the warm water _______ tropical storm development.

1. The writer wants to suggest that there are fewer incidents of tropical storms prior to the summer months. Which choice best accomplishes this goal?

    A. interacts with
    B. relieves
    C. involves
    D. triggers

The neighborhoods just east of I-40 in Clayton were among the _______ areas affected by the power outage after the storm.

2. Which choice most strongly emphasizes that the power outage was experienced by a large number of residents?

    F. particular
    G. pocket of
    H. countless
    J. numbered

These studies _________ that glass is an extremely slow-moving liquid, since so many panes of stained glass are thicker at the bottom.

3. The writer wants to remain consistent with the rest of the essay in presenting the "slow-moving liquid" theory as a distinct possibility, rather than as an accepted fact. Which of the choices best supports that intention?

    A. have confirmed
    B. exclusively show
    C. give proof
    D. strongly suggest

18.3.2 Decoding Standards

The audience members couldn't control their excitement as the curtain ________________________________.

4. Given that all of the choices are true, which one best helps the reader visualize the details of the moment?

F. rose, indicating the end of the play.
G. rose, revealing the cast standing hand in hand.
H. rose during those monthly performances.
J. rose, and the orchestra began to play.

English Tip

Giveaways: If there is a question that tells you what to look for, ignore the grammar involved and how the words sound. Pick the answer that best fits the question and move on.

1 ■ ■ ■ ■ ■ ■ ■ ■ ■ 1

18.4.1 Set One

In one of Daniel's poems, the <u>likeness</u> of the early morning air is described as a light, floral bouquet.

1. Which choice would be most appropriate in the context of this sentence?
   A. NO CHANGE
   B. appearance
   C. aroma
   D. symbol

The children <u>imitated</u> the activities they saw their family conduct at home: making dinner, driving cars, and playing music.

2. **F.** NO CHANGE
   G. matched
   H. pretended
   J. followed

Filling the bags with candy is a <u>traditional</u> part of the graduation celebration at the end of each year.

3. **A.** NO CHANGE
   B. meager
   C. frequent
   D. reliable

END OF SET ONE
STOP! DO NOT GO ON TO THE NEXT PAGE
UNTIL TOLD TO DO SO.

18.4.2 Set Two

The early cell phones were carried around in a large shoebox-sized pouch because they were too <u>strenuous</u> to be carried in a pocket or purse.

4. **F.** NO CHANGE
   G. sophisticated
   H. cumbersome
   J. ostentatious

Hannah prepared her signature meal, "Beef Braciola," for Chef Musso, who <u>tasted the dish.</u>

5. Given that all the choices are true, which one would most clearly describe an interaction between Hannah and Chef Musso during Hannah's culinary internship?
   A. NO CHANGE
   B. enjoyed the dish immensely.
   C. sampled and critiqued the dish.
   D. complimented the dish but suggested slight changes.

Fleming <u>was skilled in</u> deep-water diving and had explored the unpredictable waters of Chicuzen off the coast of the British Virgin Islands.

6. Given that all the choices are true, which one best conveys Fleming's attitude toward diving and helps clarify the kind of diving that appealed to him?
   F. NO CHANGE
   G. relished the thrill of
   H. had swum more than 130 feet below while
   J. was viewed as an expert at

END OF SET TWO

STOP! DO NOT GO ON TO THE NEXT PAGE UNTIL TOLD TO DO SO.

18.4.3 Set Three

Flames billowed from the base of the space shuttle and <u>enlightened</u> the night sky as the vessel rose from the launch pad.

7. **A.** NO CHANGE
B. illuminated
C. embellished
D. illustrated

Suddenly Amelia's mother walked through the door, <u>like a sun bursting through clouds at the end of a storm.</u>

8. The writer would like to describe the mood in visual terms to help the reader imagine Amelia's feelings. Which choice best accomplishes the writer's purpose?
F. NO CHANGE
G. bringing a sigh of relief from the girl.
H. the image making me understand the importance of the bond between them.
J. the mother's entrance having a visible effect.

Neurosurgeons at Brigham and Women's Hospital in Boston are <u>coming close to</u> the use of gamma ray beams in stereotactic brain surgery.

9. Which choice best conveys the notion that neurosurgeons at Brigham and Women's Hospital are at the leading edge of stereotactic brain surgery?
A. NO CHANGE
B. pioneers in the
C. now implementing
D. contemplating

END OF SET THREE
STOP! DO NOT GO ON TO THE NEXT PAGE
UNTIL TOLD TO DO SO.

1 ■ ■ ■ ■ ■ ■ ■ ■ ■ 1

18.4.4 Set Four

As we made our way across the countryside, Lawrence <u>spoke in quiet tones.</u>

10. Which choice would most logically and effectively emphasize the negative, hostile attitude the narrator has toward Lawrence?

F. NO CHANGE
G. asked me thoughtful questions.
H. declared his love for nature.
J. rattled on with tiresome anecdotes.

My mother warned me that if I ate too much cake, it would cause my stomach to <u>heighten</u>.

11. **A.** NO CHANGE
B. increase
C. expand
D. drop

Zinnia is a favorite summertime plant of gardeners; its large flowers come in many colors and can <u>undergo</u> high temperatures.

12. **F.** NO CHANGE
G. withstand
H. condone
J. permit

END OF SET FOUR
STOP! DO NOT GO ON TO THE NEXT PAGE UNTIL TOLD TO DO SO.

18.4.5 Set Five

The last-minute changes to the play were <u>utilized</u> the day before the first performance, just in the nick of time.

13. **A.** NO CHANGE
    B. finalized
    C. initialized
    D. privileged

Jazz music <u>can be understood quickly</u>, which gives the impression that no two performances of the same song are alike.

14. The writer wants to be consistent throughout the essay in describing jazz as a genre of music that is not as methodical as other styles. Which choice best maintains that consistency?
    F. NO CHANGE
    G. becomes predictable after repeated exposure
    H. has basic recurring elements
    J. features much improvisation

Determined to win the spelling bee, Hirst <u>made a commitment to</u> memorize ten new words each day.

15. Which choice most effectively emphasizes that Hirst was determined?
    A. NO CHANGE
    B. felt he ought to
    C. thought he should
    D. hoped to

END OF SET FIVE
STOP! DO NOT GO ON TO THE NEXT PAGE
UNTIL TOLD TO DO SO.

Sum It Up

Word Choice Part 1

Context
The circumstances that surround events or ideas

Tips and Techniques

Plug In: Try plugging in the answers if you aren't sure which one is best.

Giveaways: Pay attention to the question and pick the answer that best matches the giveaway clue.

Lesson 19

Word Choice Part 2

CAPTION:

19.1 Entrance Ticket

Read each sentence and select the best alternative or answer the question given.

Old photographs, recipes, and handwritten letters by my grandparents—these all accumulate to the love I have for my Italian heritage.

1. **A.** NO CHANGE
   B. contribute to
   C. accumulate for
   D. benefit with

My nephew showed me his souvenirs from the beach—a bottle of sand, a hermit crab, and an array of colorful seashells.

2. Which of the following alternatives to the underlined portion would be LEAST acceptable?
   F. a classification
   G. an assortment
   H. a collection
   J. a supply

Clyde's father grounded him because he was so absorbed in his new video game that he completely forgot to do his chores.

3. Which of the following alternatives to the underlined portion would NOT be acceptable?
   A. immersed in
   B. engaged in
   C. acquired by
   D. engrossed in

19.2 Learning Targets

1. Identify the words that fit the best based on clarity and meaning

2. Identify the words that do not fit because of vagueness and context

Self-Assessment

Circle the number that corresponds to your confidence level in your knowledge of this subject before beginning the lesson. A score of 1 means you are completely lost, and a score of 4 means you have mastered the skills. After you finish the lesson, return to the bottom of this page and circle your new confidence level to show your improvement.

Before Lesson

1 2 3 4

After Lesson

1 2 3 4

19.3.1 Clear and Meaningful

Order the following sets of words from weakest to strongest.

weary	tired	exhausted

1. ____________ **2.** ____________ **3.** ____________

cheerful	ecstatic	happy

1. ____________ **2.** ____________ **3.** ____________

depressed	low	sad

1. ____________ **2.** ____________ **3.** ____________

enthusiastic	excited	eager

1. ____________ **2.** ____________ **3.** ____________

19.3.1 Clear and Meaningful

1. ______________ **2.** ______________ **3.** ______________

1. ______________ **2.** ______________ **3.** ______________

1. ______________ **2.** ______________ **3.** ______________

1. ______________ **2.** ______________ **3.** ______________

19.3.1 Clear and Meaningful

When Nathan arrived in Peru, he noticed that water circled counter-clockwise when it went down the drain. This <u>contest</u> confused him since he was used to it draining clockwise in the United States.

1. **A.** NO CHANGE
   B. change
   C. difference
   D. dispute

Jerome and Maya had to <u>apply their energies to the activity of labor</u> in order the get the house ready for the upcoming storm season.

2. **F.** NO CHANGE
   G. work a long time
   H. accomplish it
   J. work hard

Staring at his sweaty hands while talking nonsense, the man knew his <u>doubtful</u> behavior would get him in trouble with the detective.

3. **A.** NO CHANGE
   B. suspicious
   C. divided
   D. tangled

The comedian's poor stage presence, bad timing, and general lack of funny material are all factors that <u>disintegrate to</u> his popularity.

4. **F.** NO CHANGE
   G. subside with
   H. disintegrate for
   J. detract from

English Tip

Consistent, Clear, and Concise: Make sure the word you choose gives the clearest meaning to the original sentence. Do not choose a word that sounds fancy. Check the meaning with the surrounding words and pick the clearest option.

19.3.2 Not and Least

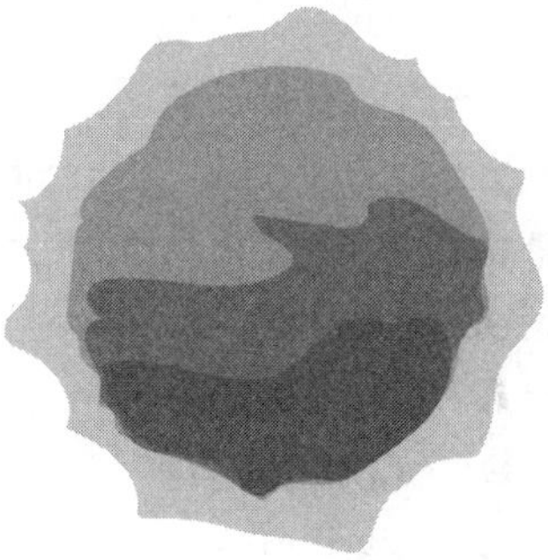

19.3.2 Not and Least

When he felt the pain in his knee start up, Greg knew he had to put on the brakes and slow his pace.

1. Which of the following alternatives to the underlined portion would NOT be acceptable?
   A. flare up,
   B. intensify,
   C. advance,
   D. increase,

Nothing completes a day in New York like going out to Central Park and watching the fireflies glittering during sunset.

2. Which of the following alternatives to the underlined portion would NOT be acceptable?
   F. sparkling
   G. twinkling
   H. glaring
   J. shining

Our little town in Maine was founded in 1764 by the many travelers who settled in the United States from France and England.

3. Which of the following alternatives to the underlined portions would NOT be acceptable?
   A. colonizers
   B. commuters
   C. explorers
   D. voyagers

19.3.2 Not and Least

In order for merchants to quickly tally up prices, the Chinese were motivated to develop the Suan Pan, which was considered to be the first calculator.

4. Which of the following alternatives to the underlined portion would be LEAST acceptable?
   - **F.** bring forth
   - **G.** come up with
   - **H.** invent
   - **J.** design

Jacob's holiday food drive would benefit the poor who would like to give their family a holiday meal.

5. Which of the following alternatives to the underlined portion would be LEAST acceptable?
   - **A.** enhance
   - **B.** help
   - **C.** assist
   - **D.** serve

Harold was ecstatic to hear that his new photographs would be included in a public display of local artists.

6. Which of the following alternatives to the underlined portion would be the LEAST acceptable?
   - **F.** exhibition
   - **G.** presentation
   - **H.** showing
   - **J.** offering

English Tip

Odd One Out: When a question contains the word NOT, LEAST, or EXCEPT, the best strategy is to find the one answer that is different from the other answers and the original underlined word.

19.4.1 Set One

Gabriel found no joy in any humor made <u>by people who were being rude about</u> others, even if it was intended to be harmless fun.

1. **A.** NO CHANGE
   B. at the expense of
   C. to deteriorate
   D. for saying bad things about

Our annual family reunion brings together the largest <u>team</u> of Meyers and Suires to be found anywhere in the continental United States. There are so many of us in one place that we have to rent out a banquet hall!

2. **F.** NO CHANGE
   G. capacity
   H. cluster
   J. concentration

Sheets of rain <u>poured</u> my brother at the bus stop—it was too late to go back for his umbrella.

3. **A.** NO CHANGE
   B. drenched
   C. absorbed
   D. watered

END OF SET ONE
STOP! DO NOT GO ON TO THE NEXT PAGE
UNTIL TOLD TO DO SO.

19.4.2 Set Two

Mom knew that she had to come up with an idea <u>by catering</u> to both me and my sister.

4. F. NO CHANGE
   G. while catering
   H. that catered
   J. and catered

It would take all she had to <u>rally</u> herself to get up and finish the race after she had tripped on her own feet.

5. A. muster
   B. evoke
   C. motivate
   D. save

The medicine provided by our mission trip would <u>benefit</u> many Hondurans and their families.

6. Which of the following alternatives to the underlined portion would be LEAST acceptable?
   F. aid
   G. improve
   H. help
   J. assist

END OF SET TWO

STOP! DO NOT GO ON TO THE NEXT PAGE UNTIL TOLD TO DO SO.

19.4.3 Set Three

My years spent in the Boy Scouts allowed me to go on many hiking <u>excursions</u> around California's mountains.

7. Which of the following alternatives to the underlined portion would NOT be acceptable?
A. destinations
B. outings
C. expeditions
D. adventures

He was surprised to learn that jazz evolved from a <u>fusion</u> of Eastern European, Creole, and Blues music stylings.

8. Which of the following alternatives to the underlined portion is LEAST acceptable?
F. blend
G. mixture
H. combination
J. group

The Internet <u>allowed</u> people to delve deeper into a wide variety of topics, all at the click of a mouse.

9. Which of the following alternatives to the underlined portion is LEAST acceptable?
A. made it possible for
B. made room for
C. permitted
D. helped

END OF SET THREE
STOP! DO NOT GO ON TO THE NEXT PAGE
UNTIL TOLD TO DO SO.

19.4.4 Set Four

Although it wasn't as glamorous as some jobs, my grandfather took pride in his profession as a janitor at the local high school.

10. Which of the following alternatives to the underlined portion would NOT be acceptable?
F. occupation
G. vocation
H. trade
J. volition

When he found the missing chapters of his grandfather's memoirs, my father bound them to keep them complete.

11. Which of the following alternatives to the underlined portion would NOT be acceptable?
A. together
B. total
C. intact
D. whole

My grandmother was well known around the community for her huge stockpile of sidewalk chalk and her wide, friendly smile.

12. Which of the following alternatives to the underlined portion would be LEAST acceptable?
F. supply
G. inventory
H. selection
J. gathering

END OF SET FOUR
STOP! DO NOT GO ON TO THE NEXT PAGE
UNTIL TOLD TO DO SO.

19.4.5 Set Five

In his disorganized garage, my father looked for the hammer and nails with no luck.

13. Which of the following alternatives to the underlined portion would NOT be acceptable?
 A. looked around
 B. searched
 C. examined
 D. glanced around

The magazine commonly featured articles about software and information technology, and Angela had finally been selected as a contributor.

14. Which of the following alternatives to the underlined portion would NOT be acceptable?
 F. gave prominence to
 G. showcased
 H. emphasized
 J. materialized

By bringing along a pocketful of treats, Karl was able to remedy the dog problem on his delivery route.

15. Which of the following alternatives to the underlined portion is LEAST acceptable?
 A. solve
 B. fix
 C. rescue
 D. alleviate

END OF SET FIVE

STOP! DO NOT GO ON TO THE NEXT PAGE UNTIL TOLD TO DO SO.

Sum It Up

Word Choice Part 2

Clear
Understandable, not confusing

Meaningful
Literally, has meaning; communicates something

Tips and Techniques

Consistent, Clear, and Concise: Make sure the word you choose gives the clearest meaning to the original sentence. Do not just pick a word that sounds fancy. Check the meaning with the surrounding words and choose the clearest option.

Odd One Out: When a question uses the words NOT, LEAST, or EXCEPT, the best strategy is to find the one answer that is different from the other answers and the original underlined word.

Lesson 20

Coordinating Conjunctions

CAPTION:

20.1 Entrance Ticket

Read each sentence and select the best alternative or answer the question given.

Jim loved his puppy, he wasn't ready for the responsibility of taking care of a pet.

1. **A.** NO CHANGE
   B. puppy, but
   C. puppy but,
   D. puppy, however

For this reason, the 1992 U.S. men's Olympic basketball team was described by American journalists as the greatest sports team ever assembled. It was nicknamed the "Dream Team."

2. Which of the following alternatives to the underlined portion would NOT be acceptable?
   F. assembled and
   G. assembled, and it
   H. assembled, it
   J. assembled; it

Although the cut on Karen's knee was small in size, but it was deep and blood loss was significant.

3. **A.** NO CHANGE
   B. size and
   C. size that
   D. size,

20.2 Learning Targets

1. Determine the need for punctuation or conjunctions to resolve errors in sentence structure

2. Determine which coordinating conjunction best fits the context of a given sentence

Self-Assessment

Circle the number that corresponds to your confidence level in your knowledge of this subject before beginning the lesson. A score of 1 means you are completely lost, and a score of 4 means you have mastered the skills. After you finish the lesson, return to the bottom of this page and circle your new confidence level to show your improvement.

Before Lesson

1 2 3 4

After Lesson

1 2 3 4

20.3.1 Conjunctions and Commas

Use coordinating conjunctions in one of three ways:

1. ______________________________

2. ______________________________

3. ______________________________

---

1. He doesn't write about fictional characters but about wonderfully familiar archetypes—the kind of people one encounters in everyday life and recognizes instantly in a short story.

Conjunction Rule: ______________________________

2. The era in which Stonehenge was erected is contested by historians, and the original purpose of the stones remains a mystery as well.

Conjunction Rule: ______________________________

3. The weeds shot up rapidly, however, and before long they had overtaken the garden, making the lettuce and radishes seem few in comparison.

Conjunction Rule: ______________________________

4. Jerry had been raised by his grandparents, so he was not only a natural with the patients in the assisted living center but also nuanced in his view of the aging process.

Conjunction Rule: ______________________________

20.3.2 Conjunctions Meanings

Conjunction	Definition
______________	____
______________	____
______________	____
______________	____
______________	____
______________	____
______________	____

20.3.2 Conjunctions Meanings

In *A Sunday on La Grande Jatte*, Georges Seurat depicts groups of people relaxing in a suburban park on an island in the Seine River with several animals are present in the scene.

1. **A.** NO CHANGE
   B. River and several
   C. River. Several
   D. River, so several

Most of the houses escaped the tornado without a scratch; none, sustained irreparable damage.

2. **F.** NO CHANGE
   G. scratch but none
   H. scratch; none
   J. scratch because none,

Where Patricia spent freely and saved little. Her mother was a penny-pincher and constantly chastised her daughter's financial decisions.

3. **A.** NO CHANGE
   B. little, but her
   C. little and her
   D. little, her

Although Mrs. Zervoudakis, our next-door neighbor for many years, never shared the recipe for her delicious baklava, but she enjoyed it when people tried to guess the ingredients.

4. **F.** NO CHANGE
   G. while
   H. and
   J. DELETE the underlined portion.

English Tip

Context Clues: Look at what is happening on both sides of the conjunction. If it's a contradiction or negative, use *but*, *nor*, or *yet*. If it's a process or explanation, use *for* or *so*. If it is just an addition, use *and* or *or*.

1 ■ ■ ■ ■ ■ ■ ■ ■ ■ 1

20.4.1 Set One

Lydia had all day to prepare for the dinner party, so not only was the food excellent, <u>and</u> also the house was spotless.

1. **A.** NO CHANGE
   B. but
   C. so
   D. yet

Thousands of stray cats prowl the streets of <u>Istanbul</u> I think most of them have selected my rooftop as their favorite sunning spot.

2. **F.** NO CHANGE
   G. Istanbul, and
   H. Istanbul, which
   J. Istanbul actually

The Montessori approach to children's education is named after Italian physician and educator Maria <u>Montessori. It</u> emphasizes independence, freedom within limits, and respect for a child's natural developmental patterns.

3. **A.** NO CHANGE
   B. Montessori, and therefore
   C. Montessori and therefore
   D. Montessori, therefore

END OF SET ONE
STOP! DO NOT GO ON TO THE NEXT PAGE
UNTIL TOLD TO DO SO.

20.4.2 Set Two

We had a long history <u>together,</u> it wasn't enough to keep us from parting ways.

4. **F.** NO CHANGE
   G. together, but
   H. together but,
   J. together, however

This afternoon Gretchen didn't sleep during her scheduled <u>naptime,</u> her mother knew she would be tired later in the day. She wasn't prepared for Gretchen's total meltdown at dinnertime, however.

5. **A.** NO CHANGE
   B. naptime, in which case
   C. naptime, because of this
   D. naptime, so

Although his adoptive parents promised that he would attend college after high school, <u>but</u> Steve later had his own ideas about pursuing an education.

6. **F.** NO CHANGE
   G. while
   H. so
   J. DELETE the underlined portion

END OF SET TWO
STOP! DO NOT GO ON TO THE NEXT PAGE
UNTIL TOLD TO DO SO.

20.4.3 Set Three

The traffic is at a standstill because of a stopped car in the left <u>lane and the result of this situation,</u> is that no one on the freeway will reach his or her destination anytime soon.

7. **A.** NO CHANGE
   B. lane, but so result of this situation
   C. lane, and the result of this situation
   D. lane and, the result of this situation

His beach bungalow was as eclectic as his artwork, featuring an assortment of mismatched furniture, colorful carpets printed with bold geometric designs, <u>and</u> various religious icons and statues scattered throughout the house.

8. **F.** NO CHANGE
   G. then
   H. if
   J. so

While my sister did well in the <u>classroom. Her</u> victories on the soccer field are what she is remembered for the most at our local high school.

9. **A.** NO CHANGE
   B. classroom and her
   C. classroom, but her
   D. classroom, her

END OF SET THREE
STOP! DO NOT GO ON TO THE NEXT PAGE
UNTIL TOLD TO DO SO.

1 ■ ■ ■ ■ ■ ■ ■ ■ ■ 1

20.4.4 Set Four

The kids swiftly lost interest in my improvised game, <u>and before long</u> I had a room full of antsy, mischevious charges on my hands.

10. **F.** NO CHANGE
    G. before long however,
    H. however, and before long,
    J. however before long

Onstage, Phil is a dynamic actor with a riveting stage <u>presence,</u> in person he comes across as quiet and reserved.

11. **A.** NO CHANGE
    B. presence
    C. presence, but
    D. presence that's

Though the Smiths continued to attend the symphony <u>performances, but</u> they felt a spark had gone out after the conductor was replaced.

12. **F.** NO CHANGE
    G. performances and
    H. performances that
    J. performances,

END OF SET FOUR
STOP! DO NOT GO ON TO THE NEXT PAGE
UNTIL TOLD TO DO SO.

20.4.5 Set Five

She not only met her deadline for the seemingly impossible project but also helped her colleagues who were scrambling to finish their work on other assignments.

13. **A.** NO CHANGE
B. but also did she
C. project she
D. project but she

B.B. King served as the unofficial ambassador for the Mississippi Delta blues; he appeared at more than 200 concerts around the world every year well into his 70s.

14. Which of the following alternatives to the underlined portion would NOT be acceptable?
F. blues. He appeared
G. blues, appearing
H. blues and appeared
J. blues, he appeared

Even the tempo changes musicians play in three-quarter, double, or common time, depending on their instrument.

15. **A.** NO CHANGE
B. changes, and
C. changes,
D. changes but

END OF SET FIVE
STOP! DO NOT GO ON TO THE NEXT PAGE
UNTIL TOLD TO DO SO.

Sum It Up

Coordinating Conjunctions

Remember the acronym FANBOYS for coordinating conjunctions.

Review the definitions you wrote for each conjunction. Keep these in mind when figuring out which conjunction to use.

For: because; introduces the cause of a cause/effect relationship
And: adds information
Nor: removes alternatives; tells what something is not, rather than what it is
But: contradicts, offers a contrast, or introduces something unexpected
Or: offers a choice
Yet: contradicts, offers a contrast, or introduces something unexpected, in a slightly more distinctive way than *but*
So: as a result; introduces the effect of a cause/effect relationship

---

Independent Clause (or main clause)
A clause that could stand by itself as a sentence

Conjunction
A word used to connect words, phrases, clauses, or sentences

Coordinating Conjunction
A conjunction that connects two items of equal importance, often independent clauses

Tips and Techniques

Context Clues: Use the entire sentence to understand which conjunction, if any, you should use.

Lesson 21

Subordinating Conjunctions

Although Jill's mom is a talented painter,...

CAPTION:

21.1 Entrance Ticket

Identify the following underlined conjunctions. Determine whether they are coordinating or subordinating conjunctions.

1. We made the cake so that our parents wouldn't be upset with us.

2. I think we should get out of here and forget about the whole thing.

3. DeAndre stayed until his parents told him to come home.

4. We decided to tell the truth once we realized what the punishment was.

5. You could have left, yet you stayed because you knew it was the right thing to do.

6. Jewel and Becca decided to study together so they can do better on the test.

21.2 Learning Targets

1. Recognize the differences between subordinating and coordinating conjunctions

2. Use subordinating and coordinating conjunctions correctly

Self-Assessment

Circle the number that corresponds to your confidence level in your knowledge of this subject before beginning the lesson. A score of 1 means you are completely lost, and a score of 4 means you have mastered the skills. After you finish the lesson, return to the bottom of this page and circle your new confidence level to show your improvement.

Before Lesson

1 2 3 4

After Lesson

1 2 3 4

21.3.1 Using Subordinating Conjunctions

1. As Thomas Edison created the long-lasting lightbulb

2. Because Rocco stayed up late watching the game

3. Although the weather improved

4. Even though LeBron James went to seven straight NBA finals

After: ______________________________

Example: ______________________________

Even though: ______________________________

Example: ______________________________

If: ______________________________

Example: ______________________________

Because: ______________________________

Example: ______________________________

So that: ______________________________

Example: ______________________________

21.3.1 Using Subordinating Conjunctions

That: ______________________________

Example: ______________________________

Though: ______________________________

Example: ______________________________

Whereas: ______________________________

Example: ______________________________

While: ______________________________

Example: ______________________________

Since: ______________________________

Example: ______________________________

21.3.1 Using Subordinating Conjunctions

after	in order that	though
although	in the event that	until
as	just in case	when
as soon as	now that	whenever
because	once	where
before	only if	whereas
by the time	provided that	wherever
even if	rather than	whether
even though	since	whether or not
every time	so that	which
if	than	while
in case	that	why

On the practice run for the upcoming car race, the Alfa Romeo driver ran the track in under thirty <u>seconds as</u> the other drivers couldn't break the minute mark.

1. **A.** NO CHANGE
   B. seconds so
   C. seconds,
   D. seconds, whereas

One would think that Benjamin Harrison, the twenty-third President of the United States, a colonel in the union army, would have little to fear. But the former president was responsible for having electricity inside the White House, even though he harbored a fear of being electrocuted. <u>Since</u> that fear, he would never touch the light switches himself.

2. **F.** NO CHANGE
   G. Because of
   H. Concerning
   J. For

It's not <u>as if</u> the preliminary hearing holds any bearing on the case, though—the verdict will be decided by the testimony of the witnesses during the actual trial.

3. **A.** NO CHANGE
   B. if
   C. whether
   D. as to whether

English Tip

Strategy: If the clause in question is using a subordinate conjunction, make sure there is an independent clause in the sentence. If not, the subordinate conjunction needs to be removed to make a complete sentence.

21.3.2 Coordinating vs. Subordinating

1. It was raining, yet I still felt it would be a good day.

2. Kenny stayed inside because he thought it would be too cold.

3. You can sit here and be upset, or you can do something about it.

4. We are going to play outside, for it is a beautiful day out.

5. Rocky wanted to go, even though I told him the store was closed.

6. Mom would be here if we told her to come.

7. Do what you want, but be mindful of your actions.

8. It isn't a bad job when everyone does their part.

English Tip

Consistent, Clear, and Concise: Sometimes the best option for a conjunction is to select no conjunction at all. Pay attention to the entire paragraph. If you cannot see a need for any conjunction or all of the options are not consistent with the paragraph, choose the concise option and remove the conjunction altogether.

21.4.1 Set One

After a recent expedition uncovered a new species in the Amazon, our investors were thrilled that their financial backing benefited everyone involved.

1. **A.** NO CHANGE
   B. Recently, an expedition that uncovering
   C. A recent expedition uncovered
   D. A recent expedition uncovering

My father likes to reminisce about "family time," which were those summer evenings, because the dinner table had been cleared and board games were set up.

2. **F.** NO CHANGE
   G. evenings after
   H. evenings, as if
   J. evenings, while

Growing up with a twin gave me the strong impression that I had a special relationship with my sibling. For one thing, we share a unique sense of humor that no one else in our family has. We quickly became best friends as we grew older, and we have stayed close, even though our careers have taken us to different parts of the country.

3. **A.** NO CHANGE
   B. close, yet even
   C. close; even
   D. close. Even

END OF SET ONE
STOP! DO NOT GO ON TO THE NEXT PAGE
UNTIL TOLD TO DO SO.

1 ■ ■ ■ ■ ■ ■ ■ ■ ■ 1

21.4.2 Set Two

The lingering discussion at the dinner party, however, would change the course of the evening, details emerged about a family fortune that had been hidden in the house and also that someone at the table knew its location.

4. **F.** NO CHANGE
   G. evening; since
   H. evening:
   J. evening, although

In the off-season, the two quarterbacks performed differently: The starting quarterback could complete passes in twenty seconds as the second-string quarterback needed almost a full minute to position himself to throw a pass.

5. **A.** NO CHANGE
   B. seconds, so
   C. seconds,
   D. seconds, whereas

While Mrs. David's accomplishments in the classroom are praiseworthy. Her talented coaching is responsible for bringing the girls' softball team to a victory at the district championship.

6. **F.** NO CHANGE
   G. praiseworthy, but her
   H. praiseworthy and her
   J. praiseworthy, her

END OF SET TWO
STOP! DO NOT GO ON TO THE NEXT PAGE
UNTIL TOLD TO DO SO.

21.4.3 Set Three

Though the coaches held each other in high regard, but their individual methods were simply too different to be able to work well with one another.

7. **A.** NO CHANGE
   B. regard and
   C. regard that
   D. regard,

Although Stanley Danwich, now a retired author, only published two critically acclaimed novels during his career, while he stated that he wished to have the rest of his work published posthumously.

8. **F.** NO CHANGE
   G. and
   H. so
   J. DELETE the underlined portion.

In 1941 in Pearl Harbor, Hawaii, where the United States naval base was attacked.

9. **A.** NO CHANGE
   B. it was there that
   C. was where
   D. DELETE the underlined portion.

END OF SET THREE

STOP! DO NOT GO ON TO THE NEXT PAGE UNTIL TOLD TO DO SO.

1 ■ ■ ■ ■ ■ ■ ■ ■ ■ 1

21.4.4 Set Four

After my scuba diving instructor made sure the area was safe to dive in, I launched into the deep blues abyss, fascinated by all the different fish swimming past me.

10. Which of the following alternatives to the underlined portion would NOT be acceptable?
F. When my
G. Once my
H. My
J. As soon as

The Bermuda Triangle has been a mystery to people of all backgrounds and interests. There were conspiracy theorists who believe it has something to do with aliens and secret government organizations to realists looking for a perfectly rational and scientific explanation, everyone can admit some bizarre events have occurred there.

11. A. NO CHANGE
B. When
C. From
D. Those

There were only a handful of these postage stamps, and a collector's chance to find them was very rare, which decidedly made them a prize sought after by many people.

12. Which of the following alternatives to the underlined portion would NOT be acceptable?
F. rare; this
G. rare this
H. rare. This
J. rare, a factor that

END OF SET FOUR
STOP! DO NOT GO ON TO THE NEXT PAGE
UNTIL TOLD TO DO SO.

21.4.5 Set Five

By these classic standards set in stone by former headmasters imbued the students at the beginning of the semester with a sense responsibility to reflect the school at all times and in all manner of situations.

13. A. NO CHANGE
    B. Regarding these
    C. These
    D. This

A little over a decade ago, Coach Bilburn was coaching college baseball at one of the most athletically acclaimed universities in the country, a young man by the name of Dale Davis tried out for his team as a freshman.

14. F. NO CHANGE
    G. Coach Bilburn coached
    H. that Coach Bilburn was coaching
    J. while Coach Bilburn was coaching

Once my best friend showed me how his four-wheeler worked, I drove it around, overcome by the freedom it gave me to go as fast as I wanted.

15. Which of the following alternatives to the underlined portion would NOT be acceptable?
    A. Because my
    B. When my
    C. My
    D. Right after

END OF SET FIVE

STOP! DO NOT GO ON TO THE NEXT PAGE UNTIL TOLD TO DO SO.

Sum It Up

Subordinating Conjunctions

Independent Clause
A clause that can stand on its own

Dependent Clause
A clause that cannot stand on its own and needs another clause to make a complete sentence

---

Conjunction
A word used to connect parts of a sentence together

Tips and Techniques

Consistent, Clear, and Concise: If there is not a need for a conjunction, go with the concise option and choose no conjunction at all.

Prepositions

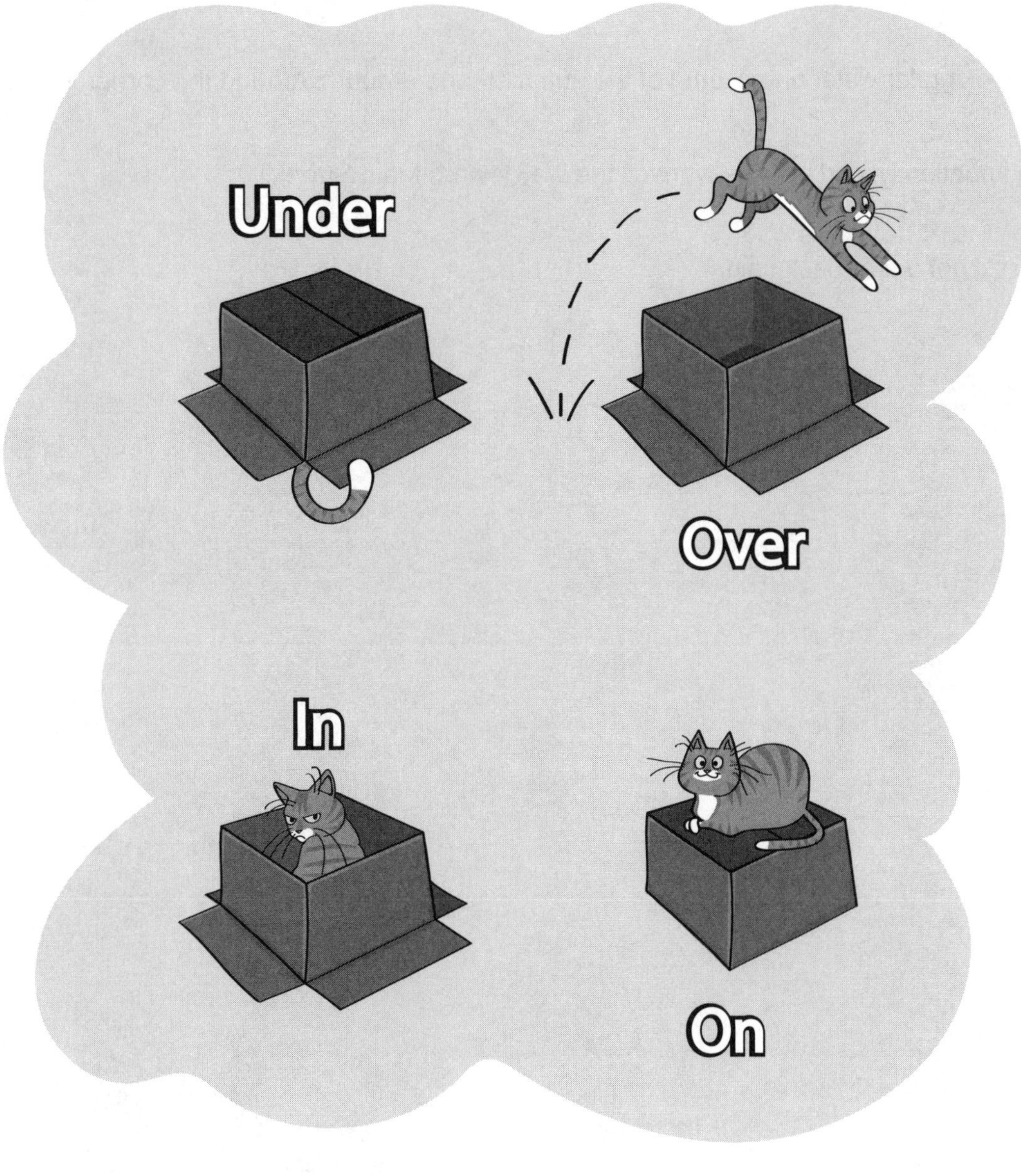

CAPTION:

22.1 Entrance Ticket

Read the passage and circle the prepositions.

Jack and Jill walked across the street to the store for water. They walked alongside the sidewalk, since the road was under construction, and across the intersection of Mayberry and Oak. They were among the many children looking for water on account of the summer-long drought. Around the corner, they found a line of kids waiting impatiently, and the line went all the way toward Main Street.

"At least we'll get a tan," Jack said.

22.2 Learning Targets

1. Identify the best prepositions to use in simple and complex sentences

2. Use idiomatically appropriate prepositions in combinations with verbs

Self-Assessment

Circle the number that corresponds to your confidence level in your knowledge of this subject before beginning the lesson. A score of 1 means you are completely lost, and a score of 4 means you have mastered the skills. After you finish the lesson, return to the bottom of this page and circle your new confidence level to show your improvement.

Before Lesson

1 2 3 4

After Lesson

1 2 3 4

22.3.1 Preposition Meaning

1.

The dog jumped onto the table. ____________________

It is a jar for cookies. ____________________

The hawk soared above the clouds. ____________________

2.

The car sped past the crowd. ____________________

She went to the library. ____________________

I saw the tiger coming toward him. ____________________

3.

We met on Sunday. ____________________

Dad gets up early in the morning. ____________________

I will call you at 1 p.m. ____________________

4.

The ball fell near the benches. ____________________

His house is at the street's end. ____________________

The teacher wrote a sentence on the blackboard. ____________________

22.3.1 Preposition Meaning

5.

The men have been arrested and charged with robbery. ______________________

Everyone blamed me for the accident. ______________________

Ben threw the ball to Jack. ______________________

6.

She is the person next to you. ______________________

The trail in the forest is narrow. ______________________

The end of the track is far away. ______________________

7.

The police wouldn't let us go through. ______________________

He walked back. ______________________

I went inside. ______________________

22.3.2 Idiomatic Prepositions

Example 1:

I spoke to your mother.

I spoke at your mother.

I spoke by your mother.

Example 2:

The dog jumped to the table.

The dog jumped on the table.

The dog jumped at the table.

Example 3:

We played with the neighbors.

We played by the neighbors.

We played at the neighbors.

22.3.2 Idiomatic Prepositions

care, forget, know, warn, write } **about**

decide, vote } **against**

classify, define, know, regard } **as**

arrive } **at**

hope, pay, prepare, provide, require, search, use, vote, work } **for**

benefit, come, derive, differ, emerge, exclude, recover, resign, save, stem } **from**

find, include, invest, involve, occur, participate, persist, result, specialize, succeed, use } **in**

approve, consist, cure, disapprove } **of**

agree, base, comment, concentrate, decide, depend, elaborate, experiment, insist, plan, work } **on**

adapt, add, adjust, agree, apply, attribute, belong, contribute, happen, lead, object, react, refer, relate, reply, subscribe } **to**

agree, associate, begin, compete, cope, deal, disagree } **with**

22.3.2 Idiomatic Prepositions

1. ______________________________

2. ______________________________

3. ______________________________

4. ______________________________

5. ______________________________

6. ______________________________

7. ______________________________

8. ______________________________

9. ______________________________

10. ______________________________

English Tip

Sounds Wrong Is Wrong: Most prepositions will sound right when used correctly on the ACT, especially the idiomatic ones. If you get stuck, try sounding out the sentence in your head with each answer choice, and if it sounds weird, eliminate it.

1 ■ ■ ■ ■ ■ ■ ■ ■ ■ 1

22.4.1 Set One

For their twenty-fifth anniversary, Louie's parents came up with a brilliant plan <u>by</u> celebrating with their family.

1. **A.** NO CHANGE
   B. about
   C. of
   D. for

Since the beginning of time, people from all cultures have attached different <u>meanings to</u> the fables they tell their children. These stories teach about everything from social etiquette to morals to falling in love.

2. **F.** NO CHANGE
   G. meanings, which they connected to
   H. meanings, to which they related to
   J. meanings because of

<u>In</u> the early hours of the morning, my grandfather would arise from bed, cook breakfast, and milk the cows, all before my brother and I even woke up!

3. **A.** NO CHANGE
   B. On
   C. At
   D. To

END OF SET ONE
STOP! DO NOT GO ON TO THE NEXT PAGE
UNTIL TOLD TO DO SO.

1 ■ ■ ■ ■ ■ ■ ■ ■ ■ 1

22.4.2 Set Two

While he searched hours and hours for his missing yearbook, he found his grandparents' love letters from during the war.

4. Which of the following alternatives to the underlined portion would NOT be acceptable?
   F. came upon
   G. came across
   H. discovered
   J. found upon

In the 1960s, the government proposed unfair voting requirements for African Americans in Selma, Alabama, by which Martin Luther King Jr. marched thousands of people in protest.

5. **A.** NO CHANGE
   B. which
   C. into which
   D. since

After my father finally declared he was lost, he merged toward the exit ramp to leave the interstate.

6. Which of the following alternatives to the underlined portion would NOT be acceptable?
   F. over toward
   G. over
   H. onto
   J. to get on

END OF SET TWO

STOP! DO NOT GO ON TO THE NEXT PAGE UNTIL TOLD TO DO SO.

1 1

22.4.3 Set Three

Troy attempted to broaden his culinary skills <u>when learning</u> how to bake the perfect soufflé.

7. **A.** NO CHANGE
   B. learning
   C. having learned
   D. by learning

On such rare occasions, he would pop open a glass cola bottle and let the fizzy memories of summer drift back <u>to</u> him.

8. **F.** NO CHANGE
   G. with
   H. before
   J. along

Goya's *The Disasters of War* prints were based <u>by</u> the actions of the French military toward the Spanish people.

9. **A.** NO CHANGE
   B. on
   C. for
   D. to

END OF SET THREE

STOP! DO NOT GO ON TO THE NEXT PAGE UNTIL TOLD TO DO SO.

22.4.4 Set Four

My mother's views were often supported <u>when</u> my father, who took pride in his wife's intelligence and wisdom.

10. **F.** NO CHANGE
G. by
H. while
J. as if

Rotwin, the ship's cynical captain, entered into a bet <u>after</u> the ship's fate—and the men's lives—in the storm.

11. **A.** NO CHANGE
B. at
C. on
D. of

On Thanksgiving, I sat across the table <u>as</u> my two little cousins and my brother Sal.

12. **F.** NO CHANGE
G. to
H. at
J. from

END OF SET FOUR

STOP! DO NOT GO ON TO THE NEXT PAGE UNTIL TOLD TO DO SO.

22.4.5 Set Five

Whenever my grandfather would go to bed, he would snore as like a sleeping giant who hadn't rested for a year.

13. **A.** NO CHANGE
B. such as
C. just as
D. like

We praised all the gods equally: Poseidon for the seas, Aphrodite for love, Themis for how firm she was in her judgement.

14. Which of the following alternatives to the underlined portion would NOT be acceptable?
F. with
G. regarding
H. along
J. about

Fromage may sound like some kind of frothy dessert, but interestingly enough, it is a French word that translates as "cheese."

15. **A.** NO CHANGE
B. by
C. with
D. from

END OF SET FIVE
STOP! DO NOT GO ON TO THE NEXT PAGE
UNTIL TOLD TO DO SO.

Sum It Up

Prepositions

A **preposition** shows a relationship between a noun or pronoun and another word in the sentence.

Tips and Techniques

Sounds Right vs. Sounds Weird: Most prepositions will sound right when used correctly on the ACT, especially the idiomatic ones. If you get stuck, try sounding out the sentence in your head with each answer choice. If it sounds weird, eliminate it.

Lesson 23

Fragments and Fused Sentences

CAPTION:

23.1 Entrance Ticket

Read each sentence and select the best alternative or answer the question given.

He then moves it to the electric stove, an appliance made to lessen gas usage in many modern homes.

1. **A.** NO CHANGE
   B. the metal appliance is
   C. it is an appliance
   D. appliance

These politically aware people, called activists, don't just talk about changing the world around them; they educate others to participate.

2. Which of the following alternatives to the underlined portion would NOT be acceptable?
   F. them: in addition, they
   G. them they
   H. them—they
   J. them. They

The town was honoring its recent high school graduates; a diverse group of students who had each overcome many personal and financial obstacles in the past four years.

3. **A.** NO CHANGE
   B. graduates, by
   C. graduates
   D. graduates:

23.2 Learning Targets

1. Recognize and revise run-on sentences

2. Recognize and revise sentence fragments

Self-Assessment

Circle the number that corresponds to your confidence level in your knowledge of this subject before beginning the lesson. A score of 1 means you are completely lost, and a score of 4 means you have mastered the skills. After you finish the lesson, return to the bottom of this page and circle your new confidence level to show your improvement.

Before Lesson

1 2 3 4

After Lesson

1 2 3 4

23.3.1 Run-On Sentences

Run-On: ____

____

____

____

The clouds part gradually the rain puddles on the sidewalk become bright, reflecting the sun like mirrors.

1. **A.** NO CHANGE
   B. part, and gradually
   C. parting gradually
   D. part, gradually,

Subject and Verb (Clause 1): ____

Subject and Verb (Clause 2): ____

To be sure he wasn't being cheated, he had the ring examined by jewelers, however, they found that the diamond was, in fact, real.

2. **F.** NO CHANGE
   G. who
   H. which
   J. they

Subject and Verb (Clause 1): ____

Subject and Verb (Clause 2): ____

23.3.1 Run-On Sentences

Employing their best defense mechanism against the approaching shark, the school of fish quickly collected themselves, swam closely together to look like one big fish.

3. A. NO CHANGE
   B. they swam
   C. swimming
   D. swim

Subject and Verb (Clause 1): ____________________

Subject and Verb (Clause 2): ____________________

Artie made his living working alternately as a painter and he was a delivery driver.

4. F. NO CHANGE
   G. as well
   H. being
   J. as

Subject and Verb (Clause 1): ____________________

Subject and Verb (Clause 2): ____________________

My kids talk all the time about how they can't wait to grow up I don't understand their rush.

5. A. NO CHANGE
   B. up, however
   C. up.
   D. up,

Subject and Verb (Clause 1): ____________________

Subject and Verb (Clause 2): ____________________

23.3.1 Run-On Sentences

DeMarcus loved video games and <u>movies. I</u> loved poetry and classical music.

6. Which of the following alternatives to the underlined portion would NOT be acceptable?
   - **F.** movies. I, on the other hand,
   - **G.** movies, while I
   - **H.** movies; I
   - **J.** movies I

Subject and Verb (Clause 1): ______________________________

Subject and Verb (Clause 2): ______________________________

The team boarded a plane in Copenhagen and took a 1,500-mile flight to Longyearbyen <u>Airport, it is</u> the world's northernmost airport with flights open to the public.

7. **A.** NO CHANGE
   B. Airport,
   C. Airport, being
   D. Airport

Subject and Verb (Clause 1): ______________________________

Subject and Verb (Clause 2): ______________________________

When fixing run-on sentences, you can:

1. ______________________________
2. ______________________________
3. ______________________________
4. ______________________________

23.3.2 Sentence Fragments

Fragment: ____

____

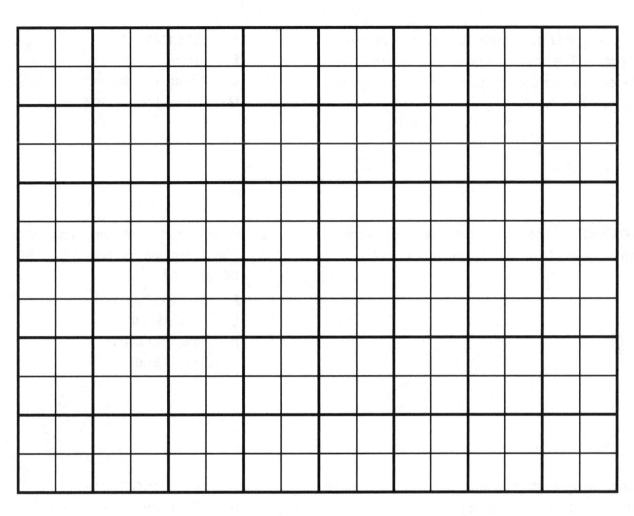

When dealing with fragments: ____

____

English Tip

Sound It Out: Read the sentence in your head. Pause where you see punctuation. If the pauses don't seem natural or if you go too long without a pause in a way that sounds awkward or unusual, you most likely have a run-on sentence.

23.3.2 Sentence Fragments

Years ago, this town was a typical example of Americana. The small businesses have since been replaced by banks, pharmacies, and high-rise apartment buildings.

1. **A.** NO CHANGE
   B. Americana the
   C. Americana, the
   D. Americana; and the

Others, feigning sleep, lie awake throughout nap time, rising instantly at the sound of the recess bell.

2. Which of the following alternatives to the underlined portion would NOT be acceptable?
   F. time and then rise
   G. time. Then they rise
   H. time, only to rise
   J. time. Rising

Pools of sweat forming on the gym floor as we trained like maniacs for the annual competition.

3. **A.** NO CHANGE
   B. would form
   C. form
   D. OMIT the underlined portion.

One of these, the dodo bird, which was hunted to extinction by man before the 18th century.

4. **F.** NO CHANGE
   G. One,
   H. One being
   J. One example is

23.3.2 Sentence Fragments

The small mosaic pieces, when viewed from a distance, appearing to be one cohesive pane of glass.

5. **A.** NO CHANGE
   B. appear
   C. appearing as though
   D. was appearing

Evidence that some video game designers have acknowledged the history of gaming is found in the recurring images of Italian plumbers, a yellow ball eating cherries, and a giant ape with a red tie.

6. **F.** NO CHANGE
   G. gaming, having been
   H. gaming,
   J. gaming being

When fixing fragments, you can:

1. ______________________________

2. ______________________________

3. ______________________________

4. ______________________________

English Tip

Sound It Out: This tactic works for fragments, too. If a thought or phrase sounds incomplete or the words sound unnatural, you may have a fragment.

1 ■ ■ ■ ■ ■ ■ ■ ■ ■ 1

23.4.1 Set One

Michael Prince went up to the podium with his speech I wasn't prepared for the flood of emotion.

1. A. NO CHANGE
   B. speech, which
   C. speech that
   D. speech.

In the suburbs, such activities are not encouraged, which led us to reconsider moving away from the city center.

2. Which of the following alternatives to the underlined portion would NOT be acceptable?
   F. encouraged; this
   G. encouraged. This
   H. encouraged this
   J. encouraged, an issue which

Gilligan likes goofing off. The Skipper really tries to fix things.

3. Which of the following alternatives to the underlined portion would NOT be acceptable?
   A. NO CHANGE
   B. off, while the Skipper
   C. off; the Skipper
   D. off the

END OF SET ONE

STOP! DO NOT GO ON TO THE NEXT PAGE UNTIL TOLD TO DO SO.

1 ■ ■ ■ ■ ■ ■ ■ ■ ■ 1

23.4.2 Set Two

My boys don't need to be reminded to show respect to their <u>elders they know</u> that.

4. **F.** NO CHANGE
 G. elders they already know
 H. elders; they know
 J. elders; knowing

Students speak loudly about issues they don't fully <u>understand; nevertheless</u>, it excites me to see that they care.

5. **A.** NO CHANGE
 B. understand, nevertheless
 C. understand: nevertheless
 D. understand nevertheless

You could probably guess <u>what</u> the rest of the party went after the stereo stopped working.

6. **F.** NO CHANGE
 G. if
 H. how
 J. DELETE the underlined portion.

END OF SET TWO
STOP! DO NOT GO ON TO THE NEXT PAGE
UNTIL TOLD TO DO SO.

23.4.3 Set Three

As we drove away from the city, dozens of evacuation sirens booming loudly from the city center.

7. A. NO CHANGE
   B. sirens, which boomed
   C. sirens that boomed
   D. sirens boomed

My mother, Marge having been the oldest of all her siblings and cousins.

8. F. NO CHANGE
   G. Marge, was
   H. Marge,
   J. Marge being

One of these is compassion, a value that many people ignore today.

9. A. NO CHANGE
   B. One of these,
   C. One,
   D. One being

END OF SET THREE

STOP! DO NOT GO ON TO THE NEXT PAGE UNTIL TOLD TO DO SO.

23.4.4 Set Four

We took the long route around the lake, and after an hour, we finally saw the campus three blocks away. Exhausted and sweaty, jogging back to our dorm.

10. F. NO CHANGE
    G. to jog
    H. having to jog
    J. we jogged

Books by Virginia Woolf, Ernest Hemingway, William Faulkner, and other modernist writers along the shelves.

11. A. NO CHANGE
    B. sitting on
    C. on
    D. line

When Jewel finally went to bed, having followed Frodo and the Fellowship across Middle-earth and had completed the *Lord of the Rings*.

12. F. NO CHANGE
    G. bed, she had
    H. bed and had
    J. bed, she

END OF SET FOUR
STOP! DO NOT GO ON TO THE NEXT PAGE
UNTIL TOLD TO DO SO.

1 1

23.4.5 Set Five

Sometimes, the children would forget about their hidden treasure—the few coins would disappear or candy would slowly become <u>dirty with</u> the changing seasons and visiting relatives, the children were preoccupied with indoor adventures.

13. A. NO CHANGE
B. dirty covered by
C. dirty. With
D. dirty because

The editor begins by reading the entire manuscript. For each chapter, all the <u>words, being</u> formatted in various fonts, differing according to the character's voice and their place in time chronologically.

14. F. NO CHANGE
G. words which are
H. words are
J. words, which are

His <u>plot—which by being a small town expelling an ancient vampire from Europe—</u>was a hit in the United States and later spawned several sequels and movie adaptations.

15. A. NO CHANGE
B. plot—that of a small town expelling an ancient vampire from Europe—
C. plot, being that of a small town expelling an ancient vampire from Europe, it
D. plot—in which it was a small town expelling an ancient vampire from Europe—

END OF SET FIVE
STOP! DO NOT GO ON TO THE NEXT PAGE UNTIL TOLD TO DO SO.

Sum It Up

Fragments and Fused Sentences

Clause
A group of words that includes a subject and verb (both independent and dependent)

Dependent Clause
A clause that includes a subordinate—*even though*, *after*, *since*, etc.

Run-On
Two independent clauses that are joined without the necessary comma and/or conjunction

---

Fragment
A sentence that does not have an independent clause

To fix a run-on sentence, you can:

- add a comma and a coordinating conjunction.
- make one of the clauses a dependent clause. Weaken the verb by adding *–ing* or a conjunction, such as *even though*, *because*, *who*, *that*, or *which*.
- add periods and semicolons.
- delete the second subject and verb.

To fix a fragment, you can:

- connect it to the main idea with a comma.
- look for a verb—some sentences need the word *is*.
- activate the verb: drop the *-ing*.
- replace *being* with *is* or *was* since it is not a stand-alone verb.

Tips and Techniques

Sound It Out: If something sounds unnatural or incomplete, determine if it is a run-on sentence or fragment.

Lesson 24

Misplaced Modifiers

Drinking some coffee, my cat jumped into my lap.

CAPTION:

24.1 Entrance Ticket

Read each sentence and answer the question given.

Late that night, Jackson's truck hydroplaned on the road <u>while delivering</u> packages to the children for Christmas.

1. Which of the following changes to the portion that is underlined would NOT be acceptable?
   - **A.** while he was delivering
   - **B.** as he was delivering
   - **C.** as he delivered
   - **D.** that was delivering

One of them was <u>for cats</u> a scratching post that looked like a castle.

2. The best placement for the portion that is underlined would be:
   - **F.** where it is now.
   - **G.** after the word *them*.
   - **H.** after the word *post*.
   - **J.** after the word *castle* (ending the sentence with a period).

To avoid having the boat capsize in the strong waves, the women reinforced the sails <u>prudently</u> to steady the ship.

3. The best placement for the portion that is underlined would be:
   - **A.** where it is now.
   - **B.** before the word *capsize.*
   - **C.** before the word *reinforced*.
   - **D.** before the word *steady*.

24.2 Learning Targets

1. Identify the presence of misplaced modifiers

2. Understand when and how to use modifiers correctly

Self-Assessment

Circle the number that corresponds to your confidence level in your knowledge of this subject before beginning the lesson. A score of 1 means you are completely lost, and a score of 4 means you have mastered the skills. After you finish the lesson, return to the bottom of this page and circle your new confidence level to show your improvement.

Before Lesson

1 2 3 4

After Lesson

1 2 3 4

24.3.1 Identifying a Misplaced Modifier

Modifying Phrase

Sentence

Combined Sentences

24.3.1 Identifying a Misplaced Modifier

Covered in flowers and colorful paper, the wedding planner had transformed the venue into something magical.

1. **A.** NO CHANGE
   B. adorning the venue into something magical by the wedding planner.
   C. transformed the venue into something magical by the wedding planner.
   D. the venue had been transformed into something magical by the wedding planner.

Bolted to the top of a high skyscraper, tourists on the observation deck are given a great view of the sprawling city.

2. **F.** NO CHANGE
   G. the observation deck gives tourists
   H. tourists visiting observation deck are given
   J. visiting tourists at this observation deck are given

Uncovered, I didn't expect to find such treasure.

3. **A.** NO CHANGE
   B. The uncovering of such treasure, but it wasn't what I expected.
   C. Out from the covers, my expectation was not to find such treasure.
   D. I didn't expect to uncover such treasure.

Cars would be parked in the alleyway that runs behind the neighborhood.

4. **F.** NO CHANGE
   G. being that they
   H. so that they
   J. since they

English Tip

Decoding: If you see a subordinating conjunction or an introductory phrase at the start of the sentence, be on the lookout for the noun that follows. If the phrase cannot logically modify the noun, then find what it is modifying and move it closer.

24.3.2 Phrase Placement

Her endurance paid off in her thirties, when Smith was awarded <u>coveted</u> the gold medal in telemarking.

1. The best placement for the word that is underlined would be:
   - **A.** where it is now.
   - **B.** before the word *awarded.*
   - **C.** before the word *gold.*
   - **D.** before the word *Smith.*

To avoid becoming redundant with his music, the lead singer called a friend <u>sagaciously</u> to collaborate on the album.

2. The best placement for the portion that is underlined would be:
   - **F.** where it is now.
   - **G.** before the word *lead*.
   - **H.** before the word *called*.
   - **J.** before the word *album*.

The scene in the poem presented the story of a young mother who, in prehistoric times, fled to the hillside to escape from a herd of stampeding mammoths <u>with her children</u> that destroyed her village.

3. The best placement for the portion that is underlined would be:
   - **A.** where it is now.
   - **B.** after the word *fled*.
   - **C.** after the word *escape.*
   - **D.** after the word *herd*.

The caravan gathered here during their travels <u>for a brief rest</u> from California to New York.

4. The best placement for the portion that is underlined would be:
   - **F.** where it is now.
   - **G.** at the beginning of the sentence (revising the capitalization accordingly).
   - **H.** after the word *caravan.*
   - **J.** after the word *here*.

24.3.2 Phrase Placement

The best design in the program was for dogs a waterpark shaped like a bone.

5. The best placement for the portion that is underlined would be:

A. as it is now.
B. after the word *program.*
C. after the word *waterpark*.
D. after the word *bone* (ending the sentence with a period).

The patriotic song is intended to invoke both the awe-inspiring beauty and the limitless ambitions during a period of manifest destiny of America.

6. The best placement of the portion that is underlined would be:

F. where it is now.
G. after the word *song.*
H. after the word *America* (ending the sentence with a period).
J. after the word *beauty.*

English Tip

Plug It In: When the ACT English test asks you where best to place a modifier, try to plug the modifier into each option. If a given placement in the answer does not fit logically or grammatically, eliminate it and move on to the next answer.

24.4.1 Set One

Anchored to a busy commercial port in the Gulf of Mexico, <u>fishermen on the shrimp trawler</u> ran back and forth across the deck to clean, sort, and secure the day's profitable catch.

1. **A.** NO CHANGE
   B. the shrimp trawler swayed as fishermen
   C. fishermen living on the shrimp trawler
   D. the shrimp trawler with fishermen

<u>Having faded away,</u> she picks up the pottery, examining it for signs of writing.

2. **F.** NO CHANGE
   G. Finally faded away,
   H. With a faded image,
   J. Although it is faded,

Because Mark is scarcely 130 pounds, the man at the table next to us doesn't believe Mark has the stomach to win the hot dog-eating contest. So Mark, who has trophies for three hot dog eating contests back at home, bets the man that he can win the <u>contest and then eat a hamburger</u> after it's over.

3. **A.** NO CHANGE
   B. contest, where he then ate a hamburger
   C. contest, and then he ate a hamburger
   D. contest and then eating a hamburger

END OF SET ONE
STOP! DO NOT GO ON TO THE NEXT PAGE
UNTIL TOLD TO DO SO.

24.4.2 Set Two

In a few weeks, when the dust had settled, the workers examined the site, revealing the results of the demolition and of the crew's thorough work. The ground was smooth, clean, and ready for new construction.

4. **F.** NO CHANGE
   G. demolition, which is the crew's
   H. demolition, of which the crew's
   J. demolition, and the crew is

No one took the complaints about the poor infrastructure seriously and insufficient funds until the bridge across the river collapsed.

5. **A.** NO CHANGE
   B. (Place after *complaints*)
   C. (Place after *funds*)
   D. (Place after *until*)

The display and sale of local farmers' produce would be held every Saturday morning at the pavilion that is behind town hall.

6. **F.** NO CHANGE
   G. being that they
   H. so that they
   J. since they

END OF SET TWO
STOP! DO NOT GO ON TO THE NEXT PAGE
UNTIL TOLD TO DO SO.

24.4.3 Set Three

Just last night I sat across the aisle from a man who was writing a novel in a grey suit in a leather notebook.

7. The best placement for the portion that is underlined would be:
   A. where it is now
   B. after the word *night.*
   C. after the word *across.*
   D. after the word *man.*

The explorers in the 1600s first encountered the now endangered species.

8. All of the following would be acceptable placements for the underlined portion EXCEPT:
   F. where it is now.
   G. at the beginning of the sentence (revising the capitalization accordingly).
   H. after the word *endangered.*
   J. after the word *species* (ending the sentence with a period).

By late autumn, the cyclists had ridden all over New England, stretching over 1,000 miles a beautiful, hilly region.

9. The best placement for the section that is underlined would be:
   A. where it is now.
   B. after the word *region* (ending the sentence with a period).
   C. after the word *cyclists.*
   D. after the word *ridden.*

END OF SET THREE
STOP! DO NOT GO ON TO THE NEXT PAGE
UNTIL TOLD TO DO SO.

1 ■ ■ ■ ■ ■ ■ ■ ■ ■ 1

24.4.4 Set Four

Frequently, we would create stories of our own, taking turns writing in a ragged journal adventures <u>about spies</u> and scary monsters.

10. The best placement for the portion that is underlined would be:
F. where it is now.
G. after the word *stories.*
H. after the word *journal.*
J. after the word *monsters* (ending the sentence with a period).

In August, Melinda received the honorable nomination <u>while reading</u> to the children living in the gymnasium with their families during the storm.

11. Which of the following changes to the portion that is underlined would NOT be acceptable?
A. while she was reading
B. as she was reading
C. that was reading
D. as she read

This ability shortens the time needed to perform <u>greatly</u> the surgery.

12. The best placement for the portion that is underlined would be:
F. where it is now.
G. after the word *time.*
H. after the word *needed.*
J. after the word *ability.*

END OF SET FOUR
STOP! DO NOT GO ON TO THE NEXT PAGE
UNTIL TOLD TO DO SO.

24.4.5 Set Five

The seamstress pulls one end through the cloth of the thread on each side of the garment.

13. The best placement for the portion of the sentence that is underlined would be:
    - A. where it is now.
    - B. after the word *seamstress.*
    - C. after the word *pulls.*
    - D. after the word *thread.*

A thousand of the bats gather under the bridge during the day for a rest and fly out over the lake at dusk.

14. The best placement for the portion that is underlined would be:
    - F. where it is now.
    - G. after the word *bridge.*
    - H. after the word *dusk* (with a period at the end of the sentence).
    - J. after the word *bats.*

The scene depicted in the painting told the story of a nobleman who, in medieval times, retreated to a house in the woods to craft a mythical dinner with his culinary books that still inspires chefs today.

15. The best placement for the underlined portion would be:
    - A. where it is now.
    - B. after the word *retreated.*
    - C. after the word *craft.*
    - D. after the word *still.*

END OF SET FIVE

STOP! DO NOT GO ON TO THE NEXT PAGE UNTIL TOLD TO DO SO.

Sum It Up

Misplaced Modifiers

Modifier

A word or phrase that adds detail or enhances another word in a sentence

Tips and Techniques

Decoding: If you see a subordinating conjunction or an introductory phrase at the start of the sentence, be on the lookout for the noun that follows. If the phrase cannot logically modify the noun, then find what it is modifying and move it closer.

Plug It In: When the ACT English test asks you where best to place a modifier, try to plug the modifier into each option. If a given placement in the answer does not fit logically or grammatically, eliminate it and move on to the next answer.

Lesson 25

Parallelism

Anna is busy answering phone calls, checking emails, and taking notes.

CAPTION:

25.1 Entrance Ticket

Select the best alternative to the underlined portion in each sentence below. If no change is necessary, select NO CHANGE.

Perhaps he is such an excellent artist because he paints—he studied classical painting techniques at Académie des Beaux-Arts—and sculpting in marble and bronze.

1. **A.** NO CHANGE
   B. but sculpts
   C. and sculpts
   D. and

The essence of joy is this: to greet each day as if it were your last, to love, and to be laughing.

2. **F.** NO CHANGE
   G. for laughing.
   H. to laugh.
   J. laughing.

I would like everyone to recognize that all people have the aptitude to take control of their own destinies and for the successes life will bring.

3. **A.** NO CHANGE
   B. the successes life will bring them can be enjoyed.
   C. for enjoying the successes life will bring them.
   D. to enjoy the successes life will bring them.

25.2 Learning Targets

1. Identify parallelism in sentences and passages

2. Use parallelism correctly by matching patterns to form correct sentences

Self-Assessment

Circle the number that corresponds to your confidence level in your knowledge of this subject before beginning the lesson. A score of 1 means you are completely lost, and a score of 4 means you have mastered the skills. After you finish the lesson, return to the bottom of this page and circle your new confidence level to show your improvement.

Before Lesson

1 2 3 4

After Lesson

1 2 3 4

25.3.1 Parallelism Errors

1. The prince loved attending balls, defeating dragons, and to ride his horse.

   Answer: ____________________

   Correct Version: ____________________

2. Hansel and Gretel gorged themselves on lollipops, chocolate, and ate gummy worms from the strange house.

   Answer: ____________________

   Correct Version: ____________________

3. Snow White had red lips, black hair, and white skin.

   Answer: ____________________

   Correct Version: ____________________

4. Cinderella's wicked stepmother enjoyed shopping, sleeping, and pedicures.

   Answer: ____________________

   Correct Version: ____________________

Parallelism: ____________________

____

25.3.1 Parallelism Errors

Jamaica's Résumé	Caroline's Résumé
Northville High School English Tutor, September-December • Helped freshmen and sophomores prepare for English tests • Volunteered at Northville High Tutoring Center • Provided feedback to parents on their children's progress • Wrote sample essay prompts for students to do as practice	*Northville High School Math Tutor, March-May* • Helped freshmen and sophomores prepare for math tests • Receptionist at Northville High Tutoring Center • Fall Award for Most Valuable Math Tutor in the center • Provided parents with progress reports based on student progress

____

____

____

____

Your Résumé

Location, Position, and Date Range: ______________________________

- ______________________________
- ______________________________
- ______________________________
- ______________________________

English Tip

Consistent, Clear, and Concise: Parallelism is about keeping the sentence consistent. If you are not sure which option is best, choose the one that best matches the part of the sentence that is not underlined.

25.3.2 Rules for Parallelism

His skill as a batter allowed the team to use him as an infielder and he was a pinch hitter when needed.

1. A. NO CHANGE
   B. as well
   C. being
   D. as

It was a varied and eclectic curriculum. In the same day, students might learn about traveling to Antarctica with the doomed Scott expedition and about programming for the latest supercomputers using specialized computer languages.

2. F. NO CHANGE
   G. how to program for
   H. of their programming for
   J. of their programming with

The car engines rev, and you can hear the crowd roaring in the stands. The visceral excitement of the race is why NASCAR is such a popular sport.

3. A. NO CHANGE
   B. also the roaring crowds
   C. and the crowds roar
   D. and the roaring crowd

Being able to walk out into the backyard and pick a fresh orange off a tree is like a person being given a precious gift from Mother Nature herself.

4. F. NO CHANGE
   G. someone
   H. a gardener
   J. DELETE the underlined portion.

The machines deafening us with their cacophony of noise and the PA system blaring out its incomprehensible racket made standing in the manufacturing area without ear protection impossible.

5. A. NO CHANGE
   B. were blaring
   C. blared
   D. blare

25.3.2 Rules for Parallelism

English Tip

What Sounds Right Is Right: A sentence usually sounds better if it uses parallel construction properly. Try sounding out the different options and then choose the one that sounds like the best fit.

1 ■ ■ ■ ■ ■ ■ ■ ■ ■ 1

25.4.1 Set One

The SUV turned out to be the better design, possibly because it built upon the success of two popular models—pickup trucks and station wagons—and combining the most popular features of the two vehicle types.

1. **A.** NO CHANGE
   B. but combining
   C. and combined
   D. and

As a mother, a wife, and besides being a brilliant engineer, she proved that a woman need not limit her horizons.

2. **F.** NO CHANGE
   G. a
   H. along with being a
   J. also being a

The kids playing in the street and the dogs wandered without collars in my aunt's neighborhood made me very uneasy.

3. **A.** NO CHANGE
   B. wandering
   C. were wandering
   D. DELETE the underlined portion.

END OF SET ONE

STOP! DO NOT GO ON TO THE NEXT PAGE UNTIL TOLD TO DO SO.

25.4.2 Set Two

For a person to try and to be failed is no shame, but to fear the endeavor is tragic.

4. **F.** NO CHANGE
   G. for failing
   H. to fail
   J. failing

Freshmen goggle at the magnificent buildings on the campus, sophomores rush to get their required classes, juniors reacquaint themselves with their classmates, and seniors view everyone with a smug attitude. Such is the first day of college after summer break.

5. **A.** NO CHANGE
   B. that goggle
   C. goggling
   D. DELETE the underlined portion

Heated oil crackles as it cooks the garlic, you can smell the aroma of sautéed onions wafting up from the pan. A kitchen is a wonderful place to be when someone is cooking.

6. **F.** NO CHANGE
   G. also the wafting aroma of sautéed onions
   H. and the aroma of sautéed onions wafts
   J. and some wafting aroma of sautéed onions

END OF SET TWO

STOP! DO NOT GO ON TO THE NEXT PAGE UNTIL TOLD TO DO SO.

25.4.3 Set Three

To build a successful corporate culture requires time, money, and to have an organization; without these, it is almost impossible to flourish in today's hypercompetitive market.

7. **A.** NO CHANGE
   B. organization;
   C. to be organized;
   D. to have organization;

She had many memories of her youth in pre-war Japan: of dressing in the finest silk kimonos and of wandering the paths among the trees at the Great Shrine of Ise.

8. **F.** NO CHANGE
   G. wandering with
   H. of her wandering to
   J. of her wandering at

Almost every orphaned child yearns to acquire the stability of a permanent family and brothers and sisters for enjoying companionship.

9. **A.** NO CHANGE
   B. the companionship of brothers and sisters can be enjoyed.
   C. for enjoying the companionship of brothers and sisters.
   D. to enjoy the companionship of brothers and sisters.

END OF SET THREE

STOP! DO NOT GO ON TO THE NEXT PAGE UNTIL TOLD TO DO SO.

25.4.4 Set Four

Her shrieks piercing his ears and her lips pecked his cheeks finally melted his resolve, and he agreed to buy her the pony.

10. **F.** NO CHANGE
    G. were pecking
    H. peck
    J. pecking

Depending on the setting of the MODE bit, the chip can function as a normal CPU or as a numeric processor.

11. **A.** NO CHANGE
    B. as well
    C. being
    D. it is

Chemical engineers refine petroleum to produce gasoline, to fabricate plastic materials engineers they alter petroleum, and organic chemists utilize petroleum reagents to synthesize pharmaceuticals.

12. **F.** NO CHANGE
    G. where petroleum is altered by materials engineers in fabrication of plastic,
    H. materials engineers alter petroleum to fabricate plastic,
    J. petroleum to fabricate plastic is altered by materials engineers,

---

END OF SET FOUR
STOP! DO NOT GO ON TO THE NEXT PAGE
UNTIL TOLD TO DO SO.

25.4.5 Set Five

Winning the lottery twice is as rare as a person getting hit by lightning three times in a row.

13. A. NO CHANGE
    B. someone
    C. a victim
    D. DELETE the underlined portion.

She cheerily explained the operation of the restaurant while correcting the uniform of a waiter, she tasted the soup of the day, and greeting longtime customers with a smile.

14. F. NO CHANGE
    G. tasting
    H. tasted
    J. tastes

In 1784, when most rooms were heated with a fireplace, Benjamin Franklin demonstrated his knowledge of physics by inventing the first iron stove and his interest in safety.

15. Which choice produces the most logical arrangement of the parts of this sentence?

    A. NO CHANGE
    B. demonstrated his interest in safety and his knowledge of physics when he invented the first iron stove.
    C. invented the first iron stove, demonstrated his knowledge of physics, and demonstrating his interest in safety.
    D. demonstrated his knowledge when he invented the first iron stove and demonstrated his interest in safety.

END OF SET FIVE

STOP! DO NOT GO ON TO THE NEXT PAGE UNTIL TOLD TO DO SO.

Sum It Up

Parallelism

Parallelism
Being consistent with the pattern of words you use

Subordinate Clause
A clause that is dependent on another clause to form a complete sentence

Tips and Techniques

Consistent, Clear, and Concise: Parallelism is all about keeping the sentence consistent. If you are not sure which option is best, choose the one that best matches the part of the sentence that is not underlined.

Sounds Right Is Right: Sentences usually sound better if they use parallel construction properly. Try sounding out the different options and choose the one that sounds best.

Style and Tone

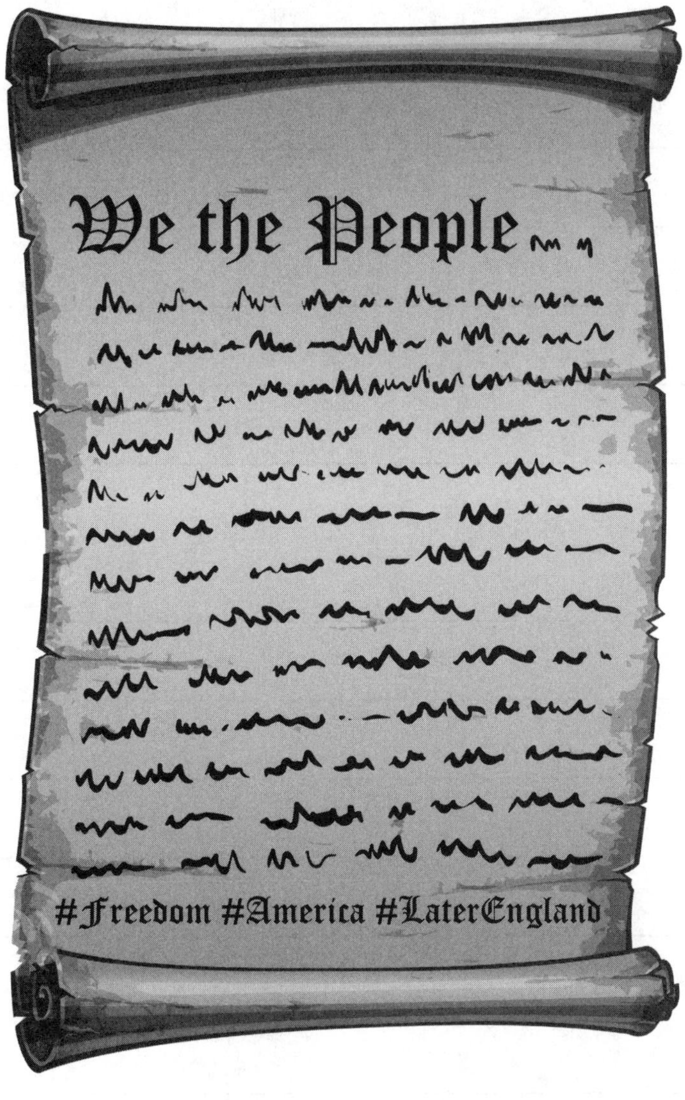

CAPTION:

26.1 Entrance Ticket

How would you define your style? How would you define the way you express yourself? Write two or three sentences in a formal tone. Then rewrite the sentences in an informal tone.

26.2 Learning Targets

1. Identify style and tone in sentences quickly and efficiently

2. Understand and analyze conciseness and repeated information as it relates to tone

Self-Assessment

Circle the number that corresponds to your confidence level in your knowledge of this subject before beginning the lesson. A score of 1 means you are completely lost, and a score of 4 means you have mastered the skills. After you finish the lesson, return to the bottom of this page and circle your new confidence level to show your improvement.

Before Lesson

1 2 3 4

After Lesson

1 2 3 4

26.3.1 Matching Tone and Style

Love battles hate, kindness overcomes fear, gentleness softens hurt, and friendly people enjoy meeting new people.

1. Which of the following options best matches the tone and style of the preceding statements in this sentence?
   - **A.** NO CHANGE
   - **B.** those who are lonely need companionship.
   - **C.** friendship lets people show affection.
   - **D.** friendship cures loneliness.

As planned, the issue really flashed its lights on unknown artists, many of whom, including Barbara Jones, became leading members of the Women's Rights Movement.

2.
   - **F.** NO CHANGE
   - **G.** issue's illustrations were first off
   - **H.** issue focused on
   - **J.** issue paid attention with

Tanya's grandmother was hired by *The Gazette* the day after she graduated college. Tirelessly, she continued working for the newspaper for over thirty years. Incredible!

3.
   - **A.** NO CHANGE
   - **B.** for over thirty fantastic years!
   - **C.** for over thirty years.
   - **D.** for—wow!—more than thirty years.

They can experience the magic of enchantment through wandering from theme park to theme park within the bounds of the resort's property.

4.
   - **F.** NO CHANGE
   - **G.** reap the benefits of magic from
   - **H.** be kept wide-eyed and maintain awe by
   - **J.** be thoroughly amazed by

English Tip

Consistent, Clear, and Concise: Each ACT English passage will maintain a consistent tone throughout. If you need to determine the best option, look at the rest of the passage. If you still are not sure, try something that fits in the middle between casual and very formal. Avoid slang.

26.3.2 Redundancy, Conciseness, and Tone

The doughnuts topped with peanut butter and honey flew off the shelf and were an instant success.

1. A. NO CHANGE
   B. were successful overnight
   C. sold like hotcakes
   D. DELETE the underlined portion

The coach thought that wearing old, faded uniforms made the athletes super bored about their performance, so he asked the school board to fund new uniforms to boost morale.

2. F. NO CHANGE
   G. really bad and boring in
   H. indifferent toward
   J. slack off

<u>26.3.2 Redundancy, Conciseness, and Tone</u>

Gran's chocolate-stuffed cupcakes <u>were yummy and</u> were the talk of the party.

3. **A.** NO CHANGE
   B. were the number-one tasting
   C. tasted wonderful and
   D. DELETE the underlined portion

The dance instructor believed that wearing "street clothes" to dance class made the dancers <u>forgetful toward</u> their routines and mandated that all dancers, even those taking hip hop classes, wear leotards and dance shorts.

4. **F.** NO CHANGE
   G. unconcerned and sloppy with
   H. totally not cool to watch during
   J. careless with

<u>English Tip</u>

Consistent, Clear, and Concise: The tone and style of the answer you choose must be consistent with the passage, but your answer choice also must be concise. Redundancy is always wrong, even if the style is perfect.

26.4.1 Set One

The girl <u>was sharp as a tack and</u> was very intelligent.

1. **A.** NO CHANGE
   B. was smart and
   C. was bright as a light
   D. DELETE the underlined portion

Sophia had been running about six miles each day to prepare for her marathon. By the end of the week, she had <u>run for—can you imagine?—forty miles!</u>

2. **F.** NO CHANGE
   G. run for forty miles. Wow!
   H. run for countless incredible miles.
   J. run a total of forty miles.

The convention will have lectures on how technology influences academia, entertainment, and <u>more!</u>

3. **A.** NO CHANGE
   B. society in general.
   C. other things too.
   D. all that stuff.

END OF SET ONE
STOP! DO NOT GO ON TO THE NEXT PAGE
UNTIL TOLD TO DO SO.

1 1

26.4.2 Set Two

It's really cool that in some places, cars are driven on the opposite side of the road than they are in the United States.

4. F. NO CHANGE
   G. You'll be shocked to find out that in
   H. In
   J. Consider, if you will, the concept that in

Sue was concerned about Davey being snowed in, but she comforted herself by remembering that he could easily experience the feeling of warmth through a combination of heating pads, blankets, and space heaters.

5. A. NO CHANGE
   B. keep warm
   C. be kept warm as bug in a rug
   D. be heated to a healthy temperature

Many species of bacteria, called extremophiles, have adapted to thrive in the most severe conditions—some can sustain the intense salinity of the deepest seas, some the high altitude and low temperatures of the Himalayas. Boiling geysers full of steam are home to still others; even the extreme heat cannot kill them.

6. F. NO CHANGE
   G. are pretty safe for others to live in;
   H. suit some all right;
   J. are okay habitats for some;

END OF SET TWO
STOP! DO NOT GO ON TO THE NEXT PAGE
UNTIL TOLD TO DO SO.

26.4.3 Set Three

Where once there had been a momentous battle scene, we now find vividly painted buildings, stately fountains, and car trails.

7. Which of the following choices best maintains the tone and style of the sentence?
   - **A.** NO CHANGE
   - **B.** jam-packed streets.
   - **C.** automobile paths.
   - **D.** bustling thoroughfares.

When I was younger, I found social situations difficult to read. Graciously, I learned to pick up on subtle cues.

8. **F.** NO CHANGE
   - **G.** Slowly, however,
   - **H.** Unfortunately,
   - **J.** In fact,

When the subject finally comes into focus, the flash often ends up ruining the photo by overexposing the picture.

9. **A.** NO CHANGE
   - **B.** magnifies the result of
   - **C.** attains the consequence of
   - **D.** results in

END OF SET THREE

STOP! DO NOT GO ON TO THE NEXT PAGE UNTIL TOLD TO DO SO.

1 ■ ■ ■ ■ ■ ■ ■ ■ ■ 1

26.4.4 Set Four

Others have followed in Dwight Yoakam's footsteps and migrated to Bakersfield, California. The traditional sound of Bakersfield-style country music has a captivating, delightful, and unique sound that means it'll be around for a long time.

10. **F.** NO CHANGE
G. allows for it to be one of those timeless things that endures for a while.
H. ensures its continued popularity.
J. makes a lot of fans really excited.

Basically, I try to go hiking every free day I can find during the summer months.

11. Which of the following alternatives to the portion that is underlined would be LEAST acceptable?
A. every weekend I can
B. prudent leisure time intervals
C. whenever I can find the time
D. anytime I can spare a day

The teacher believed that writing in pencil made the students unfulfilled with their schoolwork and required that everyone do their assignments in pen.

12. **F.** NO CHANGE
G. blow off
H. bored to tears with
J. careless toward

END OF SET FOUR
STOP! DO NOT GO ON TO THE NEXT PAGE
UNTIL TOLD TO DO SO.

26.4.5 Set Five

The performance of the new play brought to light the issues of inequality and poverty on a larger scale than ever before.

13. A. NO CHANGE
    B. shined a flashlight to illuminate
    C. put a focus toward
    D. paid attention with

Hearts break, wounds heal, friendships end, and children are becoming mature.

14. Which choice best expresses this idea in a style that is consistent with the preceding statements in this sentence?
    F. NO CHANGE
    G. kids turn into adults.
    H. people grow.
    J. the young take steps to become older.

At last, when the bus begins to slow down a lot, she knows that it is nearly time to stand up and step out onto the lively Belmont Street.

15. Given that all of the choices are true, which one provides the most detail while maintaining the style and tone of the sentence?
    A. NO CHANGE
    B. slow with a low whine,
    C. creeps to a speed of under five miles per hour,
    D. decelerate in increments to a speed at which it will be easy to exit,

END OF SET FIVE

STOP! DO NOT GO ON TO THE NEXT PAGE UNTIL TOLD TO DO SO.

Sum It Up

Style and Tone

Style

The way authors use words to establish mood, images, and meaning

---

Tone

The way authors express their attitudes through their writing

Tips and Techniques

Consistent, Clear, and Concise: Choose the answer that is concise and consistent with the passage in both style and tone.

Lesson 27

Relevance

CAPTION:

27.1 Entrance Ticket

Read the following script from a trial. In each box, write whether or not the defense had a good reason to object to the prosecution. Explain your answer.

Prosecution: Casey Lee is charged with stealing video games from Game Central. Mr. Lee, do you understand what you are being accused of?
Mr. Lee: Yes.
Prosecution: Do you understand why it is important to tell the truth?
Mr. Lee: Yes.

Prosecution: Do you enjoy playing video games? **Defense:** I object! How is this relevant to the trial?	

Prosecution: Is it true that Mrs. Lee, your mother, refused to buy you video games? **Defense:** This is absurd. This question has nothing to do with the trial, Your Honor.	

Prosecution: Is it true that you were seen near Game Central moments before there was a theft at the store? **Defense:** I object! How is this relevant?	

Prosecution: Your Honor, I want to bring in the manager of Game Central to discuss the statistics of theft in his store. **Defense:** How does this relate to the case?	

27.2 Learning Targets

1. Identify relevant and irrelevant material in terms of the focus and topic of the essay or paragraph

2. Determine the plausibility of relevant material at any point in the essay

Self-Assessment

Circle the number that corresponds to your confidence level in your knowledge of this subject before beginning the lesson. A score of 1 means you are completely lost, and a score of 4 means you have mastered the skills. After you finish the lesson, return to the bottom of this page and circle your new confidence level to show your improvement.

Before Lesson

1 2 3 4

After Lesson

1 2 3 4

27.3.1 Conciseness and Relevance

Although Wordsworth and Coleridge produced *Lyrical Ballads* as a joint effort, the first edition did not contain either of their names. The second edition listed only Wordsworth's name and also included his preface to the poems. The fourth and final edition, published in 1805, still did not credit <u>Coleridge, who endured rheumatic fever as a child.</u>

1. **A.** NO CHANGE.
   B. Coleridge.
   C. Coleridge, who coined the phrase "suspension of disbelief."
   D. Coleridge, a native of Devonshire.

The Metropolitan Museum of Art boasts permanent collections spanning more than 5,000 years of culture. Wandering through its galleries, visitors can explore some of the world's greatest art, from prehistory to the present. <u>Across the street is a diner.</u>

2. **F.** NO CHANGE
   G. (You can get a plate of lasagna at the diner across the street.)
   H. A diner serving hot meals is always open across the street.
   J. DELETE the underlined portion.

Achatz's early culinary career included time spent working in his parents' Michigan restaurants. He enrolled at The Culinary Institute of America in <u>Hyde Park, New York, the hometown of Franklin Roosevelt,</u> after graduating high school. Later, Achatz landed a position at Thomas Keller's highly acclaimed restaurant, The French Laundry, in Yountville, California.

3. **A.** NO CHANGE
   B. Hyde Park, New York,
   C. the town of Hyde Park, New York (site of the FDR presidential library),
   D. Hyde Park, New York, settled in 1742,

English Tip

Consistent, Clear, and Concise: Not enough time to figure out the best answer? If the sentence can stand alone with the shortest answer, then mark it and move on.

27.3.1 Conciseness and Relevance

The great white shark has no natural predators other than the orca. It is arguably the world's largest known predatory fish and is one of the primary hunters of marine mammals. The humpback whale, on the other hand, is a species of baleen whale. The great white is also known to prey upon a variety of other marine animals, including fish and seabirds.

4. **F.** NO CHANGE
   G. Male elephant seals reach maturity at five to six years.
   H. The New York Yacht Club is the winner of 25 America's Cup titles.
   J. DELETE the underlined portion.

27.3.2 Determining Relevance

We were halfway home when Alex cried out for his stuffed duck. We pulled over and searched the entire car, but the duck was nowhere to be found. So we drove back to the bookstore, where I volunteered to go inside and look.

1. **A.** Sure enough, the duck was wedged between two pillows in the back of the store, where Alex had been reading.
   B. Sure enough, the duck was wedged between two pillows in the back, whose tags said they'd been handmade in Germany.

Bar mitzvah (for boys) and bat mitzvah (for girls) are Jewish coming-of-age rituals. While they are joyous celebrations, they also carry a weighty significance. Under Jewish law, parents hold responsibility for their child's actions prior to the ceremony. But afterward, the child is considered accountable.

2. **F.** Pop stars are sometimes hired to perform at bar mitzvahs.
   G. The ceremony, therefore, is an important rite of passage for Jewish children.

<u>The Cherokee were already adopting modern farming techniques when Congress passed the Indian Removal Act in 1830</u>. This legislation authorized the forcible relocation of American Indians east of the Mississippi to a new Indian territory, leading to the infamous "Trail of Tears."

3. **A.** NO CHANGE
   B. The Cherokee, some of whom had excellent eyesight, were already adopting modern farming techniques when Congress passed the Indian Removal Act in 1830.

27.3.2 Determining Relevance

27.3.2 Determining Relevance

Alligators have a reputation as scary monsters, but they make vital contributions to the health of the wetlands. Alligator attacks on humans are few but not unknown. They also use their feet and snouts to clear muck from holes in the limestone bedrock, allowing them to fill with water and become oases for plants and animals during droughts.

1. Given that all the following statements are true, which one provides the most relevant information at this point in the essay?
   - **A.** NO CHANGE
   - **B.** Alligators control populations of nutria, or river rats, whose heavy grazing has caused severe marsh damage.
   - **C.** Alligators have heavy bodies and slow metabolisms, yet they are capable of short bursts of speed.
   - **D.** The baby alligator's egg tooth helps it get out of its egg during hatching time.

As a child, I used to bake cookies with my mom. She would let me crack the eggs into the mixture of butter and sugar and mix the batter until it was ready to drop by spoonfuls onto the pan. From this early experience, I developed an interest in cooking. As a teenager, I continued to learn by reading recipes in my grandmother's old French cookbooks.

2. Given that all the choices are true, which one provides the most relevant and specific information at this point in the essay?
   - **F.** NO CHANGE
   - **G.** after school, before track practice.
   - **H.** to build up the knowledge I needed for my career.
   - **J.** closely about the topics in which I was interested.

Hollywood has also contributed greatly to the general public's fear of sharks—great whites in particular. From 1975's *Jaws*, a film about a gigantic great white with a taste for human blood, to 2013's *Ghost Shark*, a film about a spectral great white that terrorizes residents of a beach town, sharks have been consistently portrayed as man-eaters in the movies.

3. Given that all the choices are true, which one is most relevant to the statement that follows in this sentence?
   - **A.** NO CHANGE
   - **B.** that was originally killed by fishermen,
   - **C.** that can materialize in the presence of water,
   - **D.** being pursued by a drunken sea captain,

27.3.2 Determining Relevance

Every June, the camp held a dance with a nearby girls' camp that all the boys were required to attend. It invariably brought about a wide range of reactions from the boys. Some of them were eager to talk to the girls, while others were intensely bashful. The smallest ones either barely registered the difference in gender or thought that the girls were dangerous and must be avoided at all costs.

4. Given that all of the choices are true, which one provides information most relevant to the main focus of this paragraph?

F. NO CHANGE
G. on a neighboring farm.
H. that generally lasted four hours.
J. called Mont Shenandoah.

27.4.1 Set One

The Major League Baseball trade deadline is July 31. It comes at a moment in the season when many teams are conceivably still in the playoff hunt, so it is always a source of intrigue. Teams who have performed unexpectedly well in April, May, and June must decide whether to upgrade their rosters for the stretch run or stand pat with the players they have. It may be a hot July 4th weekend; the trade market develops quite quickly.

1. A. NO CHANGE
   B. After what may be a hot July 4th weekend but not by much
   C. Shortly thereafter July 4th weekend,
   D. Just after the July 4th weekend,

Tim Duncan and David Robinson were known as the "Twin Towers" when they played together on the San Antonio Spurs. The nickname came not only from their height, but also from their exceptional defense close to the basket. It takes roughly five hours to drive from Dallas to San Antonio.

2. F. NO CHANGE
   G. San Antonio is about five hours from Dallas by car.
   H. (The drive time between San Antonio and Dallas is about five hours.)
   J. DELETE the underlined portion.

GO ON TO THE NEXT PAGE.

It's especially fun when kids choose to role-play as their parents. It's in those moments that you realize just how many of your unique habits they've picked up over the years. Whether it's the way you drink your coffee or how you select an avocado at the grocery store, it's always amazing to witness these imaginative little mimics you've created. <u>Most children enjoy celebrating a birthday.</u>

3. **A.** NO CHANGE
   B. Birthdays, of course, only come once a year.
   C. Different cultures celebrate birthdays differently.
   D. DELETE the underlined portion.

END OF SET ONE

STOP! DO NOT GO ON TO THE NEXT PAGE UNTIL TOLD TO DO SO.

27.4.2 Set Two

Larger fish are usually filleted. Be sure to keep your fish fresh after you catch them; this is done by storing them in a cooler or live well. Always fill your cooler with the same water from which you're fishing.

When cleaning your fish, filleting means cutting out the meat of the fish without the bones. A filleted fish has its skin and all of its bones removed before cooking. Scaling isn't necessary.

4. **F.** NO CHANGE
   G. The larger the fish, the likelier it should be filleted.
   H. The larger fish will be filleted.
   J. DELETE the underlined portion.

Scuba divers must be careful not to rise too quickly from great depths, lest they suffer decompression sickness, also known as "the bends." This painful and potentially life-threatening phenomenon is the result of nitrogen forming bubbles in the blood as it depressurizes. The bubbles can lead to heart attacks, strokes, ruptured blood vessels in the lungs, and joint pain, which is a symptom of arthritis.

5. **A.** NO CHANGE
   B. joint pain.
   C. joint pain, which can make it difficult to walk.
   D. joint pain, which has become much better understood since the 1970s.

GO ON TO THE NEXT PAGE.

Both parties are planning an aggressive courtship of Latino voters, with Democrats seeking to cement their hold on this critical bloc. <u>Organized in the 1850s, the Republican Party</u> is trying to chip away at that advantage, perhaps by nominating a candidate like Senator Marco Rubio, the son of Cuban immigrants, or Jeb Bush, the Spanish-speaking former governor of Florida.

6. **F.** NO CHANGE
   G. The Republican Party was organized in the 1850s. It
   H. The Republican Party
   J. The Republican Party, as we know it, was born in the 1850s. It

END OF SET TWO

STOP! DO NOT GO ON TO THE NEXT PAGE UNTIL TOLD TO DO SO.

1 ■ ■ ■ ■ ■ ■ ■ ■ ■ 1

27.4.3 Set Three

I used to love going to visit my grandmother at her house in Staunton, Virginia. She had a huge backyard where my brother, my cousin, and I would play for hours, losing ourselves in imagined worlds. We climbed trees, built forts, and staged attacks on each other's "kingdoms," sometimes pretending to be goblins or trolls. When my grandmother rang the bell for dinner, our invented landscapes would evaporate into the evening air as we went running to wash our hands.

7. Given that all the choices are true, which one provides material most relevant to what follows in this paragraph?
   A. NO CHANGE
   B. She lived next door to a family with a big, shaggy golden retriever named Montgomery.
   C. It took about five hours for us to drive there from Charlotte, North Carolina.
   D. Memorial Day weekend was usually reserved for exactly this occasion.

Uncle Joe loved to reminisce about his years as an ice road trucker. It was clear that he derived a great deal of pride from having been one of the few to stick with the job, which was incredibly dangerous and physically taxing. He told me that he had driven through more blizzards than he could remember. He had changed tires. He had navigated slippery, narrow roads above deep chasms, where one false move could send the rig tumbling down a mountainside.

8. Given that all are true, which of the following additions to the preceding sentence (replacing "tires.") would be most relevant?
   F. tires which had run over rocks.
   G. tires in subzero weather.
   H. tires in Alaska.
   J. tires made of rubber.

GO ON TO THE NEXT PAGE.

When you consider the twenty million people wounded during the course of the fighting, <u>much having been written about the horrors of trench warfare</u>, World War I ranks among the deadliest conflicts in human history.

9. Given that all the choices are true, which one is most relevant to the statement that follows in this sentence?
   A. NO CHANGE
   B. along with the more than seventeen million military and civilian deaths,
   C. and Henry Gunther who was killed one minute before the armistice took effect,
   D. in which France was badly damaged,

END OF SET THREE

STOP! DO NOT GO ON TO THE NEXT PAGE UNTIL TOLD TO DO SO.

27.4.4 Set Four

Octopuses, squid, and cuttlefish—all of which are characterized by bilateral body symmetry—are the ocean's champions of camouflage. They can mimic the color and texture of a rock or a piece of coral or give their skin a glittering sheen to match the water around them. Cephalopods can perform these spectacles thanks to a dense fabric of specialized cells in their skin. But before a cephalopod can take on a new disguise, it needs to perceive the background that it is going to blend into.

10. Given that all of the choices are true, which one would provide information that is most relevant and meaningful to the essay as a whole?

F. NO CHANGE
G. often portrayed as monsters in the movies—
H. a group of mollusks known as cephalopods—
J. thousands of which are sold daily in Tokyo fish markets—

The piston first travels down the cylinder, drawing in a mixture of fuel and air. The piston then goes back up toward the spark plug, compressing the mixture. At the very last second, when the piston is at its fullest reach, the spark plug sparks and ignites the fuel and air. The piston is forced back down to create power for the vehicle, and then it is pushed back up again to clear out the exhaust.

11. A. NO CHANGE
B. exhaust, which is tinted red.
C. red-tinted exhaust.
D. exhaust, which is red in color.

Tony Randazzo moved to Edgewood with his family from Italy in 2006. We started middle school together the following fall. I didn't have any classes with Tony, and he lived far away, but I saw him at soccer practice, and we would often wait together at the bus stop.

12. Given that all of the choices are true, which one provides the most relevant information with regard to the narrator's familiarity with Tony?

F. NO CHANGE
G. saw him at soccer practice, which was always a punishing workout.
H. waited with him for the bus, which was driven recklessly by Mr. Hill.
J. waited with him for the bus when my dad's car was in the shop.

END OF SET FOUR
STOP! DO NOT GO ON TO THE NEXT PAGE UNTIL TOLD TO DO SO.

27.4.5 Set Five

At first, you need to learn how to use the equipment. A good rule of thumb is to position your mouth six to eight inches away from the <u>microphone that's built to last.</u> You also need to adjust the gain on your mic to suit the volume of your voice so that the levels don't spike. And although some actors work without them, it's a good idea to wear headphones when you're starting out.

13. **A.** NO CHANGE
    B. microphone.
    C. microphone, which is constructed durably.
    D. microphone, which is built to last.

Next, the coffee beans pass through a battery of machines that sort them by size and density while also removing miscellaneous debris. A giant fan blows the beans into the air. Those that fall into bins closest to the air source are heaviest and biggest; these will end up on <u>supermarket shelves, which are frequently made of steel.</u>

14. **F.** NO CHANGE
    G. supermarket shelves. Most retail shelves nowadays are made of steel.
    H. supermarket shelves, which can be made of steel, or in some cases, wood.
    J. supermarket shelves.

Most varieties of strawberries readily produce offspring, so many farmers simply allow them to grow into a vibrant green ground cover that requires little maintenance. The plants won't bear as heavily as more intensively managed plants, but they will still produce delicious berries year after year.

In Japan, farmers now use robots to pick strawberries. These versatile machines pick one strawberry every few seconds, using imaging software to gauge which berries are ripe. When they locate a ripe one, a robotic arm reaches out and snips its stem. <u>Strawberries should be kept as cool as possible after picking.</u>

15. **A.** NO CHANGE
    B. Picked berries should be kept out of the sunshine for as long as possible.
    C. Heat and light can cause strawberries to become soft and bruise easily.
    D. DELETE the underlined portion.

END OF SET FIVE
STOP! DO NOT GO ON TO THE NEXT PAGE
UNTIL TOLD TO DO SO.

Sum It Up

Relevance

Concise
Conveying information clearly in few words; brief but comprehensive

---

Relevant
Closely connected or appropriate to the subject at hand

Tips and Techniques

Consistent, Clear, and Concise: Not enough time to figure it out? If the sentence can stand alone with the shortest answer, mark it and move on.

Lesson 28

Writer's Goal

28.1 Entrance Ticket

Read the passage below and answer the following questions.

In 1881, Ferdinand de Lesseps's laborers found themselves completely unprepared for the work ahead of them. Circumstances both foreseeable and otherwise threatened France's vision for a forty-eight-mile canal across the Isthmus of Panama to connect the Atlantic to the Pacific. De Lesseps had tremendous success in his creation of the Suez Canal through Egypt, as it had been a crowning jewel of French imperialism. Many government officials felt they could entrust him with another massive undertaking like the Suez Canal. Perhaps the greatest issue that hindered the project from the onset was that de Lesseps had begun to believe the sensationalized reputation that surrounded him after his success in Egypt. He went ahead with very little knowledge of what planning and preparation this new task would require of him.

For eight years, de Lesseps had successfully raised a great deal of capital to fund the project, but he failed to keep his promises to complete the canal in that timeframe. The project encountered many unexpected problems. From the beginning of the project, heavy rains hindered any real progress in the region. Since de Lesseps was more or less a stranger to the weather of the region, he and his men were blindsided by the intensity of the rainy season. The project was affected by the heavy rainfall, as well as by venomous snakes, spiders, and mosquitoes. Many men contracted malaria or yellow fever, and recurrent landslides from the bordering water-saturated hills also plagued the excavation of the canal. By 1884, the death toll had risen to nearly 200 casualties each month from accident and disease.

Ultimately, de Lesseps simply could not meet his deadlines, and he could not justify remaining in a part of the world that was so unknown to him. The project had proven a huge financial strain, and his men were either overworked or overwhelmed by the elements of that region. De Lesseps and his laborers abandoned the project in 1894, when de Lesseps was arrested for misappropriation of project funds. The canal would not be touched again until 1904, when the United States took up the torch and built the Panama Canal we know today.

28.1 Entrance Ticket

1. Which of the following represents the main topic of the essay?
  A. The bureaucracy involved in raising funds for such a massive project
  B. The imperialistic motivations behind a country's expanding influence
  C. The unsuccessful first attempt at building the Panama Canal
  D. Ferdinand de Lesseps's blemish on an otherwise perfect career

---

2. Suppose the writer had intended to write a brief essay that describes the process of planning and constructing the Panama Canal. Would this essay successfully fulfill the writer's goal?
  F. Yes, because it offers details about the French blueprints used for both the Suez and Panama Canals.
  G. Yes, because it explains in detail each step in the design and excavation of the Panama Canal.
  H. No, because it focuses primarily on the problems faced during the first attempt to construct the Panama Canal.
  J. No, because it is primarily a historical essay about the completion of the Panama Canal after de Lesseps's project failed.

---

3. Which of the following sentences is the least essential to the essay?
  A. The project had proven a huge financial strain, and his men were either overworked or overwhelmed by the elements of that region.
  B. Many men contracted malaria or yellow fever, and recurrent landslides from the bordering water-saturated hills also plagued the excavation of the canal.
  C. Circumstances both foreseeable and otherwise threatened France's vision for a forty-eight-mile canal across the Isthmus of Panama to connect the Atlantic to the Pacific.
  D. De Lesseps had tremendous success in his creation of the Suez Canal through Egypt, as it had been a crowning jewel of French imperialism.

28.2 Learning Targets

1. Identify critical words in both questions and answer choices

2. Process answer choices based on quality of importance and relevance

3. Quickly understand the important information and the topic in an essay

Self-Assessment

Circle the number that corresponds to your confidence level in your knowledge of this subject before beginning the lesson. A score of 1 means you are completely lost, and a score of 4 means you have mastered the skills. After you finish the lesson, return to the bottom of this page and circle your new confidence level to show your improvement.

Before Lesson

1 2 3 4

After Lesson

1 2 3 4

28.3.1 Most Valuable Phrases

1. Suppose the writer's goal had been to write a brief essay specifying the ways in which a television network is attempting to offer more programs targeted at a teenage audience. Would this essay successfully fulfill that goal?

____

2. Suppose the writer's goal had been to write a brief, persuasive essay detailing the catastrophic effects that urban sprawl has had on an endangered animal population. Would this essay achieve that goal?

____

3. Suppose the writer had been assigned to write a short essay demonstrating how a well-known athlete in a certain sport did not receive the recognition he deserved. Would this essay successfully fulfill this task?

____

---

1. Suppose the writer's goal had been to write a brief essay recognizing the advancements a certain scientist can make to a particular field of study. Would this essay fulfill that goal?
   - **A.** Yes, because the essay claims that Sir Isaac Newton's work as a scientist never would have developed without the influence of other scientists working in mathematics.
   - **B.** Yes, because the essay presents Newton as a physicist and mathematician who used his talents to become a key figure in the scientific revolution.
   - **C.** No, because the essay focuses on the process of developing the study of optics, not on a single scientist's work.
   - **D.** No, because the essay suggests that it took many scientists from different fields to contribute to the success that Newton achieved.

28.3.1 Most Valuable Phrases

2. Suppose the writer had decided to write an essay describing the moral and ethical consequences of sending a primate into space to perform a simple maintenance procedure in a dangerous area of a space station. Would this essay successfully fulfill that writer's goal?

F. Yes, because the essay explains the moral and ethical consequences of sending an animal into space in place of a human.

G. Yes, because the essay details the dangers that may arise in certain areas of the space station, which helps the reader understand the consequences of sending a primate to perform the maintenance.

H. No, because the essay does not accurately detail the dangers of space travel, so the reader has no basis for accurately judging the situation.

J. No, because the essay limits itself to technical explanations of the malfunction in the space station and the basic precautions to be taken in the future.

English Tip

MVP: Writer's Goal questions almost always appear as the last question in a passage, so watch for them at the end. If you see one, remember to focus on the MVPs in the question and answers and match them to the passage. Do not be afraid to say no if the MVPs in the question do not match the passage.

28.3.2 Summarizing an English Passage

English Tip

Take the Easy Way: Check the title of the English passage. Sometimes that makes the answer more obvious. If you are pressed for time, it is not worth reviewing the whole passage.

28.3.2 Summarizing an English Passage

The Remarkable Characteristics of a Falcon

Picture the fastest track star on the planet combined with a highly disciplined soldier, and you'll get an idea of the remarkable features of this large and agile predator of the sky—the peregrine falcon. This large animal regularly hunts in the mountains or valleys with the innate ability to make long, sharp dives to catch its prey. Unlike other birds of prey, peregrine falcons move at such high speeds that they quite literally knock the life out of their prey. The peregrine falcon's sharp talons allow it to effortlessly seize its prey with a grip that would make it almost impossible for anything to escape.

The upper beak of the peregrine falcon has a distinct notch near its tip that enables it to break or sever its prey's spinal column with more efficiency. Most animals traveling at such high speeds risk traumatic injury to their lungs, but falcons are equipped with small, bony tubercles on their nostrils that stop any sort of damage from occurring. Likewise, their third eyelid allows them to keep their eyes clear of debris and keep their senses sharp while searching for prey. These factors help the peregrine falcon survey large open spaces—largely at dawn or dusk—using a mid-air attack that stuns its prey with a clenched foot and a quick turn to catch it before it falls.

Alejandro Jodorowsky's Midnight Movie Run

Alejandro Jodorowsky could never have predicted the amount of praise he would receive from his favorite Beatle—John Lennon—when *El Topo* had a successful run as a "midnight movie" at the Elgin Theatre. This admiration convinced The Beatles' manager, Allen Klein, to dish out a million dollars to Jodorowsky, as well as provide access to larger distribution for his next film released in the United States. Acclaim from musicians and the avant-garde scene would see his work proclaimed as a significant piece of the counterculture movement.

Growing up in Tocopilla, Chile, in the 1930s and '40s, Jodorowsky recognized and cultivated his affinity for the arts from a young age. Although his disparaging father offered no affirmation for his talents, Jodorowsky drew from the characters and situations in Tocopilla to lend authenticity to his semi-autobiographical film, *The Dance of Reality.* He was constantly inspired by comics and novels that appealed to his deep love of Chilean culture—particularly Tocopilla—but his influence and worldwide acclaim would have its roots in a number of inspirations he acquired while living abroad. In his twenties, he spent time in France and Mexico City, gaining knowledge of every subject he could encounter—from acting as a mime to creating his own spiritual system he called "psychomagic." His unique vision, above anything else, would make Jodorowsky a household name among enthusiasts of cult film for generations.

28.3.2 Summarizing an English Passage

Up in the Air

Many people I know dislike airports and everything about traveling by plane, but I enjoy flying because it gives me time to daydream. A few musicians from the Midwest, newlyweds on their way to a tropical resort, and a priest wearing his crisp white collar board my departure flight. A young girl's headphones blast the latest pop hits while she stares distractedly out the oval window. I can't help but reflect that my job has made such an avid flyer of me that my network of friends reaches to nearly every corner of the world.

Sometimes, the best people you'll ever meet are the ones working to make your flight as pleasant as possible. On several occasions, I've experienced flight attendants who initiated a song or game to calm a nervous child or to ease a lull in the flight—or even just to keep people's spirits high on a transatlantic journey. I find it hilariously difficult to figure out who will be the most engaged in these uproarious social activities. Once, to my surprise, it was the suit-and-tie-clad businessman in his forties who had seemed so uptight when he boarded! You really never can tell how people will interact with strangers in unexpected social situations.

28.4.1 Set One

PASSAGE I
Golden Gloves

These days, the media covers sensational stories of boxing champions, offering them endorsements and commercial spotlights. People are not always aware of the personalities behind the scenes who set these amazing chains of events into motion. One such inspiration is W. Harry Davis, an African American amateur boxing coach who devoted his life so fully to his passions that he made national and global history.

Born in 1923 in Minneapolis, Davis was diagnosed with polio as a toddler. His mother used warm cloth wraps and massage techniques—polio treatments she had learned from a doctor relative—to breathe life back into her young son's paralyzed legs. Miraculously, Davis was free of the disease by five years old, and he went on to achieve more than any doctors thought possible.

Davis's passion for boxing began when he was enrolled at the Phyllis Wheatley Settlement House in an after-school program for continuing education. At this center, he learned etiquette and ethics, and he and his friends were exposed to jazz musicians who performed at the Orpheum Theatre. He excelled in all areas of study at Phyllis Wheatley, but it was boxing that took the strongest hold of him. He worked as hard as possible in his leisure boxing classes, and by the time he graduated high school in 1941, he held the city boxing championship title.

The Phyllis Wheatley Settlement House had been a profound influence in Davis's life, and to show his gratitude, he initiated a competitive boxing program there that would prove to be a powerhouse in the Midwest. He used what he had learned in the Phyllis Wheatley amateur boxing classes to coach and strengthen his students in both mind and body. Determined, Davis rose to fame as the vice president of Golden Gloves and cemented his legacy as the region's most successful boxing coach, espousing his iconic phrase, "don't misuse it or abuse it."

Throughout his peripheral careers as a businessman, a mayoral candidate, the creator of the *Star Tribune*, and a social justice activist through the NAACP, it remained evident that Davis maintained his passion for the sport of boxing. During the 1970s, he became involved with the United States Olympic boxing committee, which was responsible for choosing Golden Glove fighters who showed the potential to compete at the Olympic level. He took on managerial duties for the team at the 1976 Olympics in Montreal and provided for the team's wellbeing, medical care, and lodging. In 1984, the United States Olympic boxing team walked away with nine gold medals and one silver, the best record in Olympic boxing history since 1904.

GO ON TO THE NEXT PAGE.

1. Suppose the writer's goal had been to write an essay focusing on the Phyllis Wheatley Settlement House as an influence on Davis's career. Would this essay accomplish that goal?

   A. Yes, because it describes how Davis drove the American boxing team into Olympic history.
   B. Yes, because it describes how Phyllis Wheatley's boxing program taught Davis how to win boxing matches.
   C. No, because it focuses on the highlights of Davis's entire career.
   D. No, because it mentions that Davis's primary influences were the jazz musicians at the Orpheum Theatre.

2. Suppose the writer had intended to write a brief essay about W. Harry Davis's contribution to the sport of boxing. Would this essay fulfill that purpose?

   F. Yes, because the essay describes Davis's choice to come back to Phyllis Wheatley as a boxing coach.
   G. Yes, because the essay describes Davis's role in setting a significant boxing record with his Olympic team.
   H. No, because the essay focuses on Davis's civil leadership, not his boxing achievements.
   J. No, because the essay focuses primarily on specific cases of polio and how to treat the disease.

3. Suppose the writer had decided to write an essay discussing how the Phyllis Wheatley Settlement House's etiquette training influenced Davis's decision to run for mayor. Would this essay successfully fulfill the writer's goal?

   A. Yes, because the essay discusses the well-rounded education Davis received at the Settlement House.
   B. Yes, because the essay details the steps Davis took to excel and become the best student in his class.
   C. No, because the essay only briefly mentions Davis's decision to run for mayor as another of his achievements.
   D. No, because the essay limits itself to describing certain career milestones Davis made in boxing.

END OF SET ONE

STOP! DO NOT GO ON TO THE NEXT PAGE UNTIL TOLD TO DO SO.

28.4.2 Set Two

PASSAGE II

Tennis and Ice Cream

Our daughter has joined the junior tennis team at our community center. "Graceful" is a nice word often employed when talking about the sport, but there isn't much of that at this age. Parents will spend a great deal of money choosing the best racket for their child, only to see it sitting in their backyard summer after summer. Bailey is seven, and she's at the point where she can hold a racket and sometimes follow through on a serve, but her hand-eye coordination isn't so great. The only activity she and her friends seem truly interested in is keeping their ears open for the ice cream truck's distinctive tune.

Since a seven-year-old doesn't have the skill yet to hit a professionally served ball heading their way, the coach usually just lets them practice their return swings on balls served by a machine with an adjustable speed. The coach patiently stands by and offers words of encouragement while the kids swing and swing at the air. When a player finally makes contact, the ball soars up above the fence and as far away from the courts as those small arms can send it. Generally, during the first few games of the summer, the served balls simply hit the net limply and roll off the court. The coach offers a big thumbs-up, and we parents clap wildly at a job well done.

It means a lot to the kids to see their parents toughing it out in the heat with them, excited for their success. The only time the kids are allowed a break is if there is some factor outside human control—bad weather, damaged gear, a wild tantrum—that is causing problems for the players. Last week, Jorge performed a very convincing stubbed toe routine that gave him a water break and five minutes to giggle with the rest of his friends.

Apart from these kid-sized concessions, junior tennis has many of the same rules of play as the adult version. One of the most common fouls, however, happens when players lose their balance or simply forget what they've been doing all afternoon and step over the baseline—the ever-present "foot fault." They will look around quizzically for a moment, wondering why everyone is looking at them, and then they'll look down and see their feet planted squarely across that big white line. As one of the younger kids begins to grasp the notion of scoring, the rest of the kids become distracted by a playful jingle playing over a loudspeaker. It's the ice cream truck, which signals the welcome end of tennis practice for the day, and our Bailey is first in line.

GO ON TO THE NEXT PAGE.

4. Suppose the writer had intended to write an essay describing one child's experiences playing junior tennis. Would this essay accomplish the writer's goal?

   F. Yes, because the narrator's daughter Bailey is now playing junior tennis, and the essay goes on to describe Bailey's experiences at one summer practice.
   G. Yes, because it discusses the narrator's daughter Bailey's tennis abilities, such as the fact that she can sometimes follow through on a serve.
   H. No, because while it mentions that the narrator's daughter Bailey plays tennis, it also makes the point that she is more interested in listening for the ice cream truck.
   J. No, because although the narrator alludes to the tennis experiences of his daughter Bailey, it is primarily about the general features of tennis at a junior level.

5. Suppose the writer's goal had been to write a brief essay documenting the formidable qualities of tennis equipment. Would this essay successfully fulfill that goal?

   A. Yes, because it highlights the practical use of a machine with an adjustable speed for serving.
   B. Yes, because it tells readers how parents will spend any amount of money on tennis rackets to keep their kids interested in the game.
   C. No, because it fails to mention any detailed descriptions of equipment and focuses more on the rules of the game.
   D. No, because it does not include information about tennis nets or appropriate footwear worn during the game.

6. Suppose the writer had chosen to write a brief essay about how humorous he believes children can be when participating in sports for the first time. Would this essay successfully fulfill the writer's goal?

   F. Yes, because the essay compares the narrator's experience of his daughter Bailey playing tennis to the experiences of other parents.
   G. Yes, because the essay includes examples of children behaving in ways the narrator finds funny.
   H. No, because the essay focuses primarily on junior league tennis rules, which coaches must impart to their younger players.
   J. No, because the essay primarily describes the kinds of dangers present in the game of tennis and, therefore, is not humorous at all.

END OF SET TWO
STOP! DO NOT GO ON TO THE NEXT PAGE
UNTIL TOLD TO DO SO.

28.4.3 Set Three

PASSAGE III

Putting Pen to Paper

While researching for a commissioned mural project for my local arts council, I came across some pieces of calligraphy and became fascinated by the intricate relationship between visual art and writing. Calligraphy has been employed since ancient times to display words in a rhythmic, geometric, expressive visual design. Traditionally, this type of ornamental lettering style was used to bring religious texts to life in a complex and beautiful way. I became obsessed with learning about the various types of calligraphy and its evolution over thousands of years.

It occurred to me that I could use this ancient and beautiful writing style of my ancestors to tell a modern story, and I wanted to display that story in my mural. I went back and looked closely at the style of two iconic books from the Dark Ages for guidance: The *Lindisfarne Gospels* and the *Book of Kells*. After nine months of acquiring inspiration and practicing for hours each day, I finally felt I had a grasp of the proper techniques of Western calligraphy.

I asked my parents and grandparents if they had any family stories I could incorporate into the project. We decided that our family motto—*a capite ad cor*—was especially relevant to my project, since it translates to "from head to heart." The brain registers what we see and hear around us every day, but it is the heart that feels those experiences. I included allusions to jokes my grandfather often made, imagery from childhood memories, and swaths of colors and patterns that I felt would invoke feelings of love and comfort. In this calligraphic spin on modern graffiti, I was telling the story of my own life, as well as the history of my family.

It is in this way that calligraphy is able to bridge the divide between visual beauty and the written word. Every stroke of the brush plays its own small part in associating an image to a word, lending it power and depth. The words of our ancestors stay with us in the scrolls of ancient texts, ornate and alive with imagery and elegance. It is our modern-day responsibility to keep those family histories alive, whether in a mural or in our hearts and minds.

GO ON TO THE NEXT PAGE.

7. Suppose the writer's goal had been to write a brief essay describing how multiple kinds of art can be interwoven to help bring to life an artist's unique vision. Would this essay accomplish that goal?

   A. Yes, because it explains that most popular art forms in history become the foundation for an artist's career in the modern world.
   B. Yes, because it illustrates how one artist was heavily inspired by calligraphy and incorporated it into a wall mural.
   C. No, because it focuses only on historical examples of calligraphy, such as the *Lindisfarne Gospels* and the *Book of Kells*.
   D. No, because it fails to describe the history of calligraphy and visual art in non-Western cultures.

8. Suppose the writer's goal had been to write a brief essay describing the renewed popularity calligraphy was having in the visual art world. Would this essay accomplish that goal?

   F. Yes, because it details the way in which an artist used calligraphy to procure a commissioned project.
   G. Yes, because it shows how local communities are willing to finance projects that involve calligraphy.
   H. No, because it focuses on one artist who is personally inspired by calligraphy after researching the art form's history.
   J. No, because it does not examine the effect that the completed mural had on the narrator's family.

9. Suppose the writer's goal had been to write a brief essay focusing on the functions that calligraphy served in ancient times. Would this essay successfully fulfill that goal?

   A. Yes, because the essay is mainly about how the ornamental lettering style brought ancient religious texts to life.
   B. Yes, because the essay focuses on the histories of two calligraphic texts produced during the Dark Ages.
   C. No, because the essay focuses on a modern artist's view of the relationship between calligraphy and visual art.
   D. No, because the essay focuses on a specific mural, not on pieces of visual art commissioned by the arts council in the past.

END OF SET THREE

STOP! DO NOT GO ON TO THE NEXT PAGE UNTIL TOLD TO DO SO.

28.4.4 Set Four

PASSAGE IV

The Youngest Child

My Aunt Alice grew up the youngest child in a family of eight kids. Like most kids who are born last, she claimed that her voice was always drowned out by her older siblings. Close in age, the kids grew up as a close-knit unit near a military base in Honolulu, Hawaii. When my grandmother brought the kids to the commissary to have lunch with their father, Alice felt like she couldn't make her voice loud enough to be heard over everyone else. No one ever paid much attention to—or even heard—the comments she made about the food being cold or what grade she made on a test until the day she was forced to take matters into her own hands.

Aunt Alice says she was around seven when "the incident" occurred. The commissary was packed and, as usual, the family let one of the bigger kids decide where they'd sit. They were discussing their plans for the upcoming weekend, but a simple discussion soon turned into an outright yelling contest. Some of the older kids wanted to go to a beach on the north side, and some of the middle ones wanted to explore Waimano Falls again. Alice kept piping up with the suggestion that they go to the botanical gardens because it would be her birthday week, and they hadn't visited there yet. The other kids kept drowning her out, so Alice walked away from the table. It was a few minutes before her mother wondered where her youngest child had run off to. They looked all around the mess hall, but they couldn't figure out where she had gone.

Out of nowhere, my Uncle Mickey pointed to a crowd around the stage in the back of the mess hall. As the family walked up to it, they noticed Alice with one hand on her hip and the other holding a megaphone. She finally had everyone's attention—her family and hundreds of strangers. For the first time, she was being heard, and she really let them have it. She ranted about never being listened to just because she was the littlest. She reminded everyone that her birthday was coming up, that she wanted to visit the botanical gardens, and that no one could stop her from going.

It suddenly became clear to everyone that they had been rudely ignoring my Aunt Alice for too long. They were all so proud of her standing up for herself, even if it was against her own family. Alice's small voice was heard that day, and ever since then, she's been the first person to consult in family discussions.

GO ON TO THE NEXT PAGE.

10. Suppose the writer had been assigned to write a short personal-opinion essay on a specific problem faced by military bases. Would this essay fulfill the assignment, and why?

F. Yes, because the essay clearly identifies a military base in Honolulu, Hawaii.
G. Yes, because the essay describes something that was personal to the writer's family.
H. No, because the essay primarily concerns the experiences of the youngest child in a large family.
J. No, because the essay only mentions general problems encountered by military bases.

11. Suppose the writer's goal had been to write an essay focusing on how younger siblings struggle to assert themselves. Would this essay fulfill that goal?

A. Yes, because the essay describes how a younger sibling was neglected and had to take drastic action to be heard.
B. Yes, because the essay focuses on how isolated younger siblings can feel when their older siblings don't understand them.
C. No, because the essay primarily focuses on the roles each sibling plays, not on ways in which younger siblings may struggle to find their voices.
D. No, because the essay indicates that a younger sibling was able to get the attention she needed, but she went about it in the wrong way.

12. Suppose the writer had chosen to write an essay that explored the strategies employed by parents to balance a military career with raising a family. Would this essay successfully fulfill the writer's goal?

F. No, because there is not a detailed discussion of parenting strategies, but rather the essay focuses on the relationship between the narrator's aunt and her siblings.
G. No, because the essay doesn't mention how the youngest sibling was affected by having to relocate every few years for her father's career.
H. Yes, because while the essay neglects exact details about the structure of the base, it mentions that the children often joined their father there for lunch.
J. Yes, because the essay explores how the children were able to explore and live in new places like Hawaii because of their father's military career.

END OF SET FOUR

STOP! DO NOT GO ON TO THE NEXT PAGE UNTIL TOLD TO DO SO.

28.4.5 Set Five

PASSAGE V

Guitars and Social Media

Whatever happened to playing guitar? I was upset the other day when I went to pick up my kid from his friend's house and found them spacing out like zombies on their electronics. Instead of the sound of two kids trying to figure out how to play music with each other, I heard only the bright buzzing sound of a laptop.

I can understand why the Internet and social media might seem more fun than learning the guitar. Everything you could possibly want to know is at your fingertips within seconds. The Internet offers the most fun possible without really learning anything. The idea of learning an instrument like the guitar, on the other hand, sounds like a long and boring road. It can take months before you can even form a chord, so everything sounds dull at first. But after a while, the results—actually making music—are worth the time and effort.

I've told my son time and time again that the qualities that draw young people into social media cannot be fulfilling in the long run. You're not creating any real memories through fleeting conversations, and you spend more time looking at other people's pictures than living your own life. You can figure out how social media works pretty quickly, and you can gain a bunch of "likes" or stir up trouble by commenting on a controversial subject. But where is the benefit?

Learning the guitar is something unpredictable. You don't know what you're capable of creating by yourself or when jamming with friends. Even learning other artists' songs can be a sort of puzzle that takes time to master. When you finally play it perfectly all the way through, you feel overjoyed and accomplished.

It's the idea of unlocking a hidden talent or creating something never heard before that makes learning to play the guitar so appealing. That mystery will always be more exciting than seeing what your friends had for lunch. Those few seconds of reading a post or looking at a picture aren't giving any lasting fulfillment. Playing the guitar—or music in general—can help you figure out your strengths and weaknesses through a creative process. It can help you build lasting friendships with people, even if your band never makes it past the garage.

GO ON TO THE NEXT PAGE.

13. Suppose the writer had chosen to write an essay that indicates that learning guitar is superior to spending time on social media. Would this essay fulfill the writer's goal?

    A. No, because the writers admits that social media has become more popular than learning to play the guitar.
    B. No, because the writer states that social media is a successful way for people to access meaningful information within seconds.
    C. Yes, because the writer claims that learning to play the guitar takes more time to master than learning to use social media.
    D. Yes, because the writer suggests that learning guitar can lead to more personal fulfillment than social media.

14. Suppose the writer's goal had been to develop an essay that outlines the motivations and achievements of the creators of certain social media websites. Would this essay successfully accomplish that goal?

    F. Yes, because it describes the dangers of social media as a means of communication between younger people.
    G. Yes, because it explains that social media has become a way for people to network and express their thoughts.
    H. No, because it fails to mention the business models of any popular social media companies.
    J. No, because it focuses on one parent's opinion of social media and does not provide details about any social media outlets.

15. Suppose the writer had been assigned to write an essay showing how his own life experiences have made him an advocate against social media. Would this essay successfully fulfill the assignment?

    A. Yes, because the writer describes how he found his son and his friend completely obsessed with social media and nothing else.
    B. Yes, because the writer indicates that his appreciation for the guitar existed before social media became popular.
    C. No, because the writer compares playing the guitar to social media without providing any personal anecdotes.
    D. No, because the essay focuses on the writer's son and his friends learning to play music in the garage.

END OF SET FIVE

STOP! DO NOT GO ON TO THE NEXT PAGE
UNTIL TOLD TO DO SO.

Sum It Up

Writer's Goal

Informative Essay
Informs or instructs the reader

Narrative Essay
Tells a story

Descriptive Essay
Describes something or someone

Persuasive Essay
Argues for or against one side

Tips and Techniques

Most Valuable Phrases: Writer's Goal questions almost always appear as the last question in a passage, so watch for them at the end. If you see one, remember to focus on the MVPs in the question and answers and match them to the passage. Do not be afraid to say no if the MVPs in the question do not match the passage.

Take the Easy Way: Check the title of the English passage. Sometimes that makes the answer more obvious. If you are pressed for time, it is not worth reviewing the whole passage.

Lesson 29

English Strategy

CAPTION:

29.1 Entrance Ticket

Select the best alternative to the underlined portion in each selection below. If no change is necessary, select NO CHANGE.

But, the teacher opted, to offer bonus points on the exam.

1. A. NO CHANGE
   B. But the teacher opted
   C. But the teacher opted,
   D. But the teacher, opted

Although the two large dogs leapt on the cat playfully, its eyes were soon fixed on the large slab of meat on the picnic table.

2. F. NO CHANGE
   G. it soon fixed its eyes
   H. they soon fixed their eyes
   J. it was soon fixed

Franz, the youngest member of the shipwrecked family, made a great discovery.

3. Given that all of the choices below are facts, which one makes it clear that Franz was unsurpassed in his ability to recover useful objects for his family from the wrecked ship?
   A. NO CHANGE
   B. located an item that was more practical than anyone else's find.
   C. surprised his family with a discovery.
   D. was an untiring worker in his search for useful items.

29.2 Learning Targets

1. Recognize when to use appropriate strategies to answer standard ACT English questions

2. Develop a method to address difficult questions on the English test

Self-Assessment

Circle the number that corresponds to your confidence level in your knowledge of this subject before beginning the lesson. A score of 1 means you are completely lost, and a score of 4 means you have mastered the skills. After you finish the lesson, return to the bottom of this page and circle your new confidence level to show your improvement.

Before Lesson

1 2 3 4

After Lesson

1 2 3 4

29.3.1 Sounds Right Is Right

To enter into the tournament, the student or teacher have to pay $10, and all of the proceeds go to help children with cancer.

1. A. NO CHANGE
   B. teacher has to
   C. teacher must have to
   D. teacher had to

It was an intensely close match. In the end, Bruce, who was only a freshman, was victorious after beating both Geoff and Miles.

2. F. NO CHANGE
   G. end, Bruce who
   H. end Bruce, who
   J. end, Bruce; who

To this day, many people believes that the Loch Ness Monster is the surviving descendant of the Plesiosaurus.

3. A. NO CHANGE
   B. believed
   C. believing
   D. believe

Many people think it to be a myth or a hoax, some truly believe they have seen it.

4. F. NO CHANGE
   G. Although many people
   H. Despite many people
   J. Many people,

English Tip

Sounds Right Is Right: While there are some tricky questions on the ACT English test, most of the correct answers will sound correct to your ear. If you aren't sure about the rule, use the way it sounds to make as many eliminations as possible.

29.3.2 Process of Elimination

Almost every student participates and <u>are</u> really competitive.

5. A. NO CHANGE
   B. being
   C. is
   D. its

In the 1930s, a picture was taken of "Nessie," and people debate <u>the</u> authenticity to this day.

6. F. NO CHANGE
   G. its
   H. it's
   J. its'

He can grow his own food, and he knows which kinds of wild berries and plants <u>are</u> safe to eat.

7. A. NO CHANGE
   B. is
   C. being
   D. that is

Seahorses eat <u>with the use of</u> their snouts to suck up plankton or crustaceans, and they use their tails to hook onto seagrass or coral.

8. F. NO CHANGE
   G. for using
   H. with
   J. by using

English Tip

Process of Elimination: The most useful strategy you can use on a multiple-choice test, such as the ACT, is to eliminate any wrong answers you can identify, even if you don't know how to find the correct one. Look for any choice that is too wordy, contains words that are always wrong, such as "its's," or anything that is obviously wrong to you; eliminate those choices first.

29.3.3 Most Valuable Phrases

While many different kinds of sports have held their sway over the European continent throughout the centuries, soccer has been very popular in many different countries.

9. Given that all of the choices are true, which one provides the most effective evidence of the extensive history of interest in soccer in Europe?
   - **A.** NO CHANGE
   - **B.** soccer is known as *football* in almost every country in the world.
   - **C.** soccer has been played in Europe for hundreds of years.
   - **D.** soccer involves two teams of players trying to score points by kicking a ball through the opposing team's goal.

It isn't important to be very talented in order to have fun playing in front of a crowd.

10. Which of the choices best helps the writer emphasize that music is best played in front of a large audience?
    - **F.** NO CHANGE
    - **G.** practicing to get really good.
    - **H.** performing for your teacher and friends.
    - **J.** with your instrument.

English Tip

Most Valuable Phrases: When the ACT gives you a specific question about the passage, be sure to focus on the details in the question. Chances are that grammar is not the issue. If you focus on those valuable phrases, you can select the answer very quickly.

29.3.3 Most Valuable Phrases

Distance runners tend to fall into pace around the 100-meter mark during a race.

11. Given that all choices are true, which one would most effectively express the writer's viewpoint that weight training is an important part of conditioning for long-distance racing?

A. NO CHANGE
B. Weight training strengthens leg muscles and helps support slow-twitch muscle fibers.
C. Weight training is often performed every other day during training.
D. Long-distance running has long been considered the oldest sport.

Although he had never been on such a long journey alone, the boy set out across the forest in hopes of finding the rumored treasure.

12. At this point in the story, the author is trying to show that the boy had little experience navigating the wilderness. Given that all the choices are true, which one best conveys that message?

F. NO CHANGE
G. The forest was very dark the night that the boy
H. All young boys long for adventure, so the boy
J. The forest was large and foreboding, especially to a young child, but the boy

29.3.4 Consistent, Clear, and Concise

The competition was surrounded by trash talk and hype, which was from other fellow students.

13. A. NO CHANGE
    B. Trash talk and hype from fellow students surrounded the competition.
    C. The competition was surrounded in trash talk.
    D. Trash talk and hype from fellow students surrounding the competition.

They know that if anything were ever to happen, Uncle Steve would be able to guide everyone to safety.

14. F. NO CHANGE
    G. The skills
    H. He
    J. My grandmother and aunt

According to legend and myth, Loch Ness is also home to the Loch Ness Monster, or "Nessie."

15. A. NO CHANGE
    B. According to legend,
    C. Based according to legend and myth,
    D. According to, legend and myth

How much money did Joe and Susan have to spend on the home repair after she paid someone out of pocket to cut down the tree?

16. F. NO CHANGE
    G. after they
    H. after he
    J. after it

English Tip

Consistent, Clear, and Concise: Though there are many rules tested on the ACT, you can follow one simple guideline when you tackle just about any grammar question: all answers need to be consistent, clear, and concise.

29.3.5 When In Doubt, Commas Out

During our vacation to Disney World, we rode every ride, and dined at nearly all the restaurants.

17. A. NO CHANGE
B. just about every ride, and dined
C. every ride and dined,
D. every ride and dined

Eleanor Roosevelt, and Winston Churchill were both involved in the formation of the United Nations.

18. F. NO CHANGE
G. Eleanor Roosevelt, and,
H. Eleanor Roosevelt and
J. Eleanor Roosevelt and,

How much money will it cost, for all of us to be entered into the contest, and who is going to pay for all of that?

19. A. NO CHANGE
B. it cost, for every one
C. it cost for all,
D. it cost for all

The teacher announced that all students, who are tardy will be sent to the principal's office on their first offense.

20. F. NO CHANGE
G. students who,
H. students who
J. students, who,

English Tip

When In Doubt, Commas Out: One of the most common wrong answers on the ACT is an answer that contains too many commas. The test writers know that most students aren't familiar with the comma rules and tend to use too many commas. So if you don't have a specific reason for including the comma, eliminate that answer.

29.4.1 Set One

The young violinist took the stage with his instrument. I wasn't braced for the outcome.

1. A. NO CHANGE
   B. prepared for the unanticipated outcome.
   C. braced, regarding the impression, for the outcome.
   D. expecting the outcome, which I didn't foresee.

She sat at her easel and painted for hours on most days.

2. F. NO CHANGE
   G. most of
   H. much
   J. more of

The man was struggling boldly with the waves, he saw that the crew had crowded into the lifeboats and were rowing away from the sinking vessel.

3. A. NO CHANGE
   B. The man struggled
   C. That the man was struggling boldly
   D. As the man was struggling boldly

END OF SET ONE

STOP! DO NOT GO ON TO THE NEXT PAGE UNTIL TOLD TO DO SO.

29.4.2 Set Two

The only <u>healthy snack</u> we enjoyed all week was the fresh pineapple.

4. **F.** NO CHANGE
   G. flourishing pick-me-up
   H. hygienic snack
   J. vigorous refreshment

The <u>coziest</u> cottage sat near the pond and featured a porch around all sides of the house.

5. **A.** NO CHANGE
   B. most coziest
   C. more cozier
   D. coziest of

The child knew that she could enter her mother's office at any time, and someone would stop talking on the phone or typing and <u>calls her name to chats</u> with her.

6. **F.** NO CHANGE
   G. call her name to chat
   H. calling her name and chatting
   J. calls to chat

END OF SET TWO
STOP! DO NOT GO ON TO THE NEXT PAGE
UNTIL TOLD TO DO SO.

29.4.3 Set Three

Competing in the 1936 Olympics in Berlin—a city rife with ethnic discrimination—Jesse was up against daunting Nazi propaganda. He shocked the world with his athleticism, demonstrating the potential of an American athlete.

7. Assuming that all of the choices below are factual, which one best summarizes the paragraph's description of Jesse Owens's impact on the 1936 Olympics?

A. NO CHANGE
B. becoming interested in running while still a boy.
C. shattering racial stereotypes and winning multiple gold medals.
D. having matched a world record in high school track.

When he was engaged in an activity he found truly interesting, whether it was building a LEGO castle or making Play-Doh casts, the boy could not be persuaded to carry on a conversation.

8. At this point, the author wishes to give the reader a glimpse into the boy's interests. Assuming that all the choices below are true, which one best achieves this goal?

F. NO CHANGE
G. being extremely interested in his activities,
H. actions I expect him to teach his younger siblings,
J. art projects as well as building activities,

The depth limit for scuba divers is 130 feet, so a lover of aquatic life can cruise the deep ocean, observing and photographing many species of fish and marine invertebrates.

9. Which choice below best corresponds with the detail provided at the end of the sentence?

A. NO CHANGE
B. swimmer
C. thrill seeker
D. man

END OF SET THREE
STOP! DO NOT GO ON TO THE NEXT PAGE
UNTIL TOLD TO DO SO.

1 ■ ■ ■ ■ ■ ■ ■ ■ ■ 1

29.4.4 Set Four

There is serious criminal element breaking the law in my city, a town that was once a peaceful place to raise a family.

10. **F.** NO CHANGE
 G. provoking near
 H. undergoing
 J. taking control of

What was stowed in the trunks were now on the road.

11. **A.** NO CHANGE
 B. was
 C. are
 D. had been

Scientists believe that carelessness on the part of tourists may have led to the fire in the park, which developed and occurred during the busiest season of the year.

12. **F.** NO CHANGE
 G. park through happening
 H. park
 J. park, which developed, in fact

END OF SET FOUR
STOP! DO NOT GO ON TO THE NEXT PAGE
UNTIL TOLD TO DO SO.

29.4.5 Set Five

It didn't take much time, however for the affectionate German Shepherd to cuddle the rabbit and become its surrogate mother.

13. A. NO CHANGE
    B. take, much time, however,
    C. take much time however,
    D. take much time, however,

Being quiet about your special fishing holes, is one of the secrets of the sport.

14. F. NO CHANGE
    G. quiet, about your special fishing holes,
    H. quiet about your special fishing holes
    J. quiet, about your special fishing holes

Myths and lore were often celebrated by early Hawaiians, who used drama, in their signature dance, the hula.

15. A. NO CHANGE
    B. drama in their signature dance,
    C. drama, in their signature dance
    D. drama in their signature dance

END OF SET FIVE

STOP! DO NOT GO ON TO THE NEXT PAGE UNTIL TOLD TO DO SO.

Sum It Up

Tips and Techniques

Sounds Right Is Right: The ACT usually gives you a correct answer that sounds right, so use your ear if you aren't sure.

Process of Elimination: Make sure to eliminate as many answers as you can as you work through the test. Even if you don't know what's right, you can usually find one or two that you know are wrong.

Most Valuable Phrases: If a question asks you to do something really specific, make sure you first find the key words and then go to the passage to find the best answer.

Consistent, Clear, Concise: Keep in mind that a good rule of thumb for any question is to keep it consistent with the rest of the passage, clear in meaning, and short and to the point.

When In Doubt, Commas Out: If you aren't sure whether to use a comma, don't use one.

Lesson 30

English Pacing

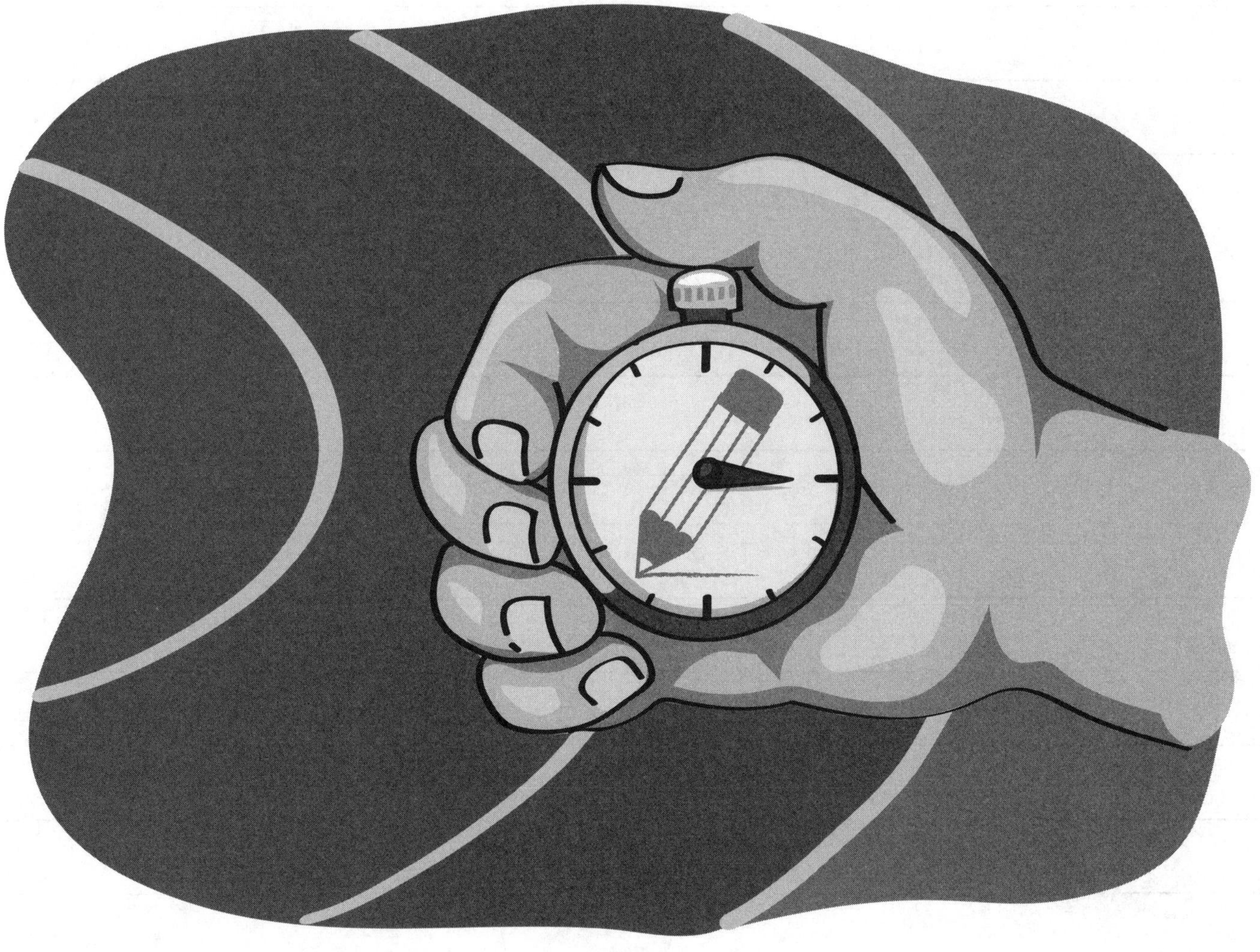

CAPTION:

30.1 Entrance Ticket

What are your goals for the English section of the ACT? How do you plan to achieve them? What might stand in your way? Answer these questions in complete sentences.

30.2 Learning Targets

1. Set a personalized pacing goal for the English test based on ACT scoring tables

2. Follow a personalized pacing plan for the English test

Self-Assessment

Circle the number that corresponds to your confidence level in your knowledge of this subject before beginning the lesson. A score of 1 means you are completely lost, and a score of 4 means you have mastered the skills. After you finish the lesson, return to the bottom of this page and circle your new confidence level to show your improvement.

Before Lesson

1 2 3 4

After Lesson

1 2 3 4

30.3.1 Setting a Pacing Plan

Scale Score	Raw Score (correct answers)	Scale Score	Raw Score (correct answers)
36	75	18	43
35	74	17	41
34	73	16	38
33	72	15	35
32	71	14	33
31	71	13	31
30	69	12	29
29	68	11	26
28	67	10	24
27	65	19	21
26	63	8	18
25	61	7	15
24	59	6	12
23	57	5	9
22	54	4	7
21	52	3	5
20	49	2	3
19	46	1	0

30.3.1 Setting a Pacing Plan

Goal Scale Score: ____________________

Overall Goal Raw Score: ____________________

Target Raw Score (1–15): ____________________
Actual Raw Score (1–15): ____________________

Target Raw Score (16–30): ____________________
Actual Raw Score (16–30): ____________________

Target Raw Score (31–45): ____________________
Actual Raw Score (31–45): ____________________

Target Raw Score (46–60): ____________________
Actual Raw Score (46–60): ____________________

Target Raw Score (61–75): ____________________
Actual Raw Score (61–75): ____________________

English Tip

Mark and Move: As soon as you are stuck on a question, eliminate what you can, mark your best guess, and move on. You probably won't have time to revisit these questions, but if you have extra time, go back and check your work. Since the difficult questions are mixed throughout, you should be prepared to use this technique quite often.

1 ■ ■ ■ ■ ■ ■ ■ ■ ■ 1

30.4.1 Mini-Test 1

PASSAGE I

Attempts: ______ Correct: ______

Grandmother's Scarves

[1]

When I was very young, my grandmother would <u>sew, knit and crochet.</u> (1) She made <u>my siblings and I</u> (2) scarves for the winter. She liked to use our favorite colors in the <u>scarves she made for us, sometimes</u> (3) she would combine multiple colors to create more diverse patterns.

[2]

My grandmother's handmade scarves came in handy in the winter when it would snow <u>owing to the fact that</u> (4) they were warm. When I would get ready to go outside in the cold, my mother would always remind me of the scarf my grandmother <u>has made</u> (5) me. My siblings and I would play outside or go sledding wearing our scarves around our necks.

[3]

One <u>year, Nana</u> (6) tried to teach some of the grandchildren how to knit and crochet. She let everyone pick out the colors of yarn they wanted. We

1. **A.** NO CHANGE
   B. sew and knit and crochet.
   C. sew, knit, and crochet.
   D. sew, knit and crochet,

2. **F.** NO CHANGE
   G. my siblings, and I
   H. my siblings and me
   J. me and my siblings

3. **A.** NO CHANGE
   B. scarves, sometimes,
   C. scarves. And sometimes,
   D. scarves. Sometimes

4. **F.** NO CHANGE
   G. and
   H. for the reason that
   J. because

5. **A.** NO CHANGE
   B. made
   C. makes
   D. make

6. **F.** NO CHANGE
   G. year; Nana
   H. year. Nana
   J. year—Nana

GO ON TO THE NEXT PAGE.

all laughed as each <u>other's</u> [7] fingers fumbled over the needles and yarn.

[4]

<u>Hence,</u> [8] my grandmother remained patient. After a few days of lessons, some of my cousins were able to knit and crochet on their own.

<u>The scarves were not very long, but they were good to start.</u> [9] My grandmother was very proud to share her talents with her grandchildren.

[5]

My grandmother's <u>scarves means</u> [10] a lot to me because they remind me of all the wonderful things she <u>does</u> [11] for us while we were growing up. She <u>was always</u> [12] there to make us smile with her warm welcomes and unceasing love. I am a better person <u>today, because</u> [13] I grew up with her in my life.

7. **A.** NO CHANGE
B. others's
C. others'
D. others

8. **F.** NO CHANGE
G. Therefore,
H. Nevertheless,
J. Although

9. **A.** NO CHANGE
B. Although the scarves were not very long, they were a good start.
C. The scarves were a good start even if they were not as long.
D. The scarves were not very long, but the cousins had a good start.

10. **F.** NO CHANGE
G. scarves meant
H. scarves mean
J. scarves, mean

11. **A.** NO CHANGE
B. did
C. had did
D. had does

12. **F.** NO CHANGE
G. were always
H. is
J. are

13. **A.** NO CHANGE
B. today, since
C. today because
D. today therefore

GO ON TO THE NEXT PAGE.

One day, when I become a grandparent, I hope to give my grandchildren the same amount of love and care that my grandmother gave me. [15]

14. F. NO CHANGE
G. day when
H. day, when,
J. day when,

15. The writer is considering adding the following sentence to Paragraph 1:

> My grandmother made us these scarves to show us how much she loved us.

Would this addition help the writer's piece?

A. Yes, because it makes the passage flow more smoothly and fits with the overall theme of the passage.
B. Yes, because it would give the reader a better visual idea of the writer's grandmother.
C. No, because it is irrelevant to the rest of the passage.
D. No, because it is stylistically different from the rest of the passage.

END OF MINI-TEST ONE

STOP! DO NOT GO ON TO THE NEXT PAGE UNTIL TOLD TO DO SO.

1 1

30.4.2 Mini-Test 2

PASSAGE II

Attempts: _____ Correct: _____

Ride a Bike

[1]

Each and <u>everyday</u> [16] carbon dioxide emissions from automobiles <u>affect</u> [17] our atmosphere and <u>attribute</u> [18] to the deterioration of the ozone layer. <u>Using public transportation is a significant way to decrease daily carbon dioxide emissions.</u> [19]

[2]

For instance, imagine if all the people <u>who ride</u> [20] the subway in New York City tried to drive to work. They would sit in traffic all morning, alongside the thousands of people who already drive, with their <u>vehicles release</u> [21] fumes into the atmosphere.

16.
- F. NO CHANGE
- G. every-day,
- H. every day
- J. every day,

17.
- A. NO CHANGE
- B. affects
- C. effect
- D. effects

18.
- F. NO CHANGE
- G. contribute
- H. attributes
- J. is contributed

19.
- A. NO CHANGE
- B. It is important for public transportation to reduce the number of people driving cars.
- C. Public transportation increases carbon dioxide emissions, as well as the number of cars on the roads.
- D. The use of public transportation will significantly decrease the number of people driving.

20.
- F. NO CHANGE
- G. whom ride
- H. that ride
- J. which ride

21.
- A. NO CHANGE
- B. vehicles releasing
- C. vehicles released
- D. vehicle releasing

GO ON TO THE NEXT PAGE.

[3]

That being said, the most environment-conscious way to travel from point A to point B is to ride a bike.
22

22. How would omitting this phrase change the sentence?

F. It would remove an unrelated detail.
G. It would affect the tone of the overall paragraph.
H. The writer would improve conciseness and clarity.
J. The sentence would lose meaning.

[4]

Riding a bicycle has many benefits. Not only is it good for the environment but it also helps the rider stay fit. In a country with obesity rates at an all-time high, physical activity should be a top priority. Riding
23

23. A. NO CHANGE
B. environment and
C. environment, but
D. environment, yet

a bicycle instead of driving a car is great exercise that works multiple muscles at one time. Bicycling also exercises the
24

24. F. NO CHANGE
G. exercise works
H. exercise working
J. exercise, and working

heart making the rider altogether more physically fit.
25

25. A. NO CHANGE
B. heart, which makes,
C. heart and makes
D. heart, and making

[5]

While on a bike, the rider is more aware of his or her surroundings then when driving a car. Too many people drive while distracted, whether they are texting, changing the radio, or eating. A cyclist
26

26. F. NO CHANGE
G. than during driving
H. than while driving
J. then while driving

GO ON TO THE NEXT PAGE.

is significantly less likely to be distracted on the road. If more people rode bicycles, there would be fewer
27

27. A. NO CHANGE
B. being significantly
C. are significantly
D. is more significantly

accidents and fatalities because people who ride bikes are safer when compared to drivers.
28

28. F. NO CHANGE
G. bike riders are generally safer than
H. people who ride bikes are safer then
J. people who bike are compared to

[6]

Why wouldn't you choose to ride a bike instead of driving a car? A car can definitely get you to your destination faster—but at substantial risk. A bike, on the other hand, is environmentally friendly, good for your health, and safer than a car. [30]
29

29. A. NO CHANGE
B. health while
C. health and,
D. health while,

30. Which of the following choices is the best way for the writer to make a more convincing argument for the passage as a whole?

F. NO CHANGE
G. The writer could include a paragraph about the financial benefits of riding a bike.
H. The writer could mention famous bike riders.
J. The writer could describe a city where a lot of people ride bikes.

END OF MINI-TEST TWO
STOP! DO NOT GO ON TO THE NEXT PAGE
UNTIL TOLD TO DO SO.

30.4.3 Mini-Test 3

PASSAGE III

Attempts: _____ Correct: _____

Religious History in Rome

[1]

Rome, known worldwide as the heart of Christianity, housing Vatican City and the Pope. For thousands of years, however, people worshipped the gods and goddesses of Roman mythology. Through their worship, the Romans were able to make sense of the world around them and build the unique culture the Roman Empire.

[2]

Rome today still has roots in these traditional values as evidenced the prominent architecture that continues to stand in the city, such as the Pantheon and various pagan statues.

[3]

The reformation of Rome from the ancient Roman religion to Christianity happened within only a few generations with or without the consent of the Roman public.

31. **A.** NO CHANGE
B. Christianity because it houses
C. Christianity, is home to
D. Christianity; housing

32. **F.** NO CHANGE
G. although,
H. therefore,
J. however;

33. **A.** NO CHANGE
B. culture; the
C. culture, the
D. culture of the

34. **F.** NO CHANGE
G. Rome, today
H. Rome today,
J. Today, Rome

35. **A.** NO CHANGE
B. values, as evidenced by
C. values, that can be seen
D. values, as evidence by

36. **F.** NO CHANGE
G. generations, with
H. generations; with
J. generations with,

GO ON TO THE NEXT PAGE.

[4]

When Christianity first came to Rome, implemented largely by Emperor Theodosius in 391 C.E., not all Romans accepted the conversion. [37] Many people in Rome, particularly the senatorial elites, protested the removal of pagan non-Christian altars and statues. While Christianity was sweeping across the nation many Romans were asking not only for more respect for traditional altars; but freedom of religion.

[5]

Hence, religious tolerance was not implemented until many years

37. The writer is thinking about removing the following information:

> implemented largely by Emperor Theodosius in 391 C.E.,

If the writer would delete this, how would it affect the essay?

A. It would have no effect on the essay.
B. The essay would lose historical context.
C. The essay would lose irrelevant information about a Roman emperor.
D. The essay would lose the writer's opinion about a Roman emperor.

38. **F.** NO CHANGE
G. elites',
H. elite's,
J. elite;

39. **A.** NO CHANGE
B. pagan and non-Christian
C. pagan, non-Christian
D. pagan

40. **F.** NO CHANGE
G. nation the Romans
H. nation; Romans
J. nation, many Romans

41. **A.** NO CHANGE
B. altars but
C. altars but also for
D. altars but for also

42. **F.** NO CHANGE
G. However,
H. Therefore,
J. Although

GO ON TO THE NEXT PAGE.

later, the Roman protests against the removal of pagan altars
43

was revolutionary at that time in history. [45]
44

43. A. NO CHANGE
B. later the
C. later; the
D. after Roman

44. F. NO CHANGE
G. were
H. continues to be
J. is

45. Suppose the writer intended to write on the history of ancient Roman mythology and gods. Would this essay as a whole have fulfilled her intention?

A. Yes, because the essay covers religion in Roman history.
B. Yes, because the essay mentions religious tolerance in ancient Rome.
C. No, because the essay focuses more on the introduction of Christianity than specific Roman gods.
D. No, because the essay does not mention the Roman goddess Athena.

END OF MINI-TEST THREE

STOP! DO NOT GO ON TO THE NEXT PAGE UNTIL TOLD TO DO SO.

30.4.4 Mini-Test 4

PASSAGE IV

Attempts: ______ Correct: _____

Zion National Park

[1]

In a plateau region of Utah that was once a desert, lays a beautiful national park which span nearly 150,000 acres. The Zion National Park features the Virgin River, which engraves it's long trail through Navajo sandstone. One of the features of the park is Zion Canyon, a narrow gorge so deep that sunlight barely reaches the bottom.

46 — "desert, lays"; 47 — "park which span"; 48 — "it's"

[2]

Along the floor of this canyon which contains vegetation, it is abundant. The park sits at an intersection of ecosystems, which allows a variety of more than 800 different kinds of plants to flourish at any one time. [50]

49 — "Along the floor of this canyon which contains vegetation, it is abundant."

46. **F.** NO CHANGE
G. desert lies
H. desert, lies
J. desert lays

47. **A.** NO CHANGE
B. park which spans
C. park, that spanning
D. park, spans

48. **F.** NO CHANGE
G. one's
H. its
J. the

49. **A.** NO CHANGE
B. It is quite abundant at the floor which is this canyon containing vegetation.
C. Vegetation along this abundant canyon floor is contained.
D. Vegetation is abundant along this canyon floor.

50. The author is considering adding a sentence here to convey relevant information concerning vegetation variety. Assuming all of the following are true, which addition best accomplishes this goal?
F. The widest plant diversity in Utah can be seen at Zion National Park.
G. Zion National Park also has hanging gardens.
H. A lot of flowers can be seen in the spring and summer.
J. A lot of these plants were useful to the Native Americans who once inhabited the area.

GO ON TO THE NEXT PAGE.

[3]

The terrain rises nearly a mile high then different vegetation can be seen with changes in elevation. The park is home to a variety of animals, that can be seen, by hikers and other nature lovers. Along the river, live bank beavers and many different birds. Throughout the rest of the canyon, birds such as eagles, hawks, falcons, and vultures can be spotted. Foxes, deer, and mountain lions also live within the park.

[4]

The Zion National Park being a popular site for climbers even though the sandstone makes it a challenge. The same techniques and gear that would work on granite do not work on sandstone because the rock is too loose.

[5]

There are many hiking trails throughout the park that visitors can explore at a leisurely pace. Hiking is a great alternative to climbing for those who are inexperienced.

[6]

The climate at Zion National Park changes throughout the year and at different elevations. Visitors must be prepared for fluctuating

51. **A.** NO CHANGE
B. high, then
C. high, and
D. high and

52. **F.** NO CHANGE
G. animals, that can be seen
H. animals. That can be seen
J. animals that can be seen

53. **A.** NO CHANGE
B. Along the river, live bank beavers and many different birds:
C. Bank beavers and many different birds, live along the river.
D. Bank beavers and many different birds live along the river.

54. **F.** NO CHANGE
G. Park is
H. Park was
J. Park,

55. **A.** NO CHANGE
B. make
C. would make
D. had made

56. **F.** NO CHANGE
G. park where visitors
H. park; and visitors
J. park, visitors

57. **A.** NO CHANGE
B. elevations, and, visitors
C. elevations; therefore, and visitors,
D. elevations, and visitors

GO ON TO THE NEXT PAGE.

temperatures, <u>thunderstorms and even</u> wintry snowstorms.
58

The best time to visit the park <u>being</u> spring or fall. [60]
59

58. **F.** NO CHANGE
G. thunderstorms, and even,
H. thunderstorms and even,
J. thunderstorms, and even

59. **A.** NO CHANGE
B. would being
C. is
D in

60. To enhance the logical progression of the essay, the last paragraph should go:

F. before paragraph 2.
G. before paragraph 3.
H. before paragraph 4.
J. where it is now.

END OF MINI-TEST FOUR
STOP! DO NOT GO ON TO THE NEXT PAGE
UNTIL TOLD TO DO SO.

30.4.5 Mini-Test 5

PASSAGE V **Attempts: _____ Correct: _____**

German Brother

[1]

When I was a freshman, there <u>were</u> 61 two foreign exchange students attending our high school. My school was very small, and all of the students had known each other since the first <u>grade, so having</u> 62 two new students from a different country was intriguing.

[2]

Both of the foreign exchange students were boys. <u>One, named Zuka,</u> 63 was from Georgia, and the other, named Bjorn, <u>he was</u> 64 from Germany. [65]

[3]

Halfway through his year at my high <u>school, Bjorn</u> 66 came to live with my family because he did not get along with his host family.

61. A. NO CHANGE
 B. was
 C. is
 D. be

62. Which of the following alternatives to the underlined portion would NOT be acceptable?
 F. NO CHANGE
 G. grade. To have
 H. grade. So to have
 J. grade. Having

63. A. NO CHANGE
 B. One named Zuka
 C. One was named Zuka,
 D. One, were named Zuka,

64. F. NO CHANGE
 G. was
 H. is
 J. he is

65. The writer is considering adding a sentence to the preceding paragraph in order to provide more information about the exchange students. Which of the following sentences best accomplishes this goal?
 A. Both boys were seniors in high school.
 B. At the time, Germany had stricter laws than Georgia.
 C. Some people thought that Georgia was the state in the U.S. rather than the country.
 D. I had always wanted to learn German.

66. F. NO CHANGE
 G. school; Bjorn
 H. school. Bjorn
 J. school, Bjorn,

GO ON TO THE NEXT PAGE.

It was not a good fit for Bjorn. Over the rest of the year, Bjorn
67
became like a brother to me.

[4]

At first, he was very quiet and shy in his new home, but eventually he opened up to my family and fit in perfect. Since Bjorn was the same age as my older
68
brother, he was able to relate to him easily, and they became close friends. He told us all about Germany and we helped him break
69
down the language barrier. The single most important German phrase that he taught us was "Ich liebe dich", which is German for *I love you.*
70

[5]

Bjorn had left at the end of the summer after
71
graduating from our high school. He has yet to return to the United States, but he keeps in contact with my family and I over the Internet.
72

[6]

One day when I travel to Germany, he will be my
73
host and help me navigate the new culture, just as we

67. **A.** NO CHANGE
B. The first family was
C. They was
D. It were

68. **F.** NO CHANGE
G. in perfect!
H. in more perfect.
J. in perfectly.

69. **A.** NO CHANGE
B. Germany. And
C. Germany; and
D. Germany, and

70. **F.** NO CHANGE
G. "Ich liebe dich," which
H. "Ich liebe dich" which
J. Ich liebe dich, which

71. **A.** NO CHANGE
B. left
C. had gone
D. leaving

72. **F.** NO CHANGE
G. my family, and I,
H. us, my family
J. my family and me

73. **A.** NO CHANGE
B. One day, when,
C. One day, when
D. One day when,

GO ON TO THE NEXT PAGE.

did for him. He will forever be in my heart and a part of my family. [75]

74. F. NO CHANGE
G. had did
H. done
J. were doing

75. Which of the following details could the writer add to the last paragraph of the passage in order to improve the development of her conclusion?

A. Mention what happened to Zuka.
B. Give details about when the writer expects to visit Germany.
C. Explain the differences between the cultures of the United States and Germany.
D. Discuss the language barrier the writer might face in Germany.

END OF MINI-TEST FIVE

STOP! DO NOT GO ON TO THE NEXT PAGE
UNTIL TOLD TO DO SO.

Sum It Up

Tips and Techniques

Goal Score: Remember to have your goal raw score in mind on the day of the test. You should know exactly how many questions you need to get correct.

Pacing Plan: Have your plan in place before you take your ACT English test. Know how many minutes you will spend on each section and how many questions you need to attempt in order to get to your goal score.

Notes

Notes

English Glossary

Adjective
a word or phrase that modifies a noun

Adverb
a word or phrase that modifies an adjective, verb, other adverb, or word group

Ambiguity
unclear; can be interpreted more than one way; not precise

Antecedent
the noun a pronoun replaces

Clause
a phrase that includes a subject and a verb

Clear
understandable, not confusing

Comparative
an adjective or adverb that express a higher degree of a quality

Concise
providing information clearly and in as few words as possible without losing meaning

Conjunction
a word used to connect words, clauses, or sentences

Context
a way of looking at something as it relates to the surroundings; perspective

Contraction
a word that takes the place of two other words by combining them into a shortened version with an apostrophe (the apostrophe replaces the missing letters)

Coordinating conjunction
a conjunction placed between words, phrases, clauses, or sentences of equal rank

Dependent clause
a clause that cannot stand alone because it is not a complete idea

Fragment
a sentence that is incorrect because it does not have an independent clause

Independent clause
a clause that can stand alone as a complete sentence

Linking verb
a verb that links the subject with the rest of the sentence; does not show action

Main Idea
the central topic of a paragraph or essay

Meaningful
literally, has meaning; communicates something

Modifier
a word or phrase that adds detail or enhances another word in a sentence

Noun
a person, place, or thing

Parallelism
being consistent with the pattern of words used

Parenthetical elements
words or phrases that are not essential to the meaning of a sentence

Possessive noun
a noun that expresses ownership

Preposition
a word that shows the relationship between a noun or pronoun and another word in the sentence

Pronoun
a word that replaces a previously mentioned noun (antecedent)

Purpose
the reason an author writes a sentence, paragraph, or essay

Redundancy
unnecessarily repeating words or ideas

Relevant
closely connected or appropriate to the topic at hand

Run-on
two independent clauses that are joined without the proper comma and/or conjunction

Style
the way authors use words to establish mood, images, and meaning

Subject
a person, place, or thing doing the action in a sentence or phrase

Subordinating conjunction
a conjunction that connects a dependent and independent clause

Superlative
an adjective or adverb that expresses the highest degree of a quality

Synonym
a word or phrase that is close to or exactly the same meaning of another word or phrase

Tone
the way authors express their attitudes through their writing

Transition
a word or phrase used to link two ideas together

Verb
a word that expresses an action or a state of being

Verb tense
the form a verb takes to indicate when the action took place

Contributors

Chief Academic Officer
Oliver Pope

Lead Content Editor
Lisa Primeaux-Redmond

Assistant Content Editor
Allison Eskind

Layout
Jeff Garrett, Elaine Broussard, Shannon Rawson, Eric Manuel

Art
Nicole St. Pierre, Eliza Todorova, Roland Parker, Kayla Manuel, Anne Lipscomb

Lesson Writers
Lisa Primeaux-Redmond, Allison Eskind, Stephanie Bucklin, Nick Sweeney, Lori Martin

Question Writers
Jillian Musso, Lisa Primeaux-Redmond, Thomas Whittington, Pam Braud, Erin McAdams, Emily DeYoung, Anthony Mabrey, Tyler Munson, June Manuel, Allison Eskind, Nick Sweeney, Lauren Pope, Peter Frost, Karen Gatto, Wade Heaton, Michael Laird

Proofreaders
Kristen Cockrell, M. Jason Brown, Chrissy Vincent, Dan Marchese, Rhett Manuel, Catherine Tall, Jerelyn Pearson, Liz Baron, Jordan Sermon, Megan Reitzell, Michael Laird

Interns
Kaitlyn Mattox, Rashaud Red, Jamaica Rhoden, Chelsey Smith

ACT® Mastery created by Craig Gehring